I0540359

Belonging to Bethlehem

Belonging to Bethlehem

Stories from the Christmas City's
Jewish Community

Jennifer Lader

©2026 by Jennifer Lader

All rights reserved. No part of this publication may be reproduced or transmitted in any form or by any means, electronic or mechanical, including photocopying, recording, or any other information storage and retrieval system, without the written permission of the author or publisher.

All individuals interviewed for this book were informed of the nature and intent of this project and agreed to speak with the author; wherever practicable, they had the opportunity to review their stories as presented here.

Regarding archival or group photos, to the best of our ability, wherever feasible the author reached out to as many people as could be identified to obtain approval to be pictured in this book.

Printed in the United States of America
Published in Hellertown, PA
Cover design by Gary Lader, original artwork based on a photo taken from the Broad Street Bridge in Bethlehem, looking south

Library of Congress Control Number 2025925658
ISBN 979-8-89420-074-3
For more information or to place bulk orders, contact the author or the publisher at Jennifer@BrightCommunications.net.

In memory of my parents, a storyteller and a reader,
who, in so many ways, made this book possible

"When we first came to town in the 1950s,
there was a man, very old, very learned, at the Center when
I went up to buy candles.
He thought it was so wonderful that I wanted to light the
Friday night candlesticks.
He said, 'Now, do you know the story?'"
—Betty Diamond of Bethlehem

Contents

1. "How Lovely Are Your Branches": Arriving in Bethlehem — 9

2. "Above Thy Deep and Dreamless Sleep": Meeting at the Crossroads — 17

3. "*Campanas de Belén*" (Bells of Bethlehem): Becoming Us — 39

4. "All is Calm, All is Bright": Building Places for the Young People — 76

5. "Morning Star, O Cheering Sight": Fitting In, Standing Out, Finding Belonging — 112

6. "O Come Ye to Bethlehem": Arriving Survivors — 143

7. "Like a Diamond in the Sky": Women of the Jewish Community — 161

8. "*Adeste, Fideles*": Honor, Fidelity, Commitment of the Men, and More about the Community — 198

9. "Field and Fountain, Moor and Mountain, Following Yonder Star": Weathering Changes — 238

10. "O Morning Stars, Together": Sharing Our Story — 277

Acknowledgments — 283

Sources Cited — 285

Index by Last Name — 292

About the Author — 300

Bethlehem, Pa.

"Broad Street, at Christmastime Bethlehem, Pa.," circa 1940s, Lehigh University Postcard Collection, [LUPC0253], Special Collections, Linderman Library, Lehigh University, Bethlehem, Pa. Artist: Bethlehem artist and printer J. Carroll Tobias.

Chapter 1
"How Lovely Are Your Branches"
Arriving in Bethlehem

I arrived in the Christmas City of Bethlehem, Pennsylvania, with my husband and our three young sons at that time of year when a 30-foot fir tree graces the plaza outside the library and city hall. We'd found an older house fronting onto two streets, including one called Prospect; our move-in day was in late December 2004, a cold and snowy time. We kept our coats on to weather the immediate boiler repair, reassembled the baby crib, and eventually settled in. At night from the boys' bedroom, we could see the 91-foot high "Star of Bethlehem" shining on our new city from South Mountain, though we didn't yet know what that star meant to this place.

For my children, everything became an opportunity for fun. The plumber told me, "My kids used to climb over my head, too, just like yours are doing with you." I took to writing about my small and constant companions, turning ordinary happenings into stories, such as the time one of my sons lost his glasses in a leaf pile and the day another skipped school for what to him was a very good reason.

Though invited to join a writers group, I found it too uncomfortable to read my work, or even speak, in public. Then one day, I heard about an eyeglasses coupon in the *Bethlehem Press*. After four failed convenience store stops, I ended up at the offices of that weekly newspaper to pick up an issue.

"I'm a writer," I said, feeling more like a pretender. Yet the office manager introduced me to the editor. We scheduled a meeting, though it took me a while to realize it was actually a job interview. For the occasion, I checked out a library book on writing for newspapers and wrote my first article, about a traveling python exhibition at our school, Calypso Elementary.

To my surprise, the editor entrusted me with a camera and assigned me to cover the city's schools and my neighborhood. Eventually, I became a columnist. One of my favorite stories that I shared with readers involved our inflatable kayak on one of Bethlehem's historic canals and an unrelated dentist appointment, with my oldest son, Jacob, finding the common thread and christening the boat "The Root Canal."

In 2010, after a day spent walking through the downtown looking for holiday gifts to the tune of piped-in music of seasonal favorites—"O Christmas tree, O Christmas tree, how lovely are your branches!"—I arrived home to a message from the editor. He asked me to write something for Hanukkah about Bethlehem's Jewish community. I had converted to Judaism a few years after marrying my Jewish husband, and we'd been attending services at the local synagogue and become members there. I agreed to the assignment.

After visiting a man in his 90s who grew up in Bethlehem, it seemed the story would focus on how there had once been a group of thriving Jewish-owned shops on the South Side of Bethlehem. For me, this history came as a surprise. By the time I had arrived in Bethlehem, the South Side evidenced poverty and empty storefronts. This was the aftermath of the demise in the 1980s and '90s of Bethlehem Steel—for years the city's main employer—and the growth of suburban malls.

"Part of the Fabric of Our City" ran on the front page on the first of December. After organizing my notes into a slim file folder, it was time to move on. But then, what had started as a newspaper article became a lot more than that as my first interviewees referred me to others in the community, prompting me into the "snowball" method of researching. I decided to take a closer look at this community to see if there was a deeper story. Plus, something about the people drew me to them.

As my younger sons entered their grade school years, I spent hours sitting with people in their kitchens, listening to their stories, and chronicling their lives. Some recollections, they said, were "off the record," and I always honored that. These new acquaintances welcomed me into their homes, sharing lore like threads running through generations: arrivals, departures, life in times that were hard for this country, and forging the bonds of community.

I sensed that I was looking for something, but I wasn't sure what. Born in the 1960s, I had noticed the shift away from joining religious and secular institutions by people my age and younger. At the same time, I was raising three young people born in the late 1990s and early 2000s. We were at the beginning of the digital age and increasing social isolation, whether by choice or not. America had long since cycled through the age of anxiety, the subject of W. H. Auden's famous 1947 poem, to the age of depression. Now, evident in many in the 2000s, anxiety was resurging. Would any of us someday tell the kinds of stories of resilience and finding connection that I was hearing?

At the same time, my husband and I intended to someday pay for college. Once Jacob reached middle school, I felt I had to say no to further pursuing this project and return to the workforce in a more substantial way. In 2012, on the strength of being "in town for the day," I secured an appointment at a movie studio in a nearby city. My wish was for a job; my hope was for one that would build out my writing practice, still in its infancy. That visit set me on a path I hadn't yet imagined.

The morning of the appointment, I discovered the studio had recently moved into a gothic-style former church. The young man who greeted me at the front doors led me up a narrow, spiral staircase toward the second floor's once-sacred space. I'd seen churches turned into restaurants, apartments, even an accounting firm (the irony!), but here was something new. In the second-story office, rows of computer monitors held more young men spellbound, their eyes fixed on glowing screens. The producer at the heart of it all greeted me with a smile more like that of a movie star. We sat at his desk in the center of the massive work room.

"We have people with credits a mile long trying to get in here," he said. "What are your credits?" Well, mine were a string of $15 stories for the *Press*. Although the producer was kind, even encouraging, I still walked out of there feeling disappointed.

I had just been privy to a raft of talented individuals at work telling stories of real people. The problem was, this required a lot of technology, all foreign to me, and as noted, I had very little experience. But something clicked in my mind on the drive home: Almost anyone could pick up a pen and record a story; in fact, I already had. It came to me that there must be something here in the project I'd seemingly put on hold, I just needed to understand what I was looking at ... and beginning to find out for myself.

The more stories I collected and shared, the more I realized that the life stories of individuals are not only personal but also are threads that weave people into a larger tapestry. Bethlehem's Jewish community was small but tightly knit. Unlike some historic communities, it wasn't based primarily on family relationships; instead, feelings grew out of friendship and shared experiences. Of course, my job search needed to continue, but so did the story-gathering.

Then one afternoon I was chronicling the Bethlehem Jewish community as it was in the 1970s. My interviewees,

Henry and Isabel Schiff, were paging through a many-decades old "ad journal" from the synagogue, the cover of this combination annual fundraiser/congregational directory softened by time. The Schiffs even offered to lend their *Brith Sholom Ad Journal, 1971* to me. Their sharing and trust made me feel as though I were part of their family.

"We've been waiting for someone to do this," another community member, Edith Blinderman, said of my story-finding project. This was both good news and bad news; the stories and sometimes the archival materials of these generous souls were now in my hands and, seemingly, on my shoulders. What had started as (I thought) an oral history of the Jewish community of the Christmas City soon turned into an exploration of memory, culture, and belonging. The more I listened and researched, the more it became clear that people connect with one another through sharing their stories and being part of each other's stories.

After about 10 years of this, I had an "ah-ha moment" echoing the one famed mythologist Joseph Campbell experienced, which led to his 1949 book, *The Hero with a Thousand Faces*. Campbell had carried around James Joyce's novel *Ulysses*, studying the plot night and day, while also looking at creation stories, folk tales, and the like. Eventually Campbell realized, "They're all the same story!" Something like that happened to me, too, except the story I found in Bethlehem again and again was about belonging.

~

In Bethlehem, stories matter. The past is valued and talked about. The city's Moravian founders, a Christian sect, had a tradition of memoir writing they called *Lebenslauf*. Their archives now provide windows into the personal lives of thousands of their 18th- and 19th-century congregants that help us better understand those lives and their descendants today. Many secular traditions in Bethlehem relating to music and the arts span decades if not centuries.

This project also mapped to my roots in anthropology, which I'd studied in college. The works of pioneers like Ruth Benedict, Margaret Mead, and later Barbara Myerhoff show how culture, life story, and everyday life interact. My project opens a window into a particular place, group of people, and span of time through a collection of stories. It also charts how my life changed because of this story-gathering experience. The result is neither a scholarly historical analysis nor a study of small town (or city) Jewish life. Instead, my purpose is to faithfully share the lives and world of the people of this one community *as they see them*.

When I was a child, I learned from my grandma how to quilt. It seemed to me that the same process could work with storytelling. To discover the elements of this community's story, I pieced together the up close and personal life story narratives shared by the people of this place—a quilt of stories.

I wasn't an outsider, yet I wasn't fully inside either, and I doubted I ever would be. My birth family was far away. I had grown up in another religion. This Jewish community and this city valued long-time residence. Yet, reminiscent of Meyerhoff describing a Jewish senior center, I am of the same culture in some ways.

Like Zora Neale Hurston, another of my anthropology (and writing) heroes, I was turning my gaze on what was close to me. She famously described working among her own people, Black Floridians, practicing an unfamiliar folk song, for example, until it became part of her. Similarly, the more I immersed myself in this project, the more the community's story became my own.

For every person I spoke with, there are probably three more that I did not get to interview. So this is one way to tell the story, and I had lots of help. The nearly 100 people I interviewed were more than just *participants* in this project. They were my *collaborators* on a story that wasn't mine alone;

nor was it theirs alone. In fact, no one person could offer even a semblance of the full story. So they opened their lives and hearts. They didn't dictate; they encouraged me to find the story that wanted telling.

Although I gathered many more stories than would ever be practical to publish, and I love them all, this book shares a century of stories, lives, and community—from the 1890s to the 1990s. Many of the people interviewed were in the final years of their lives. Now they "belong to the ages" because they've passed on. For some people in the Jewish community of the Christmas City, sharing their stories with me became their parting gifts. Now it's my honor and privilege to share them with you.

The Star of Bethlehem shining from South Mountain, overlooking
Main Street, Bethlehem, Pennsylvania, 2008. Photo by and (c)2008
to Derek Ramsey (Ram-Man), GFDL 1.2, via Wikimedia Commons.
Used with permission.

Chapter 2
"Above Thy Deep and Dreamless Sleep"
Meeting at the Crossroads

One Sunday morning of April 1893 in South Bethlehem, 500 Christian men skipped church and gathered in the street to witness something never before seen in this town. Already dressed in their best black suits, the men noted the undertaker's horse and carriage standing in the street outside the Gilles home. Inside, the undertaker Mister Kinney sat idle in the front room. This being a Jewish home, his presence was a mere formality. In keeping with the family's religious practices, he wouldn't be allowed to participate in the washing of the deceased or any other preparation for the burial of Yehoshua Gilles, the now-departed head of household and father to several grown children.

At half past 11 a.m., pallbearers carried their burden through the front door and down to the street. The Widow Gilles and her daughters followed. In front of them gaped the 500 townsmen. Soon enough, however, the funeral carriage, its burden set in place and the double rear doors firmly shut, creaked into motion. Slowly, it rolled past dirt-hewn side streets. At every boarding house and inn along the way, pipe-smoking men spilled out of windows thrown open to the mild spring day. Curiosity overcame the better angels of all who heard, "It's the first Hebrew burial, come and see!"

The horse proved up to the task of climbing the long, muddied hill, with the cortege coming to a stop on the road immediately below those acres in which previous generations of Bethlemites already rested. The various denominational sections of the burial ground lay separated only by low fences over which a man could easily step and under which animals could and did burrow. As the walkers merged with those already assembled to watch the grave digging, Fountain Hill cemetery became "black with people." There were at least 1,000 observers on hand, the *Bethlehem Times* later reported, adding, "It took from 12 to 2 to complete the grave and the last funeral rites. Several men of about the same height as the deceased lay down to see if [the grave] were long enough." (Source: "Burial Ceremonies of Mr. Gilles")

The body was then laid to rest "like Sir John Moore, simply in its shroud"—a reference to a British military officer, thereby sanctioning the simplicity of this typical Jewish burial. However, what happened next received a less refined description and one deeply in error: "A bowl of the blood of a lamb was on hand. Part of this was sprinkled over the corpse and the rest poured into the foot of the grave." Meanwhile, the throngs grew increasingly unruly. "Several times the vulgar curiosity of the crowd overcame their good behavior and their crush was so great as to interfere seriously with the work of the burial. They were ordered away but would not leave until the ceremony was over.... There was a good deal of talk about the funeral [the next] morning. The Christians who didn't go to church out of curiosity to attend it exploited (made a good story of) what they saw."

The newspaper account not only captured the rowdiness of the crowd but also perpetuated a dangerous piece of misinformation: Pogroms would have been happening at exactly this time of year in Europe, when Passover and the Christians' Easter coincided. These state-sanctioned murderous outbreaks were fueled by false but pervasive ideas about the making of the Passover matzah, replicating the bread that did not have time to rise when Moses led the Jews from Egypt. Pogroms were violent rampages in which non-Jews brutally attacked and even killed their Jewish neighbors. In Europe, pogroms had been happening for eons, and in turn-of-the-century Russia, worse times were just ahead.

Most of the Jews who survived these onslaughts and emigrated to the United States were so traumatized that they refused to talk to their own children and grandchildren about what they witnessed or even where they had come from. One who did, however, was Irving Berlin, a Jewish immigrant from Russia and composer of some of the best loved selections in the American songbook, including "God Bless America" and "Dreaming of a White Christmas." Though known for stirring nostalgia, his earliest memory was of watching from a ditch in Russia while his village was burned to the ground.

The *Times'* mistaken narrative would have reawakened trauma among the Jewish immigrants. So a few days later, the following description of a letter penned by Yehoshua's son, Max, appeared in the newspaper, "The funeral had been in accordance with the old-fashioned Orthodox method and had been correctly described by the *Times*. Only the blood was his poor father's own blood, taken from him by doctors in their efforts to save him. Since it was part of himself, it had to be poured into the grave with him, where it belonged. Mr. Gilles thanked the people for the interest taken in the funeral, which the family construed to be respectful and kindly. The money [donated] was given to the poor...." (Source: "The Late Josiah Gilles")

Such details of the funeral magnify the importance that attended "the first full-fledged Jewish funeral ceremony in this town." Would the Christian townsmen under any other circumstance have been so very interested in the sendoff of this proprietor of a tea shop located on the Philadelphia Pike (now Wyandotte Street)? Nor did this represent the sudden discovery that there were Jews in the town. On the contrary, there was widespread awareness because of a recent series of articles detailing the infighting of some of the town's Jews. No, this funeral represented something else altogether.

Writer and social critic bell hooks, who eschewed capitalization of her pen name, described the significance of the earth itself in her writings about belonging to her native Kentucky. She valued a connection with nature and the physical attributes of a place, right down to a familiarity with its dirt. A Black woman who grew up in the Southern United States in the 1950s, she described her home state, where she experienced such a connection with nature, as the only place where she felt "a true sense of belonging." (Source: hooks, page 58)

In the Bible, Abraham purchases a cave for his wife Sarah's final resting place in a land where he is at the same time invited to settle. Years later, in Egypt, their grandson Jacob extracts a promise from his son Joseph to bury him in that same land of their forefathers. This is not unusual. Around the world, one of the hallmarks of belonging to a place is having ancestors buried there. Belonging begins to take root.

~

One hundred twenty years later, Herb Gilles heard of this project and shared what he had uncovered of the story of his great-grandfather Yehoshua Gilles's life in Bethlehem. Herb also shared his personal story: He had returned to this city from Philadelphia where he was born and raised. Herb arrived in Bethlehem in the 1960s to work as a chemical engineer, first at the company Air Products and then at Bethlehem Steel.

"We always knew from the time I was little that my great-grandparents were here," Herb said. It was possible for Herb to piece together his family story, set in the 19th century, because a new technology had been in play—the daily newspaper. The era in which Yehoshua's multi-part story was chronicled in print for all to read saw an explosion in ways to communicate. There was a sevenfold increase in daily newspapers. These papers described events in language that locals found highly readable and even entertaining. (Source: Schlereth, page 182) Decades prior to the advent of radio, let alone television, and a century before the Internet in people's homes, daily newspapers peered into the personal lives of the people written up in its pages in detailed fine print, the Victorian version of social media.

In writing his letter to the newspaper, Max Gilles embraced and made use of that new technology. He took up the mantle of leadership of this little band of Jews; he spoke to the townspeople in their language, that of newsprint. Max's action not only explained his father's burial but also conveyed his hope that it was possible to influence whether and how much someone belongs to a place. His carefully worded letter to the newspaper set a conciliatory tone because he, too, was now vested in Bethlehem.

Max's letter indicated a new status of the Jews of Bethlehem, one that was a little more polished and self-possessed than newspaper readers had previously witnessed. As evidence of what came before, Herb gave me photocopies of articles published by the *Times* in 1891-93. In contrast to Max's poise, these accounts showed not one but *two* small groups of Jews trying desperately—and fitfully—to cleave into one.

~

Though usually a quiet man, Herb Gilles radiated enthusiasm about what came to light when he and his brother, Barry, looked into the family history. Herb was a scientist who evaluated data with care, and he had found sources worth taking seriously. It turned out that two years before the funeral described above, Yehoshua, Max, and others had raised $72 in donations and founded a synagogue called Talmud Torah (various spellings given).

Yehoshua had immigrated from Lithuania in about 1870 and settled in South Bethlehem sometime in the intervening

20 years. He served on a synagogue board of trustees, its governing body. Meanwhile, a different group of Jews founded "Breeth Sholam" (Hebrew for Covenant of Peace, later spelled Brith Sholom).

Those two groups didn't coexist easily. Appearing under the headline "From Rival Synagogues," a February 25, 1892, article opens, "Two score of Jews packed themselves into Squire Krauskopf's office yesterday afternoon." The squire was a magistrate; at issue was a business dispute involving a Russian Jew named Smerrien, whom the paper portrayed as "rather accomplished and well educated," a woolen mill agent "who came to America on account of the persecution suffered by his race."

Smerrien was suing a man named Adleman for $90 over a breach of contract regarding goods to be purchased and sold. The article goes on, "The Adleman crowd say it is a malicious prosecution," because Adleman had previously served an eviction notice on Smerrien. The story closed, "The religious prejudices of the Jews entered into the case. The plaintiff belongs to the Breeth Sholam Congregation and the defendant and his crowd to the Tolmuth Thur [sic]."

Then there is this from May 2, 1892, nearly a year before Yehoshua's passing: "The South Bethlehem Hebrews have buried their animosities and merged into one congregation." Yehoshua was identified as a leader in this effort. By April 3 of the following year, however, the two groups had again split; the newspaper indicates that they celebrated Passover at separate locations. Two weeks later, Yehoshua was dead of heart disease. Ironically, the alarming press coverage may even have had a role in bringing the Jewish congregations together again. There's nothing quite like a perceived threat to pull a group together. As British and diaspora Israeli sociologist Nira Yuval-Davis wrote, "The emotional components of people's construction of themselves and their identities become more central the more threatened and less secure they become." (Source: Yuval-Davis, page 14)

The two congregations united into one, dubbed Brith Sholom Talmud Torah Congregation, which continued as its name until the mid-1920s. Services were held for the first few years in Sloyer's Hall on the Philadelphia Pike, aided by the arrival of Reverend Isaac Gershon Resc (later referred to as "Rabbi Reis"), who also served as *shochet* (one who ensures meat is kosher). Coming together was a process and one that could not be accomplished single-handedly. This took years and started with these Jews' forebears across the river in the *other* of "the two Bethlehems" (there were originally Bethlehem and South Bethlehem) which also later merged into one.

Coming Together: Early German Jewish Settlers and the 1897 Synagogue

Several German Jews preceded Yehoshua and his Eastern European contemporaries and laid the foundations of community and belonging. They lived mainly on what is now the North Side of Bethlehem and set up shops in both Bethlehems. Rabbi William Frankel chronicled this early community in the *Brith Sholom Ad Journal, 1955*:

> There were Ferdinand Reis and Adolph Reis, who operated a men's clothing store at 73 S. Main Street, 1873 to 1877. Lewis Reis, brother of Ferdinand and Adolph, bought the store in 1877 and married Miss Tillie Friedman of Philadelphia. Judah Salomon owned a men's store selling hats, caps, and clothing, located at 111 S. Main St., Bethlehem, and is mentioned for the first time in the 1883 [city] directory. In the 1870s, he was permitted to bury his child in the Easton Hebrew Cemetery.

This was pre-childhood vaccines. Killer epidemics were not unusual, and Bethlehem outbreaks included smallpox. The next time Judah and Alice Salomon went through the loss of a child, their seven-year-old year old Harry "was one of the first ones to be buried on the Brith Sholom Cemetery in Salisbury Township, now Fountain Hill"—no doubt much more quietly than Yehoshua's "full-fledged" interment a few years later.

Most of the North Side German Jews never affiliated with the new congregation established in South Bethlehem by the Eastern European Jews, who in the United States were typically looked down upon by German Jews as is well documented, but Rabbi Frankel wrote: "One German Jew, Isaac Price ... settled on the South Side. He married Miss Frances Salomon, youngest daughter of Judah Salomon, on January 2, 1887." Given the prevailing prejudices, the Prices' choice was remarkable.

Within a few years, the couple had two children, Berton and Alfred. This family had established more of a geographic connection with the Eastern European Jews by living in South Bethlehem. They also got involved in the building of the Brith Sholom Talmud Torah synagogue; however, Isaac died in 1898, just a year after the new building opened.

The "1897 Synagogue," as this early house of worship and communal gathering place came to be called, measured 46 by 31 feet and almost 30 feet in height. The main entrance was on Wood Street (now Carlton Avenue), with the cornerstone also being on Wood Street, near where it intersected with Walnut Street and bearing the inscription "Brith Sholom Talmud Torah, 1897." A distinctive feature of the building, though not unusual for a synagogue, hinted at its fraught history: *Two* domes topped the building.

For the July 1897 cornerstone-laying, Adolf Friedman of the congregation planned to give the speech, but he had a cold so his brother David gave the speech for him—in

German. The German Jews spoke the language, and many of the Eastern European Jews would have spoken Yiddish, a related language. Likewise, many of the local non-Jews were Pennsylvania Dutch, descendants of German immigrants and a major ethnic group in the region that also spoke a dialect of German. It seemed that German would do just fine for most.

According to an article published by the congregation years later, the day following the cornerstone-laying, the *Bethlehem Globe* newspaper opened its coverage of the story with the words, "The antisemitic propaganda of recent years has evidently not affected the Bethlehems, for the large audience at the ceremonies yesterday afternoon was composed of Christians as well as Jews."

The "1897 Synagogue," as it is still remembered today, although the photo might have been taken in the early 1900s—note the utility pole in the foreground.

In the press coverage, it was noted that "a policeman kept the crowd from pouring into" the area and "the absence of Hebrew women was especially noticeable, only two or three attending." As with Yehoshua's funeral, few Jewish women ventured into this crowded, chaotic public scene. But at least one young Jewish woman in Bethlehem during this decade alternately searched out and created ways to take an active part and belong in her community. I learned about this young woman more than a century after her arrival in Bethlehem.

The Jewish Rapunzel

When a 2013 rabbi search committee needed a chairperson, Steve Bergstein's name soon surfaced, and he accepted the weighty responsibility. He had previously agreed to talk with me about the story of his great-grandmother, whom he knew and spent time with into his college years. She had immigrated to Bethlehem as a teenager in the late 1800s with her parents Morris and Suzy Glasawitzki and seven siblings. But when I met with Steve in his law office in nearby Allentown, my first question had to do with his chairmanship of the search committee.

"Why you?" I asked.

"I'm old," Steve quipped, then offered what to him seemed a more plausible answer, familiar to anyone who volunteers regularly, that he was "there" and "willing." Steve got it right the first time. Although he was not old in the sense of age, he was old in the way that matters most to Bethlehem's Jewish and general populations: Several generations of his family had lived in or near the area. Of course, I was also there that day to learn more about his great-grandmother. This quest led me to the home of Steve's mother, Marilyn Bergstein.

I sat with Marilyn in the living room of her apartment in neighboring Allentown. Behind her on the wall was a large photo portrait of an elderly Jewish lady with a radiant smile of childlike joy. That was Rachel.

Rachel "Ray" Glasawitzki Cohn: From Marilyn Bergstein

My grandmother was the Jewish Rapunzel. She never cut her hair in her life. When she took it down, it would go to the floor. I probably knew my grandmother better than any of the other grandchildren, and this I know: She was born in 1874 in that part of Poland that was always switching [being seized first by one nation-state and then another].... My grandmother was the oldest and had several siblings. Her youngest sister was Winnie, and they were very close. They came to the US when my grandmother was 12 or 13 years old and they lived in Bethlehem near the steel company.... As a teen, my grandmother served as a kosher meat runner for the Jews of Bethlehem. She would get on a streetcar—that was what she called it—and go to Philadelphia. She was small but feisty and would bring back kosher meat because most of the Jews who came over were very observant. As time went on in the US, she never once changed her allegiance to Judaism or observances or made exceptions. She was pretty rigid. However, she did change her name.

Shortly after they arrived in Bethlehem, my grandmother's mother died very suddenly. Her father remarried soon after. My grandmother was about 17 years old by then. She did not get along with her stepmother and was looking for a way out. Her way out would be to get married. My *zayde* (grandpa) was 25 years older than she was. He had a hardware and mining supply business in Hazleton [in the nearby Pocono Mountains, coal country]. Someone arranged for them to meet. His name was Jacob Cohn.

My grandmother signed her checks "Ray." I remember very, very vaguely when she was naturalized, so I must have been a really little kid when she went to take her test. She never really learned how to spell; she taught herself. When I think about what she did ... Her husband, my grandfather, died, leaving her with five little kids!

All of my cousins and I—there were nine of us—got a charge out of talking with my grandmother because it was like an education. She wanted her kids to speak English. When she spoke Yiddish or Polish, they would ask her, "Why don't you tell me what that means?" and she said, "No, in America, you have to speak English."

She was very charitable, very selfless. She saved every penny and never kept it for herself. You could have picked up her personal belongings in one hand. She was the first to get in line for giving to Hadassah (a Jewish women's organization supporting hospitals and summer camps) or anything Jewish. It was kind of ingrained in her. She had no patience with people who didn't give as she did.

She always raved about the fact that she'd seen the complete evolution in transportation, from horse and buggy to cars to a man on the moon, which happened right before she died. In her later years, she visited her cousin who was a gadget lover and had a tape recorder. The cousin said, "Don't say anything until I tell you." Then the cousin turned on the tape recorder and started asking my grandmother questions. The cousin replayed the tape, and my *bubbe* (grandma, Ray) sat there absolutely silent. Finally, she asked, "So who is the lady with the accent?"

Rachel "Ray" Glasawitzki Cohn, circa 1960s
Contributed photo.

Growing a Sense of Belonging

Like the German-speakers at the cornerstone-laying, Ray's story shows how people can *both* be who they are *and* belong with the other people around them. Ray accepted and used technology like the streetcar in ways that enhanced belonging—even if the technology was not fully understood. Max Gilles did the same thing in writing to the newspaper.

Researcher Elspeth Probyn wrote about how movement, being, and longing are all part of belonging. That's evidenced in these stories, for sure. But these Bethlehem stories go further. The activity, building, and doing of these early individuals actually seem to have driven belonging for whole groups of people. They were the tip of a very big iceberg; more than that, they had a choice to help other people, and they did.

Ray's story is just one of many because, between 1880 and 1924, some two and a half million Eastern European Jews came to the United States. Life in Europe had become increasingly difficult throughout that time due to poverty and pogroms, which reached their height in Russia between 1903 and 1906. While the majority of Jewish immigrants in this period remained in New York, about 25 percent were like the Glasawitskis in that they moved to outlying areas such as Bethlehem or the rest of the country, where they were a very slim percentage of the population. Today Jews number about two percent of the US population. Those who came to Bethlehem around the turn of the century arrived individually or as families, with many of the men at first working as peddlers in rural areas. One of them was Morris Black.

Going Strong: Morris Black and Sons

Sometimes connectedness and a sense of belonging happen as naturally as the next step in a dance. Morris Black arrived from the east, not yet married, with a pack of goods on his back. In Bethlehem, he established a building supplies store. Today, Morris Black and Sons, a company that has grown and changed over the years, is still going strong. In a 2011 interview in his home, Morris's grandson Ron Black of Bethlehem, said, "My grandfather was one of the founders [of the 1920s iteration of Brith Sholom] in Bethlehem. He was bar mitzvahed on the boat. His older brother Ike came first and brought his brothers and sisters in 1898. His father, Eli, and mother, Nellie, arrived here, settling in [nearby] Easton, where the Jewish community had gotten its start in the 1830s. That's where Morris met his wife, Rebecca Perleman, at a synagogue dance. She came with her sister; they rode in a wagon for a weekend to spend with friends and family. It was between 1905 and 1908. [Morris and Rebecca] moved to the South Side of Bethlehem, under the Hill-to-Hill Bridge. Later they moved to 7th and Prospect to raise their three sons, Benjamin, Samuel, and Leonard."

Ron's wife, Linda, said, "Bethlehem has been a wonderful place to raise children. [For me,] coming from Philadelphia, this was a step back in time; it was a culture shock. But I got used to how comfortable it was. Before, I would never have thought to take a walk around the block... This was a great community to come to; the Sisterhood was active; there was a gymnasium on the South Side. I used to drop the kids off and go up to the kitchen. The luncheons! The girls went out of their way with the food, the entertainment, the cultural activities. Though getting more children into the community has been the problem."

"There's been a big turnover here. I'm one of the few left," Ron said, referring to his cohorts born and raised in Bethlehem, the remaining grandchildren of turn-of-the-century immigrants.

Linda said, "This is 'O Little Town of...' It was [such] a small town the first time Ron brought me here and drove into Bethlehem. I asked, 'Where's the downtown?' He said, 'That was it.'"

Linda's comment was memorable because she was the first of many people in this project to hint that living in the Christmas City has a particular meaning to its Jewish population.

From the Bethlehem artist and printer, J. Carroll Tobias. "Christmas Lighting-Hill to Hill Bridge," Lehigh University Postcard Collection, [LUPC0317], Special Collections, Linderman Library, Lehigh University, Bethlehem, Pa. Reprinted with permission.

Leaving Europe Behind: Leon Roth

For some, the journey to belonging is nowhere near as smooth as a ride through town. The Roth family immigrated in the 1930s and established themselves in the construction industry with the help of Morris Black. That was harder than it sounds. Leon Roth recalled his family's struggles in a speech for his "second bar mitzvah," held at Brith Sholom.

What follows is excerpted from his speech, which Leon had mailed to my friend Betty Diamond. It is shared with permission of his daughter Karen Kuhn, whom I reached by phone on the seventh anniversary *(yahrzeit)* of Leon's passing.

Leon was born in 1916 in the Carpathian Mountain area of Czechoslovakia. "I did not enjoy childhood," Leon said in his speech. Each year, beginning at age six, he traveled with a group of boys to one of "about six different towns for *cheder*" (the "ch" is pronounced as a guttural h) as religious school was known at the time—likely the only form of schooling the boys ever received.

"There were only three Jewish families in our village, and there was no *cheder* there," Leon said. "We poor boys went to a village with boys from three or four other villages. A *melamed* (Hebrew for teacher) was hired to teach us. The teacher was usually a youngster of about 20. He was not a good *melamed* unless he used a stick to hit the students. [At night,] I slept with one family, but I ate in a different home every day. That was called *essen teg* (Yiddish for eat a day). I ate only if the family had food. Most of all, I remember the hunger and the cold."

Leon was the ninth of two boys and 11 girls, four of whom died as babies from simple childhood diseases. The family had no electricity, running water, or even changes of clothing. Leon said, "If we had shoes, we wore them only in the winter. My parents had it very hard; what they endured is beyond description, but most important to them was to teach their children to be a *mensch* (Yiddish for a good, down-to-earth person) and share or give to the poor or to anyone who was in need. Their motto was, 'Don't wait to be asked for help; offer.' As poor as we were, my parents took in orphans. They refused to talk about their hardships."

When the opportunity arose, Leon's father immigrated to America. Just before Leon's 13th birthday, his father returned to Czechoslovakia for a visit. It was then, in a village called Hostovice, that Leon became a bar mitzvah—a little early because his father was going back to America in 1928. Two years later, in December of 1930, Leon, his mother, and siblings followed. "We arrived in New York on January 1, 1931," Leon said. "Sometimes words can be hopelessly inadequate. The adjustment was not easy."

Leon's father brought the family to Bethlehem, where, when Leon was a young man, "Mr. Morris Black gave me credit unlimited, as I had nothing when I started the masonry business. Mr. Black knew my father well. I remember him pressing his little finger and saying, 'If you are that much like your father, I will give you anything you want.'" Leon went on to earn the respect of his Jewish and non-Jewish business associates and customers.

Leon married Lila, whom he credits with helping him become "a complete *mensch*." He said, "She never complained about helping our parents, especially my parents. We had very little ourselves, but we shared it. That is something we learned from our wonderful parents. We did without, but we did not wait to be asked." The couple had two daughters and later several grandchildren. Leon's mother-in-law lived with the family for nearly 13 years. Of that time, he said simply, "I was fortunate to have two beautiful women in my home."

As Leon explained in his speech, "The Biblical lifespan of a person is three score and 10 years. Since I have lived 13 years longer than 70, age 83 is time for my second bar mitzvah." Leon closed his speech with the words, "God bless America."

Manufacturing a Sweet Success Story: Sam Born

For still others, belonging happens by invitation. Around the time Leon Roth arrived in the United States, Sam Born and his brothers-in-law Jack and Irv Shaffer moved the Just Born Candy Company from Brooklyn, New York, to Bethlehem. The company had started in chocolates, about which Sam had learned the hard way. In the early 1900s, Sam, who was brilliant from the start, traveled at a young age from his birthplace in Ukraine to study at Berdychiv, one of the premier *yeshivas* (Jewish theological seminaries). His son Bob, who was age 86 at the time we first spoke, said, "I'll give you stories of the man after whom I try to model my life. He died at 69; I'm a little older than that now, but I would still like to be as good as he was." What Bob shared shows the complexity of belonging. The social fabric includes not only the community in which someone lives and the ways they earn a living, but also the family into which they are born or otherwise join.

"After my father finished at Berdychiv, he went home to Vinnytsia in Ukraine," Bob said. "When he got there, he heard that the tsar's army was going around recruiting Jewish bootblacks.... He had no inclination to shine any Russian officer's boots, so he paid as much as he possibly could to a chap on the underground railroad, who spirited him out of Ukraine. He got as far as Paris and then he ran out of money. He was dead broke."

In Paris, Sam got a job at a candy factory. Factories were on the rise, though major efforts to increase efficiency were still in their infancy. Sam's employer gave him a paddle for mixing batches of candy, and Sam used it.

Bob said, "What he learned about making candy, you could put under one fingernail. But he was able to eat and to squirrel away some money, with the ultimate goal of getting to America. He knew quite a few languages: Russian, Polish, Yiddish, Hebrew, Italian, and now French. The only language he didn't know was English. He had arrived in the United States in 1910 at the age of 19 to discover that there was a glut of Russian rabbis in the communities here. They didn't need any [more]."

Sam noticed a number of little candy factories around New York with Jewish owners. "Them he could communicate with," Bob said. "So he went around to them saying, 'I am a candy consultant. What I do is this: If you have a problem and I help you, you pay me. If I don't help, then you don't compensate me.' All right. This was agreeable. So he went to a factory and they said, 'We have a problem with our fudge. It's too soft.'

"'Fudge.' He had never heard this word. He went to the factory, and it was too soft, and he couldn't help them. Again and again at the factories, the fudge was too soft. 'Sorry, I can't help you.' At the fourth factory, the fudge was too hard. That night, he ate!

"He had put two and two together and made five. He [had] learned the trade and [so] started out across the country, to Chicago and on from there. One year later, he was in San Francisco, and the mayor was giving him the keys to the city and making him an honorary member for [inventing] the first automatic lollipop machine."

Sam went back to New York and set up his business serving candy, pastries, and tea in the front of the shop and making the goodies in the back. "Soon, he had five of these places," Bob explained. "To manage the finances, he hired a lawyer, who disappeared after five months, taking the money with him. People told Sam he would have to file for bankruptcy. But he didn't." He just worked harder and smarter than ever before. "My father, he couldn't get it through his thick Jewish skull that one day, you owe people money, and the next day, you owe nothing," Bob said. "So he worked at making candy, and one year later, he paid back 100 cents on the dollar.

"Now Bethlehem had 400 people from a closed-up candy company out of work, mostly women who had been hand-dipping the chocolates," Bob said. "The mayor was looking for a way to fill [the factory space], Avondale Dairies was looking for a chocolate maker [because chocolate makers purchase a lot of milk], and PP&L [Pennsylvania Power and Light] was looking for another customer. They [or their representatives] found my father in Brooklyn."

Then-Bethlehem Mayor Robert Pfeifle courted the company, and the time seemed right to go from a smaller operation in New York to a factory in Bethlehem. "The thing that made the difference is that there was rail service that came right to the factory," according to a family member. "The raw ingredients could be brought right here. At that time, a lot of chocolate manufacturers—and we were one— came to the East coast because of the dairy cows [on nearby farms]."

In 1932, Sam moved to the Bethlehem/Allentown area with his family, including his brother-in-law, Jack Shaffer, establishing Just Born candy company in Bethlehem. Sam's other brother-in-law, Irv Shaffer, "stayed put in New York [but continued to be involved]," Bob said. "They were a triumvirate 'til I got into the act. Then it was the four of us. That's the story."

~

Over the years in Bethlehem, these families and others became able to help the Jewish community grow and also to benefit other people in the city. As Bob's son, Ross Born, said, "We believe that a strong and successful business requires a strong and successful community. They go hand-in-hand, which is a good reason for us to care about the health and vibrancy of our Lehigh Valley community."

Those early immigrants and their descendants became givers and not just receivers of the bounty because what started as a will to survive grew into the ability to contribute to others. They belonged, both in the Jewish community and Bethlehem, and in the Lehigh Valley at large.

Among 100 or so of Bethlehem's "men prominent in the commercial, professional, political, and social activity of Bethlehem" in the 1918 publication, "Men of Bethlehem" were at least two Jews. Furniture store proprietor Theodore Goodman and "one of the leading businessmen" Abraham Refowich were featured along with the likes of Charles Schwab (Bethlehem Steel founder), Eugene Grace (eventual and longtime President of Bethlehem Steel), and Archibald Johston (first mayor of Bethlehem). Courtesy of the Bethlehem Area Public Library.

Chapter 3
"Campanas de Belén" (Bells of Bethlehem)
Becoming Us

Like us, the land we live on constantly shifts toward or away from belonging. Some 500 to 300 million years ago, the world's ancient continents collided to form the supercontinent Pangaea. From deep in the Earth rose the Central Pangea Mountains. Weathering and geological events gradually separated parts of these mountains and opened a great divide between them—the Atlantic Ocean. The once-united range continued to drift apart. As a result, today we have, on one side of the water, the Scottish Highlands and on another, the Atlas Mountains in northeastern Africa. On the North American side, we have the Appalachian Mountains that step down like a clamshell to the eastern seaboard of the United States. In one part of that clamshell is a minor impression bounded by the Blue Mountains to the north and South Mountain at the other end, cradling Bethlehem.

These are the generations on the land that is now Bethlehem; it will be a story familiar to many peoples. The Lenni Lenape people speak of migrating to the land that is now Eastern Pennsylvania, and beyond to the east coast of today's New Jersey 10,000 years ago. The tribal name means "Men of Men" and "Original People." They traveled for generations and "finally they came to the land where the sun rose, and they knew it was their home." (Source: Alexander)

After maybe 500 generations, in the mid-1600s, Swedish, Finn, and Dutch fur traders arrived. The Lenape blended the new arrivals into their society through marriage and trade. But this could only work for so long. More waves of settlers arrived, eventually changing the way the land was seen and used.

In 1682, William Penn arrived with a land grant from the faraway king of England. Penn encouraged newcomers, offering freedom of religion for "everybody who believed in God." (Source: www.ushistory.org). In line with his Quaker beliefs about fairness, he apparently sought to purchase the granted land, a process he started via a treaty, though one he never finalized.

Meanwhile, Penn's invitation brought many English, Welsh, Dutch Quakers, and French Huguenots to the colony. German-speaking Mennonites, Amish, and Lutherans from Catholic German states immigrated; collectively, they came to be known as the "Pennsylvania Dutch." The early promise of religious freedom might even have brought one Jew.

View of Bethlehem–A Moravian Settlement, Published Dec. 29, 1798. The artist Isaac Weld includes himself in the drawing, at lower left. Used with the permission of Historic Urban Plans, Inc., Ithaca, New York.

But in 1741, it was the Moravians who founded the city of Bethlehem. They were a Christian sect originating in the historic country of Bohemia, for a time controlled by Prussia and now part of the Czech Republic. On Christmas Eve of that year, some of these founding Moravians crowded into a manger to recall the first Christmas. At that moment, their visiting Saxon benefactor Count Nicholas von Zinzendorf named the settlement "Bethlehem."

"The Moravians' mode was one of hard work and self-reliance, of taking care of their own," said Rabbi Jonathan Porath, who lived in Bethlehem as a child in the 1950s.

"The Moravians have a history of being open to diverse groups," said Ann Goldberg, who taught in Bethlehem's public schools. "They coexisted with native peoples, although they may have tried to convert them."

Jerry Hausman of Bethlehem also shared that back in the 1700s there was a Swede with a name that "sounds Jewish." Isaac Martens Ysselstyn and his wife, Rachel, built up a farm on land that later became the South Side site of Union Station and Bethlehem Steel (Source: Frankel). In the 1950s, Rabbi William Frankel investigated the frequency of the names Isaac and Rachel historically in Sweden. Finding they were little used, he wrote that the couple could have been Jewish. The Moravians called Ysselstyn "a friend" (Source: Levering), suggesting that he was not one of them but that his ways were compatible with their own. When Isaac died, Rachel and her daughters joined the Moravians.

That was not a peaceful time because in 1737, William Penn's sons Richard and Thomas decided with others to finalize that land purchase their father had initiated. In it, the Lenape had agreed to relinquish the amount of land a man could walk in a day and a half. However, the brothers hired three fast runners and obtained close to 1,000 square miles in the Eastern portion of what is now Pennsylvania. This was further extended in the surveyors' subsequent maps to cover

1.2 million acres. This maneuver was viewed as spurring violence between the Lenape and the Moravians and other European settlers and, ultimately, the French and Indian War of the 1750s. The Lenape lost the land they had lived on for so long. Many in the tribe either moved or were moved, except for those Homeland tribal members who remained and still live in the area. (Source: Alexander)

Pennsylvania then came to fill a pivotal role as one of the 13 colonies of Britain, with the Declaration of Independence being signed in the state and as home to the Liberty Bell, so named in 1839 by abolitionists in recognition that there was freedom for some but not yet for all. The bell was housed in the Lehigh Valley during the 1777 British occupation of Philadelphia. Pennsylvania became a state in 1787, the second to ratify the US Constitution. All this and more is part of the cultural legacy of the people who today live in Bethlehem.

View of the Lehigh Valley. South Bethlehem Historical Postcard Collection, [SCMS 0250], Special Collections, Linderman Library, Lehigh University, Bethlehem, PA, 1907.

By the mid-1800s, Bethlehem's canals and railroads made the area an attractive place to establish businesses. After several iterations in the second half of the 19th century, in 1904 a company that began as an ironworks became Bethlehem Steel Corporation. Known to many as "the Steel," the company was a top steel producer, second only to US Steel in Pittsburgh, and the top shipbuilder in the country.

To accomplish its mission, the Steel hired laborers from around the world. They came from Lithuania, Hungary, Czechoslovakia, Poland, Ireland, and Italy to join the Pennsylvania Dutch. Some Jewish men from these same countries also worked at the Steel. Workers settled with their families in the surrounding town, which was rapidly filling with people yet had an overall amicable atmosphere as its inhabitants all looked to make better lives for themselves and their children. And it all depended on the rising fortunes of the Steel.

Furnaces, Bethlehem Steel Works, South Bethlehem, Pa., undated. Lehigh University Postcard Collection, [WPC WPC0201], Special Collections, Linderman Library, Lehigh University, Bethlehem, Pa. (1–). (n.d.). (1–).

Several Jewish merchants who peddled their wares in Eastern Pennsylvania found enough of a customer base to open retail shops in Bethlehem or nearby cities or towns. Some, like Morris Black, Leon Roth, and Rachel Cohn of the previous chapter came directly to Pennsylvania from Eastern Europe. Others, like Aaron Potruch and Sarah Phillips, who appear later in this chapter, stopped off for a time in New York. An exception was Martin Schwalb, who came to Bethlehem via Mexico.

Bethlehem native Nevin Mindlin recalled, "My great-uncle Martin Schwalb owned a shop called The Hub. A relative had sent the family [in Europe] a visa two times. They sold off the first one for a doctor, then for the second there was a roof collapsing [so again they needed the money]. There wasn't going to be a third [chance]. So he went to Mexico instead, where he carried wood and water for a while. Then somebody spotted him some money for getting set up in Juarez. When he came to this country, he came as a Spanish-speaking Mexican citizen to Bethlehem."

Following the Great War and the Spanish flu pandemic of 1918-20, the new decade was a boom time for US cities. The Steel once again needed workers and the clang of its machinery and rumble of equipment could be heard far and wide. The historian M. Mark Stolarik found evidence that by 1917 there were 64 ethnic groups represented in Bethlehem's South Side. He writes that it was estimated that a third of the population was Irish, a third of German descent including Pennsylvania Dutch, and a third Eastern and Southern European.

Latinos from Mexico had begun arriving in South Bethlehem. Migrating Black Americans from Southern states also came in pursuit of jobs. (Source: Tatu) These new arrivals were assigned to the coke works, the worst of the Bethlehem Steel jobs, and to the blast furnaces. Immigrants from Puerto Rico arrived in later decades. The city's population grew from less than 13,000 in 1910 to more than 50,000 in 1920.

The Great Depression of the 1930s hit the city hard, however. Bethlehem needed a way back to its former sense of prosperity and felicity. In 1937, far into the bleak days of the Great Depression, a now unknown individual at the Bethlehem Chamber of Commerce declared, "Why not make Bethlehem, named at Christmas, the Christmas City for the entire country?" The city then raised the star on South Mountain that can be seen from much of Bethlehem and christened itself "Christmas City USA." That's how Bethlehem became known as the Christmas City, despite its winter snows being tinged with the soot of the Steel's roaring blast furnaces.

In a sense, the city's people, who had come from all over the world to find a place to live and work, then had a unifying symbol—a star to guide their journey to connection with this place. Why did that matter? Because we are all of the earth, I suspect that for an answer we could look to those shifting mountain ranges. All of the people on Earth originated from a relatively small population in a limited part of the world. As the world's population grew and differentiated, we drifted apart, at times turning against each other. But Jewish-American psychologist Abraham Maslow showed us in his Hierarchy of Needs: Smack in the middle of his five-tiered pyramid is Belonging, something all humans need if we are to feel satisfied with our lives.

Wanting to belong is the motivation, both social and hard-wired into us, to be emotionally close with other people and to be accepted by them. Although we inherently want to be together with other people, that can be difficult. At times, we can be like those mountain ranges, quietly drifting apart. If we're lucky, we find places to gather and people who welcome us—or who we can welcome. What the stories of Jewish Bethlehem highlight are the many ways every day that we all shape our own and each other's sense of belonging.

From the Hotel Bethlehem, Marion Brown Grace, a Bethlehem native and wife of Bethlehem Steel President Eugene Grace threw the switch that lit up the first iteration of this star on December 7, 1937. It shines from South Mountain each evening and can be seen from up to 20 miles north of the city. Photo courtesy of Carley Wright.

Working Here in Bethlehem: Ervin and Shirley Gross

My neighbor Shirley Stein heard about this project and suggested I speak with brother and sister Ervin and Shirley Gross. So one day, I sat down with pen and notebook and called the telephone number of Ervin and Shirley, who shared a home. While their phone rang, I mentally rehearsed how I might explain the project to these two people whom I had never met. But it was easy because the two Shirleys had already talked. The siblings readily told me of their family's experiences at the Steel. I felt both that they had been waiting for someone to ask and that they would not have been open to speak with just anyone.

What follows are excerpts of my questions (in italic) of Shirley (S) and Ervin (E) and their replies while handing the telephone back and forth between them. Their story shows many points at which their family lost or gained a sense of belonging.

I understand your father, Julius Gross, worked for the Steel.

S: He was in the pipe shop at first, but after a while he thought it would be a better thing—because of the manual labor, you know, coming home with greasy clothes—if he opened a butcher shop. So he quit and opened a kosher one. This was after the war, in '45 or '46, for about two years.... But the people didn't come to the shop. I don't know why; my mother and father kept it very clean. He sold the meat market to Henry Adler, someone in the Jewish community, and went back to the Steel as a repairman.

One thing I remember is that a lot of the men at the Steel spoke Pennsylvania Dutch, and what they didn't know was that my father spoke it, too. He'd be quiet for a while, then start talking to 'em. They were kind of flabbergasted. He was raised here on a farm in Saucon Valley and learned how to speak this. It was close to Yiddish, too. He really worked hard for the Steel, fixing whatever was broken. He got pretty greasy. He would fix the roller lines. My dad could have got a better job, maybe as a foreman; he never wanted it. Maybe he didn't want to tell those guys what to do. You'd have to be kinda tough ... on the tough side. My brother was a material supervisor right out of high school—

E: I was 17, and they wouldn't take me! I had to wait until I was 18.

S (in the background): He expected to get a job at the mills, too.

E: First they sent me to the labor gang and said—.

S (laughing): He's not too tall! They said he wouldn't even be able to pick up a jackhammer. They wouldn't hire him but sent him over to the general foreman who said, "We're not gonna put you there." They put him in the office, ordering materials, doing payroll. That foreman knew the whole Gross family; my father's brother worked for the Steel, Harry Gross. So the foreman hired my brother right away. That's how he got in the Steel.

I've heard that's where everyone wanted to work.

S: That's right, unless you had a business or a profession. There wasn't too much else. I don't think there were too many Jews working out in the plant.

E: They worked up at the Research Center. Leo Pozefsky worked there [as a ceramics engineer].

Why do you think there weren't many Jews in the plant?

S: It's not the type of work they went in for, I guess. My father must have started in 1936 or '37, before the war. They were hiring because the war was coming, and they made steel for the ships, the battleships. He was laid off for a while in the Depression. The whole family would drive past; if smoke was coming out, we knew they were working again. There was a big strike, too. My father stayed in the plant; he didn't go out. He didn't belong to the union, so stayed in for safety or to keep it going. My aunt used to throw kosher sandwiches over the fence. He would park his car at Aunt Esther's, that's another aunt, because the union guys were looking for him. They would wreck the car if they found it. I guess they were trying to get everyone to join the Union. There was a lotta nasty business to be wrecking cars.

My father was lucky he got back in. He'd lost all his seniority, nine or 10 years, with the Steel. He thought it'd be hard to get back in, but he had a good record. He was lucky; a lotta people they wouldn't do that for.

S: I was 18 years old and went in the sales department, plate sales. I started as a file clerk and kept going. That's what they used to do; start you at the bottom, where you stay until you learn. When I started, there was one room, all typists. There was filing to do and there were two of us and they didn't need two. Naturally—she was older than me—she was gonna keep that job. I went in the plate sales department, and there were about five men working there. They were gonna have me go in the back and do filing, but the supervisor said, "Why do that to her? Don't do that. Bring her out here, and we'll train her."

I became a schedule clerk. Remember, there was no computer. I had to do it all by hand. Then I was preparing orders, dealing with the district offices, just like the Pony Express. The orders would go into the district office, then they would send them to me. I handled Sparrows Point, where they made the plate steel for ships and bridges. Bethlehem was structural steel, [and the plant in the town of] Steelton was rails. Johnstown is another plant I should know. Fabricating was Steelton and Burns Harbor. I handled the orders for fabricated steel according to their specifications. It was a lot to keep in your head. [When the end came,] I had 30 years. My brother had 41. Things just got bad.

Bethlehem Steel strikers wrecking any cars they could find of those who continued to work through the strike. These photos are undated but are likely from the 1941 strike by the Steel Workers' Organizing Committee, precursor of the United Steelworkers of America. Courtesy of Bethlehem Area Public Library.

Why do you think the Steel failed in the end?

S: They didn't modernize the Bethlehem plant. Maybe if they did, it would've kept up.

There are Rules and There are Exceptions: From Gordon Goldberg

My father went to Broughal on the South Side; it was an elementary school then. He dropped out of school after the sixth grade, which wouldn't have been all that unusual at the time. He was big for his age and was able to get a job for Bethlehem Steel. During the first World War, what they called the Great War, he was a machinist and had women working for him at that time.

Charles Schwab was really the founder of Bethlehem Steel. He was ruined as a result of the Depression. He lost his fortune and committed suicide. The Bethlehem Steel people don't like to talk about it.

I had two uncles who worked for Bethlehem Steel, from the 1930s through retirement. There was one in Central Tool. He married my mother's youngest sister. Weisenberger was his name. Then there was Sam Berger.

The plant and corporate were quite separate. You have to differentiate between the two. Corporate was white, Anglo-Saxon, Protestant. You would not find Catholics or Jews in the corporate side. My father helped get my Uncle Sam Berger a job; he used his connections somehow. My Uncle Sam worked in "industrial fasteners."

Do you mean as a laborer?

No! This was on the corporate side as an executive. He did well, he was second-in-command in the department and, by the end of his career, he was asked to become head of the division and did.

Postscript: Charles Schwab was a Catholic — another exception; as Gordon's story shows there were many.

51

The Haze in the Air was Red: Sam

Growing up in the 1950s and '60s, Sam (who requested his last name not be shared), lived with his parents on the South Side, across the street from the Steel. He said, at sunup, "You could not see out of the window. At a certain time, they would do a reversal and blow out the blast furnaces. Everyone kept the windows shut. The haze in the air was red, and you couldn't see the sidewalk. On the window sill would be iron filings. You could take a magnet, run it along there, and pick them up. People either kept the windows shut or woke up early and shut them. There were no pollution warnings! The place was always covered with grit—a red, rusty grit. [For a kid,] it was cool to see the red flame shooting out of the top of the furnace. It was a Bessemer converter, and it was destructive. They'd use one and melt everything inside, then move on to the next one while they rebuilt the last one."

Besides the Steel's impressive smokestacks, its physical plant included machine sheds, furnaces, train trestles, and loading and unloading sites. Its fiery output could not be contained; the whole city lived with the effects of its processes. But the Steel offered steady wages for men (and later women), nonstop 24/7 operation, and a lifelong test of endurance, whether from the multi-thousand-degree heat of the furnaces or the height of the trestles, the dangers of molten metal and polluting sediments, and even the pecking order of all its employees from top to bottom.

"When they were making steel, it was a round-the-clock thing," Sam explained. "That went on until it all went south. Then they moved to the BOF—Basic Oxygen Furnace. That took the place of the Bessemer."

In the days when the Steel was still going strong, some of Sam's family members were among the steelworkers: His maternal grandfather, who had immigrated from Hungary,

The Bill Weiner Collection

Steel Works, Bethlehem, Pa., 1908. Lehigh University Postcard
Collection, [WPC0195], Special Collections, Linderman Library,
Lehigh University, Bethlehem, Pa.

worked for Bethlehem Fabricators and a maternal uncle
worked for the Steel as a laborer.

~

Years later, Sam worked for a local radio station that
often produced the big name acts that routinely appeared
at the Roxy, an art deco theatre in the nearby town of
Northampton that was a magnet for big music names. One
day, singer-songwriter Billy Joel came to the Roxy. It was later
reported in local papers that was where he came up with the
words for his hit song, about a steel factory closing down.

The song opens with a steam whistle reminiscent of the
one used to signal the start of the work shift at Bethlehem
Steel and other mills and factories. Though Joel may have
begun writing about his hometown of Levittown, New York,
and an entire region facing economic hard times, he named
the song "Allentown," for the city abutting Bethlehem to the
west. The thing is, there wasn't a steel mill in Allentown. It

was Bethlehem that grew up around the Steel and to which the Steel belonged. And in many ways, Bethlehem belonged to the Steel, but things changed. In the song, the steelworkers are standing in the Bethlehem unemployment line. And that's exactly what happened.

"I stayed for 35 years at Bethlehem Steel and eventually worked my way up to handling squads of men doing building work for New York City high rises," remembered Henry Schiff. "I got a diploma from the International Correspondence School. I took courses at night and at the community college. In 1976, they decided to get rid of my division. Bethlehem Steel didn't want us anymore."

~

My husband, our three sons, and I arrived in this city in 2004, a mere one year after the final dissolution of the Steel, yet its demise had been a gradual process. Nor was that process complete. The Steel's superstructure was pelted by rain, ice, and sun of many a season. Wind-blown seeds took root in crevices of the Steel's dormant hulks and wrack of rusted metal. They slowly cracked the shell of this fallen giant in a silent eruption from gutter and smokestack of new, green life. It was, nevertheless, a chilly echo of the Steel's fiery, productive life. Likewise, only gradually did we come to understand that the rundown state in which we found the city's South Side hardly hinted at what this district had felt like in its heyday.

Taking a walk along the South Side's Third Street in the early to mid-1900s, according to longtime Jewish Bethlemite Zelda Levin, it was possible to see that "for every 10 businesses, nine of them were Jewish." A reverse-phone book analysis suggests the number of Jewish-owned businesses might have been a little less than Jews and non-Jews alike suggested, but it's true enough that Bethlehem Steel paid employees livable wages, enabling them to support a thriving business district. The sociologist and anthropologist Jill A. Schennum wrote about how strides in compensation at the Steel helped build a financially secure working class in her book, *As Goes Bethlehem*. Those wages, combined with the up-and-coming technology of advertising, helped stoke the local economy.

The goods on offer in South Side shops—an array of clothing, furnishings, sports equipment, and sheet music—ensured a more enjoyable life and supported a climb toward the middle class for Steel families. Sales of these goods also resulted in income that led to better lives for the shopkeepers' families—quality clothing, music lessons, education—a chance for their children if not for themselves to enter the middle class. When Zelda and her husband, Gus Levin, each opened shops in the mid-1950s, they continued a tradition that traced back to 19th-century Jewish immigrants in Bethlehem.

In the 1920s, the South Side teemed with people. "We would be open on Saturday nights," Bethlehem native Robert Kroope recalled. "The sidewalks were packed; you couldn't get through." Store owners forged a special connection with their customers. Robert particularly recalled of his father, Nathan, who owned Kroope's, a clothing store, "The customers spoke their language, and he learned it from them, not just English, but Hungarian, Russian, and Italian, too."

Besides clothing stores like Kroope's or Podber's, which was owned by Bethlehem native Anna Podberesky and her husband, Isadore, there was everything from pharmacists and grocers to jewelry stores and movie theaters. Palace Theatre owner Jacob Beilin's daughter, Esther Hirshberg, recalled, "We were in the movie business. All of my family is from Reading, but my father had an opportunity to buy a theater in Bethlehem on Third Street on the South Side. There were five movie houses; some of them started with vaudeville."

The Palace Theatre, owned by Jacob Beilin, was just one of many South Side Jewish-owned businesses that many who grew up in Bethlehem remember fondly. Circa 1950s. Courtesy Bethlehem Area Public Library.

Just as Jacob Beilin knew movies, Abram Philip knew retail; his family had owned a shop in Lithuania. In the 1880s, he settled in Bethlehem, opening a pawn shop. Along the way, he changed his name to Abraham Phillips and married Sarah Joseph—niece of America's only chief rabbi, Jacob Joseph, of New York City. One of Abraham and Sarah's 10 children, Maurice, as an adult transformed his father's pawnshop into Phillips Sporting Goods at 13 W. Third Street, a much-loved Bethlehem establishment.

Maurice's brother, Sol, opened Phillips Music and Appliance Store at 24 E. Third Street. Like other store owners, Sol extended credit to his customers. "Customers bought on credit and paid weekly," explained Nan Bratspies, whose family owned and operated Goodman's Furniture. "When there was a strike at the Steel, we 'carried' the customers. You knew they would make good." Phillips, Goodman's, and other shops were rewarded for their trust when the customers kept coming back in better times.

The South Side was considered *the* place to shop; it was bustling in the '50s and '60s. Betty Diamond, who with her husband, Eugene Diamond, owned the Fabric Center at Fourth Street and Brodhead Avenue, recalled, "A lot of mothers stayed home, and they sewed. The children got a new suit of clothing for school and holidays. We were deluged with trays of cookies from our customers at Christmastime. You got to know them, to learn their stories. It was nice."

The couple even went to a Greek wedding as a result. Betty later learned that Eugene gave a customer the fabric for her wedding dress, calling it a wedding gift, because he knew it was difficult for the family to afford.

Rabbi Allen Juda, who moved to Bethlehem in the 1970s, said of the shopkeepers, "They wanted independence." He noted that their vocation came with a price because of the responsibility to open the doors each day: "They couldn't go far from their stores."

The wedding photo of Abraham and Sarah (Joseph) Phillips on
December 25, 1891. Courtesy South Bethlehem Historical Society.

Even though the shopkeepers desired financial self-sufficiency, they very much needed other people, and not only as customers. Robert Kroope recalled seeing Jewish entrepreneur and builder Aaron Potruch come often to Kroope's to visit with Nathan, who would sometimes cosign loans for Aaron's construction company. Whether friendship or business came first might have been beside the point. As Robert put it in reference to another such acquaintance, "Jacob Beilin was my father's partner in business and in cards, in everything. They never had a paper between them. It was all done on a handshake." Those social and business ties also knitted the shopkeepers together. Despite the responsibilities that came with it, that handshake did provide a measure of freedom: to invest, take a chance, and make mobility—physical, economic, and social—available to their children if not to themselves.

In many cases, Jewish children born and raised in early to mid-20th century Bethlehem went to college before it was commonplace to do so. This mirrored the nationwide phenomena among Jewish families compared to the general society that the sociologist Marshall Sklare studied and wrote about in his 1958 book. These educated young people then entered a wide range of professions, either in the Lehigh Valley or elsewhere.

Today, a parking lot has replaced Kroope's. Goodman's Furniture store, which stood empty under a faded sign for many years, has been adapted to new uses and the sign taken down. The name of another shopkeeper, Anton Sell, can be found only in the floor tiles at the entrance of his former store—"SELL." Yet the South Side was once a world unto itself, and in its diverse neighborhoods, it was a place to grow up and forge belonging.

Jennifer Lader

Making Lox and Eggs: Robert Kroope

Robert Kroope had plenty to say about his mother, who he recalled "knew all the Jewish practices and taught us," and about his friends, who "mostly were not Jewish." Family and friends represented two parts of one world that is Robert's own. He was born in 1917 at St. Luke's Hospital on the South Side. I met him for the first time when he was 91 years old, in his room at an assisted living center. Rabbi Juda had come along to introduce us.

Robert explained that his parents came to Bethlehem in the 1910s from Lithuania and Russia. He said that his mother, Martha, was a good-natured woman, who moved to the nearby small town of Northampton because she had a sister there. Robert described his father, Nathan, as charming. "He had a big smile, a big greeting for people. He was glad to be alive and told everybody so."

Robert said that his father came to Bethlehem "under inducement of a job." He began by working for someone else and then opened his own store. "Kroope's was a retail store.... We had a ready-to-wear shop. We sold sheets, pillowcases, blankets."

Bethlehem was growing, and Robert witnessed a strong drive in the senior Kroope to make a living, "to preserve independence, not to depend on others for a handout."

Nathan bought his property on East Third Street on the South Side in 1914, just a few years after he arrived in this country. Nearby, one of the Blindermans had a barber shop, the other a junkyard. There was Finkelstein's Jewelry, Ben Goodman's Furniture Store. Frank Stone had a store that sold children's wear and clothes for all. "Whatever sold, they stocked," Robert said.

Shops were crowded onto Third Street, which ran from the loftily situated Church of the Nativity eastward all the way down the hill and out to the Steel. On the surrounding streets and radiating southward from the river and west toward the nearby borough of Fountain Hill were the residential neighborhoods. Jewish families lived interspersed among immigrants of other religious, ethnic, and national origins, rather than in any one neighborhood.

Like many other parents at the time, Martha and Nathan experienced their share of tragedy: Their first two children died just days apart, apparently from influenza, in December of 1913: Louis, shortly after his third birthday and Ida, at exactly 18 months of age. It wasn't until four years later that Robert arrived, in 1917.

~

Robert grew up on Montclair Street, part of the steep, crowded residential hillside near Lehigh University, also found on the South Side. When Robert was very young, he loved to look out his home's big, sunny front windows. "Across the street from our house was the German Catholic School.... I would go over and play in the schoolyard. I learned 'Hail Mary' and came home and recited it to my parents.

"My father went over to the nuns and asked, 'Do you know this is a Jewish boy?' The nun said, 'That's all right. He can come back as long as he's well-behaved.' So I'd go over and play at recess, then come home and have some lunch and take a nap."

Robert's siblings eventually joined him at his window: May, Eugene, Hilda, and Arlene. "My mother kept those girls so well-dressed, they were like fashion plates," Robert said. Nathan and Martha acted with purpose and taught their children to do the same.

Robert's words are a study in contrasts. Although at one point he claimed that Jewish children were accepted on the playgrounds, in the next breath he added, "If they called us names, we turned around and fought. My mother said, 'Stand up for your rights. Don't be afraid to slug it out.'"

The second time I met with Robert, he said, "My mother kept us home. We didn't mingle much." And so here is the tension: Robert acknowledged that, on the playground, they did mix with other children, though it was important to be separate in some ways, "so that [the non-Jewish children] knew we are Jewish, and we don't play ball on the Sabbath." And although his mother didn't mind him "fraternizing," he said, "She wanted us to know all of the ways.... Her father was a rabbi or something. He showed us. He didn't live with us, but was somewhere around."

In Robert's experience, it was expected that a young Jewish person would find a Jewish spouse. He found his wife at the railroad station in Bethlehem the day that Sylvia Garfinkel came in on the same train as Robert's parents. "I took her to a dance, or to a party or something when I took her out," Robert recalled. "She was a sharp dresser, a good-looking dresser, had her hair this way and that, perfect. We just had a good time. She loved to kiss me, and I loved to kiss her. She'd say, 'Bobby, it feels the way it should feel.' We had light, very nice conversations. We had hot chocolate sometimes, and we always had corned beef on rye." Robert's parents liked Sylvia from the moment they saw her. Robert and Sylvia raised two sons and a daughter.

By the time I met Robert for the third time, he had recently turned 94 and was noticeably weaker than when we first met. We visited for a while and then I asked him just two questions. First, I asked him his earliest memory: "Going to public school, I guess. I went to public school with all the other boys, all the gentile boys. I was the only Jewish one in the class." True to form, he called his school years, "Great! We knew how to defend ourselves.... We never gave it a thought."

When I asked Robert his fondest memory, he immediately answered, "Having breakfast with my family and our friends came in." In each of our three talks, Robert made a point of saying, "Nothing was missing from our table." It seemed at first that he referred to staying ahead of Depression-era financial struggles. Yet Robert was able to attend college during the Depression. Tellingly, he said his father was "liberal on money and feelings and the friends you brought home. We were allowed to bring our friends home. We were allowed to have them sit down to a dinner, to a meal, just to be nice."

Robert's precise words expanded my view of what a table from which nothing was missing meant for him: not only would there be food, but also friends. Several times, he elaborated regarding his friends. "Background meant nothing, as long as they were good and decent, that's all." He said his mother "would cook everything you liked. Everything was prepared and brought to the table that you should enjoy. There was always enough for everybody."

This, it seems, was Martha's way of "getting along."

During the last few minutes we were ever to spend together, Robert said, "My mother always invited everybody to sit down at the table.... [Our gentile friends] came in, they sat down, and we didn't serve bacon and ham. She made scrambled eggs, and sometimes she made lox and eggs."

"The Border was Always Changing": Edith Blinderman

When someone I had gotten to know through this project told me that I should go see Edith Blinderman, this was the last thing I expected.

"I like to be bad," Edith said in her best Betty Boop impression as she welcomed me into her apartment. We soon settled down at her kitchen table to talk together.

"My name is Edith Podberesky Blinderman," she began. "My mother was a Frankel." Thus she provided her

Bethlehem credentials, for Edith is no newcomer. Edith's grandfather, a widower and immigrant known in this country as John Frankel, brought two children with him to America and here married Lena, who had come from Eastern Europe. "Or it may have been closer to Germany," Edith said. "The border was always changing, you know." Lena gave birth to nine more children, including Anna, who would become Edith's mother.

"My mother's father ran some kind of Army-Navy store called Cheap John's in Bethlehem," Edith began. Anna grew up on the South Side going to public schools. At a party in town, she met Isadore "Pat" Podberesky, who later recognized her walking in New York, where she had gone to work for a cousin. Like his father-in-law, Pat was an immigrant.

"He came from Vilna," Edith said. Though he was the child of a poor Jewish family, he was admitted to the tsar's music academy because of his talent on the violin. He had the same teacher as Jascha Heifetz, another Jewish immigrant to the United States, who was considered one of the greatest violinists of all time.

"[My father] got out as they all got out, kind of snuck out, rather than go in the Russian army. Then there were pogroms. In the US, Pat joined his brothers and sisters. He brought his mother and father out. Also upon arrival in the United States, Pat "went in the service," Edith said. "When was the war—1917? They put him in an orchestra right away in New York. There he stayed as 'bombs burst in air.' He never went overseas but played in an officer's club. They liked to have their music."

After the war, Anna and Pat married and lived in New Jersey. Pat played music in the theaters and for the silent movies, and he had to travel a lot. Anna didn't like that life and wanted to get him out of the business. "She wanted to open a store, and she had family in Bethlehem," Edith explained. "In those days, [families] wanted to stay close. When she

Edith Podberesky at about four years old, on Bethlehem's South Side.
The photo is dated August 8, 1930. Contributed photo.

was pregnant with me, my mother came to Bethlehem to be with her mother. I was born here." That was in 1926. "My mother went back to New Jersey for a short time and decided she wanted to open a store, so she came back."

Anna and Pat opened the business together on Fourth Street and called it Podber's. The family lived above the store. Later they opened a second store on Third Street. Drawing on his classical musical training, Pat got a job playing dinner music at the Hotel Bethlehem. He also dealt with the bank for Anna and handled the vendors and the buying trips to New York City.

Anna was successful in the shop especially because her demeanor was a draw for women customers.

"When women came in, they didn't want to talk to a man," Edith said. "Also my mother would call customers when something nice came in and say, 'I have a dress for your little girl. Let me put it away for you.' Also my mother was very good-natured. She kept a little book and on payday she hoped they would pay a bill. She hadn't the nerve to ask them, though. She would send me and my father out.

"I remember going to a yard, and I was afraid of the dog in the yard. A woman came out, and she knew who I was and wanted to know what I wanted." Here, Edith's little-girl persona comes to the fore: "My mother asked if you could pay on the bill," she said in a singsong voice. Then switching to her regular voice, she added, "Imagine!"

Growing up, Edith visited her friends, whose families had come from Italy and Hungary.

"I didn't like Jewish food," she said. "I wanted something different from what I had at home. My mother would [keep] kosher in the house, a lot of them 'kept' at home. I thought everyone didn't eat [certain foods] like that. At my friend's house, I would smell Italian food and would sometimes eat there. The Hungarians are wonderful bakers.... I liked everything, except what my mother cooked. When I think

about it, I didn't feel comfortable in a Jewish environment....
It's not so unusual. A lot of [Jewish] kids lived in gentile
neighborhoods. There were no Jewish kids." Edith didn't
have a Jewish friend until junior high, when Gus Levin's
sister, Natalie, became her friend. "As I got older, I had more
Jewish friends, but I still had gentile friends."

One day when Edith was 15, she got a bit of soot in her
eye.

"I had long eyelashes, and they would pick up a cinder
and it would get into my eye," she said. "In those days, you
would go to a druggist who would roll your eye back and
take it out with a Q-tip. Now you'd have to go to a specialist.
I went to Abe Blinderman."

At that time, in the early 1940s, most of the young men
were in the service for World War II, so Edith and her friends
wrote hundreds of letters to them.

"It was a big deal, writing to guys," Edith said. "Almost
everyone you knew was in the service. I knew lots of them.
Any fellow I ever dated was in the service." So when Abe,
the pharmacist, asked, "You want to write to my brother?"
Edith said yes.

In the meantime, Edith said, "I went to Penn State where
they roomed you with your own kind. And you know what?
I don't think it was such a bad idea. My roommate was
Jewish, and the other two in our group were the same, also
Jewish. It was okay with me. By that time, I was comfortable
[being with other Jewish young people]. We had something
in common, and it wasn't just religion. We had grown up in
the same kind of environment."

Even so, Edith said, "At Penn State, I was dating
everything that moved." The boys weren't necessarily Jewish,
but she did plan to marry a Jewish man "mostly because of
my parents," she said. "In those days, they were adamant
and you wouldn't want to go against that."

Edith said she went to college "to get away from Bethlehem." However, Edith said, "I kind of ran my own life. I would go to New York shopping and 'charge it' to my mother. Or [my mother] would say, 'Go to Hess Brothers' (a world-famous department store in Allentown). They were wonderful, the perfect place ... I wanted to go into fashion and retailing. Penn State didn't have anything to offer; I went there one year. Then I went to Tobé Coburn in New York, in fashion and merchandising." This was a notable, rigorous school. There were no excused absences from classes. In those days, women had to wear hats and gloves every day. After finishing at Tobé Coburn, Edith was employed at Hochschild Kohn's, a famous department store in Baltimore.

By that time, pharmacist Abe's brother Marty Blinderman was through the war and back stateside. "Then he went to OCS, they called it officer's training, and became a second lieutenant," Edith said. "He finally came home on leave. He'd always be taking me out."

Other family members shared that after the war, Marty could have gone to Lehigh University on the GI Bill, but he wanted to get married and start a family, so he went into business with his father instead of going to college.

In July 1946, Edith and Marty married, while the rabbi was "on summer break."

"In those days, with so many soldiers returning from the war and getting married, there was a housing shortage," Edith said. "You didn't plan your wedding until you found an apartment, so everything was last minute. 'Now we can get married.' We got married in the sanctuary of Temple Beth El in Allentown [by the rabbi there]. The rabbi at Brith Sholom was mad at me. 'You could have called me,' he said."

The wedding being held at Beth El was extraordinary because the Bethlehem and Allentown Jewish communities didn't really mix.

"I don't think Allentown recognized Bethlehem, that it was on the map," Edith said. "I'd see someone at Hess's, and they'd ask, 'What are you doing over here?' It wasn't even 10 minutes from my house!"

Marty grew up in a rural area outside Bethlehem. "My father-in-law went out to North Dakota with a program that was re-settling Jewish immigrants on the land," Edith explained. "After becoming a farmer and returning east to New York City, he married and bought a farm in the Lehigh Valley." Growing up during the Depression, Marty and the other children walked to a one-room elementary school. The family's farm was later sold and the land eventually became Lehigh University's athletic field. After the war, Marty went into the scrap business in Hellertown with his father, Harry Blinderman, and then branched out on his own.

Although Marty was a hard worker, Edith said, "I didn't work after I got married and I always wanted to go out to work, but every time I brought it up, my husband had some excuse. Now that I think about it, in his mind, it meant that he wasn't making enough. I said, 'Marty, I want to know if I'm worth 50 cents an hour.' He said [if I worked], it would put us in a higher tax bracket. He did make a good living."

Five months after Edith and Marty got married, Edith's mother died at just 46 years old of a brain tumor. Edith's much younger sister, Dolly, was just eight years old, so Edith took her in and raised her.

South Side Mainstays: The Phillips Family

Mel Phillips was born in 1926. I visited him at his apartment where he and his wife, Elaine, lived and Elaine sometimes chimed in.

"My grandfather had a pawnshop. It had three balls outside. That's how people knew it was a pawnshop," Mel explained. "It was where Lehigh Pizza is now. Even after

A plaque honoring the 145 young adults of Brith Sholom who mobilized for World War II. Nathan Sonnenfeld is shown (on the left in this Philadelphia Inquirer photo on the opposite page that ran February 28, 1944) loading a 60mm mortar, a weapon used for close-in support of ground troops. Nathan was later killed in action, as indicated by the star shown on the plaque next to his name, as well as five other names.

G WORLD WAR II

MAX MOZER	ROLAND L. SIGAL
HARRY MOVITZ	JACKSON SIGMON
ARTHUR NEUMAN	RUTH SILBERMAN
JACK NEWMAN	DR. WM. SILVERMAN
LEONARD NORMAND	HARRY SIMON
BERNARD D PACHTER	LILLIAN SIMON
FLORENCE PACHTER	WILLIAM SMITH
MAURICE PHILLIPS	ARTHUR C. SOLOMON
MELVIN PHILLIPS	MARTIN SONNENFELD
SHIRLEY PHILLIPS	NATHAN SONNENFELD ☆
NATHAN PISAREV	SIDNEY SOSNOW
SOL POSNER	ALBERT SPEAR ☆
DAVID REFOWICH	MILTON SPILBERG

Inquirer Photo

MORTAR Staff Sergeant Nathan Sonnefeld, of Bethlehem 60-mm. mortar as Private First Class Charles Cantrell st., Philadelphia, crouches down on the other side of th

למולדתם

my uncle turned the pawnshop into a sporting goods store, he still had a corner where he sold watches and things like that. Eventually he got rid of that. They sold guns, fishing equipment.... For a few Saturdays, I even worked there!"

On the Sabbath?

"My grandparents were Orthodox[1], but my uncle wasn't," Mel said. "I came to work once in overalls on a Saturday, and my grandmother was insulted because I was wearing overalls! It's just what you wore to go to work; it's what people wore!

After that, you left town for a few years, working elsewhere?

"Then Uncle Sol called and said Gus Levin had just left [his job working for my uncle's business, Phillips Music Store], and my grandfather Phillips said he thought I'd like working there.... My Uncle Sol had married Sadye, who we called Suzie [pronounced with a short "u" sound], and Aunts Rose and Helen worked there, and for a short time Sol Berman, Frances's husband."

Around that time, Mel went to visit his sister, Ruth, at Penn State.

Elaine Phillips continued the story, "I got a call from [my friend and former roommate] Ruthie, 'My brother's coming up.' It was a fraternity weekend. She said, 'I want you and Mel to meet.'"

"That was the last chance we would have had to meet because then it would have been summer," Mel said. "I took the train and got up to Penn State. Elaine and I met May 24, got engaged on September 4, and married January 28 [of 1951]. It was an eight-month whirlwind."

---

[1] Jewish Orthodox religious life includes strict observance of Shabbat (no driving, working, turning electricity on or off, or handling money on the Sabbath and holy days) and keeping kosher (never eating milk products and meat products together, only eating meat of animals allowed by Torah (such as beef or chicken) and prepared in the manner allowed, and never eating foods like pork or shellfish that are forbidden).

Phillips Sporting Goods, 13 W. Third Street, Bethlehem. Courtesy
South Bethlehem Historical Society. Mid-century newspaper ads
advertised their fishing equipment, baseball supplies, sneakers, rifles,
"ammo," and luggage.

After Mel and Elaine were married, Mel spent his working years at the music shop.

"We sold everything that [had to do with] musical instruments," Mel said. "My aunt sold records, sheet music. We sold phonograph needles. There are hundreds of different kinds. We had three listening booths on the first floor where our customers could try records. We had one player piano. Our biggest customers were Lehigh University students. The Phillips family took over Third Street! Morris was on one end of Third Street (Phillips Sporting Goods), our store was in the middle, and my father's shop was on Polk Street—Phillips Home Furnishings."

"A lot of people don't know about that store. My father had a nice business and a potbelly stove. The store was shaped in a U, and he sold everything from window screens to sleds, to carpeting to beds, living room furnishings, and lamps. I used to go to furniture shows with him. He went out of business in 1950, after 20 or 30 years in business. Then he helped Uncle Sol in his store."

"But even before that, during the first World War, my father worked in the office at Bethlehem Steel," Mel continued. "My mother, Rose Kohler Phillips, was born in Charleston then grew up in Knoxville. She came to Bethlehem to visit her cousin Morris Glazier. She met my father, who worked for Morris as a bookkeeper, and that was it."

After World War I, Jewish organizations flourished, such as youth groups like the Young Men's Hebrew Association (YMHA) and of course the 1897 Synagogue. It felt like too many organizations to support, and the people wanted a sense of unity. Morris Glazier was instrumental in the community's next step of bringing Jewish families together in a single gathering place and creating a niche so that the little community could have a greater sense of belonging in Bethlehem.

The lot at Brodhead and Packer avenues, circa early 1900s, where the Brith Sholom Community Center was later built; now the site of Lehigh University's Harold S. Mohler Laboratory. Courtesy Lehigh University Special Collections.

Chapter 4
"All is Calm, All is Bright"
Building Places for the Young People

One day, after driving up the long slope of South Mountain and coming over the rise into Bethlehem from the south, I descended along the road into Bethlehem that early settlers like Yehoshua Gilles knew as the Philadelphia Pike, today's Wyandotte Street. I turned right and eventually ended up eastbound on Packer Avenue, stopped at a light where it intersects with Brodhead Avenue, the southwest corner of Lehigh University. There to my right, a building loomed, its facade featuring a huge set of tablets, smooth as a sidewalk and painted a dull brick red. By their shape, the tablets could only be likenesses of the Ten Commandments that Moses brought down from the mountain.

Far below these wordless replicas, on the sidewalk near my car, a college student opened a glass door and walked into what I discovered on an inquisitive return visit was a university lab. But for many years, that building housed a Jewish congregation and more. The current purpose, such a departure from the original one, combined with the blank-faced tablets, made me think, *This building has a story to tell.*

The Brith Sholom Community Center

On my return visit and now wielding my camera, I made my way inside and along narrow corridors lined with pasteboard walls, wondering what was behind them. Nothing hinted at the underlying story—until I reached the back stairwell. Its honey-colored, plain wood railing was polished smooth from

76

the hands of children, parents, and grandparents—hard workers, entrepreneurs, and survivors. Week after week, they climbed those stairs up to the sanctuary on the building's fourth and top floor. I followed in their footsteps, and I initially met with disappointment.

In the place of the sanctuary that I had seen in old photos, resplendent with ornately carved dark wood, I saw two classrooms divided by more pasteboard. The spot where the ark and the Torah once held pride of place had become the province of a movie screen, aimed at by a projector stationed at the back of the room. I wondered, *What would happen if I pressed the projector button? What story reel would play across that screen?*

Something caught my eye—maybe because of the glimmer of sun through the stained glass windows along the wall to my left. An opaque, golden lion, the symbol of Jewish strength, stood watch behind the window shades that masked but didn't quite hide the building's heritage.

~

Red Letter Day in History of Jewry in City: Ideal Weather Prevails for Breaking of Ground for Jewish Community Building

by Clifford Frey

Bethlehem Globe-Times, Monday, March 31, 1924, page 1

An excerpt:

With appropriate exercises, the ground for the Brith Sholom $100,000 Community Center building at Packer and Brodhead avenues was broken on Sunday afternoon in the presence of a large gathering.

Rabbi Landman, of Easton, said "...[It] is an experiment ... fraught with great opportunities for the Jewish residents of the community. The social, educational, and religious activities are to be banded together under one roof so that the next generation will be able to live the Jewish life based on the Jewish traditions and be better Jews and better American citizens than they would otherwise...."

Then began the formal ceremony of breaking ground.... The officers and directors of the Brith Sholom Community Center are: Aaron Potruch, president; Ben Goodman, first vice president; Morris Black, second vice president; Anton Sell, treasurer; William Bernstein, recording secretary; Herman Alofsin, executive secretary; Harry M.

Aaron Potruch, first president of Brith Sholom, breaks ground for Brith Sholom, with the original board and community members looking on. This and other Brith Sholom photos in this book courtesy of Congregation Brith Sholom.

Goodman, Isaac Kaplan, Samuel Wiesenberger, J.G. Beilin, John Hartman, Frank Stone, Morris Glazier, Robert Long, B. F. Tauss and Abe Glaser, directors.

Esther Hirshberg's father, Jacob (J.G.) Beilin, was one of the founders of the Brith Sholom Community Center. Born in nearby Reading in the 1910s, Esther came to Bethlehem as a child with her family when Jacob bought the Palace Theatre, which had opened sometime prior to 1912, at 206 E. Third Street on the South Side.

"I remember my parents taking me to services in the 1897 Synagogue," Esther said. "The women sat separate from the men. When Aaron Potruch saw the community was worshipping in such an unattractive place—and it was very Orthodox—he wanted to do something. A little group of men got together. Whether there was a lot of money, I don't know. They would meet at my father's office on the second floor. Glazier's had furniture, Kroope's had dry goods, and Silverman, shoes. They would gather together and talk things over."

At the time, there were more than 200 Jewish households scattered through the South Side and in nearby boroughs and even farms, likely numbering a little more than 1,000 people. (It was just a few too many to make it into Lee Shai Weissbach's 2005 book on small Jewish communities of under 1,000 people.) Bolstered by these numbers, the men obtained land, formerly deeded to a Mr. Hess in Allentown, and scheduled a groundbreaking, even going so far as to order a silver-plated shovel. They invited the mayor and hired a photographer.

"I'm in the picture!" Esther said. "My sister and I are in the picture. I was in my early teens. I'm wearing a hat, if you look at the picture."

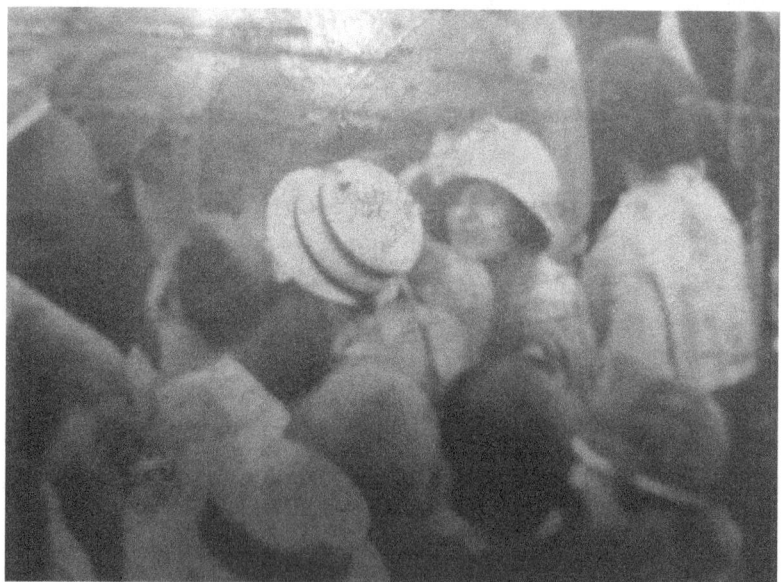

Cornerstone-laying ceremony, Brith Sholom Community Center,
Bethlehem, June, 1924: Finding the girl in the hat seems a tall order,
but a close look reveals there really is one girl wearing a hat who stands
out, lower right of group photo. She peeks out from across the years,
showing just how to be an individual in a crowd.

Notwithstanding the all-male demographics of the first board of directors, the story goes that everybody helped. "The young people did their duty in contributing to the fund because they realize that this building will serve them primarily," President Aaron Potruch said in a speech he gave in June of 1924 for the cornerstone-laying. The women organized a Sisterhood. They sewed curtains for the building.

Carol M. said, "The women would do all the catering in-house. They would make [so many] tiny blintzes, and my mother never wanted to see another mini-blintz. I don't know if anyone got notice, but the women were always busy behind the scenes."

Aaron, Esther, Jacob, and the rest of the community probably never imagined what the Brith Sholom Community Center would come to mean in their lives.

"It was a very impressive structure," said Rabbi Allen Juda, who arrived in Bethlehem in 1975. "Four stories with a huge sanctuary on the top floor that sat 600. There was a gym and a pool on the first floor. On the second floor were the social hall, the main office, the rabbi's office, and the gift shop. The third floor was the library, some classrooms, and the junior congregation room. On the fourth floor were several classrooms, the sanctuary, the daily chapel, and the apartment. In an earlier time, the maintenance person lived there as part of the compensation."

During the years between the first and second world wars, synagogue centers—or *A Shul with a Pool* as David Kaufman titled his 1999 book on the phenomenon—were the chosen model to offer something for people at every stage of life.

Bethlehem native Gus Levin recalled the community center during his childhood, "It was like heaven. We could run up there any time; we didn't have to be transported like kids today. We could play up there, go to Hebrew School up there. It was great, especially during the summer. My family moved to Montclair Avenue, so it was just a few streets over.

"There was a kind of indentation in the front [of the building]. We played out there with a hard rubber ball. If you hit the corners on [just the right] angle, it would go way out. [The indentation was filled out in a remodel years later.] We had teams [based on country of origin]—the Litvaks and the Hunkies ... the Poles ... We had five or six three-man teams.

"Another thing: There was the pool. We didn't know how good we had it! We'd go in the morning to the Center and play, go swimming. We were also great Ping-Pong players, we thought."

Both boys and girls had access to the Center, although whether the girls also ran up there anytime they wanted was inconsequential to Gus, who said, with a grimace, "Girls aren't that important when you're 12."

Brith Sholom Community Center, circa 1925, with the front steps and the porch, with its low wall, labeled.

Jerry Hausman, another Bethlehem native, added, "The Center was our home. Sunday mornings, my father would take us up there. It was a family tradition to spend the day there, playing basketball and swimming. We'd have a catered dinner on Sunday afternoon."

Sunday dinners were prepared by a professional caterer who worked out of the kitchen, rather than by the women of the congregation, so the women got to sit down and partake, too.

Adults in the community enjoyed the kosher meals and visiting over Sunday lunch. Yet they could never totally relax.

Esther Hirshberg ("the girl in the hat") said, "The Center was always out of money. For many years, my father held the big March Ball, with the men in tuxedos and the women in gowns. Outside people from the community came, too. There would be paid ads in the program. Everyone dug in their pockets. There were a lot of fundraisers. They were always going around for card parties, raffles. I was too young to be interested. There was a lot of activity. It was a huge, huge building. It's amazing when you think of it. It was difficult because it wasn't a wealthy community."

Challenging though it was to provide adequate financial support, people were willing to go all out because the Center was also a spiritual home, the place that finally gave heart to a cohesive community. As Phil Moskowitz put it years later, "There was a feeling of warmth."

When I met with Isabel Schiff, who came to Bethlehem when she got married soon after World War II, she showed me a photo of the early sanctuary, which in addition to the rows and rows of seats for congregants facing the ark, featured rows of seats along the left and right sides of the room.

Isabel's husband, Henry, explained of these seats along the side, "I'm going to say three steps up from the [main] floor was for people who wanted to sit separately, in the Orthodox custom. The left side was for women, and the right side was for men. A lot of 'em would not come to the synagogue unless they were separated."

Esther recalled something that seemed unusual for such an Orthodox-leaning or even a Conservative synagogue. "You'll be shocked to know that when Rabbi Signer was there, when I was very young, there was a half Reform[2], half Conservative[3] congregation and we had an organ."

Though unheard of now because Orthodox and Conservative synagogues do not have musical instruments being played during a Sabbath or holiday service (though there is plenty of singing), according to Rabbi Juda, organs were common in Conservative congregations of that era. (He also described the early days of the synagogue as more somewhere between Conservative and Orthodox— "Conservadox" —rather than Reform, so there are varying points and opinions.)

Esther traced the use of the organ not only to group preferences but to particular individuals: "Do you know about Dr. and Mrs. Maysels?" she asked me. "He was a doctor on the South Side, and she was very much musically

---

[2] A religious movement that arose in early 19-century Germany with the aim of reinterpreting (or reforming) Judaism in the light of Western thought, values, and culture where such a reinterpretation does not come into conflict with Judaism's basic principles (Source: Oxford Reference). There is a value on assimilating into the general culture, American society in the case of the United States, with less emphasis on keeping kosher or strict adherence to tradition.

[3] A form of Judaism particularly prevalent in North America that seeks to preserve Jewish tradition and ritual but has a more flexible approach to the interpretation of the law than Orthodox Judaism (Source: Oxford Dictionary). Brith Sholom is Conservative.

The 4th floor sanctuary at the Brith Sholom Community Center, said to seat 600. Those who grew up there speak of it as having a "kind of warmth."

inclined." Dr. Alexander Maysels gave an organ to Brith Sholom in memory of his wife, Clara. "I guess they don't like to talk about it now," said Esther of the congregation in general. "There was a choir, too. The service used to be beautiful. Oh yeah, they had an organist! Then gradually, gradually, the majority of people didn't want it."

When Ira Lehrich, another Bethlehem native, looked back on the early days of the Center with the eye of the builder he became, he said, "It was built with gas lights. It was one of the first community-center-and-synagogues in Pennsylvania built at that time. Allentown's was just a community center. But the Center in Bethlehem was built into the hillside, and it was never built properly. There was no elevator, and the sanctuary was on the top floor."

To help with the operating costs of such a large building, "they opened the pool and the gym to the public," Rabbi

Because this was the only indoor pool, many non-Jewish people in
Bethlehem fondly recall having learned to swim at the Center.

Juda said. (Reportedly, back then the city had no other public
pool.) "I can't tell you the number of non-Jewish people on
the South Side who told me they learned to swim there, [but
it was a lot]."

Despite all the people coming and going, the Center did
not meet some of the municipal codes of today, of course,
for safety and accessibility.

Bethlehem native Jean Mindlin Deutch said, "Harold
Glazier, Gus Levin, and my brother played basketball there
when they were kids. When Harold was a teenager, he fell off
the exterior balcony, [which had no safety railing] and broke
his wrist.

As for the older members in the congregation who would
have had to climb three flights of stairs to attend services,
Jean said, "They walked! We had quite a few elderly. They
still made it. Where there's a will, there's a way."

Jean Mindlin Deutch, second from left, shown at her confirmation, circa 1940.

One of Bethlehem's Brightest: Aaron Potruch

In the mid-2010s, I attended a Bethlehem gallery show entitled "Postcards of Old South Bethlehem." In one of the 1920s-era postcards, two young men stand outside a shop. Above them a sign on the building reads: "Rooms to let. See Potruch."

Aaron Potruch was an energetic Russian Jew who arrived in Bethlehem in the 1910s and changed the face of the city before somewhat mysteriously disappearing into obscurity— and appearances mattered to him. He spearheaded the community center project, made large donations to fund it, and became its first president.

"He was a natural born leader," said Robert Kroope, who was a child in the 1920s when the Center was built. "He spoke English very well ... was a very well-dressed man, not very tall. ... He and his wife had four boys: Max, Louie, Freddie, and Bobbie [Robert]."

First Brith Sholom President Aaron Potruch gives a speech, circa 1924

Aaron was a builder, but he was also a visionary. He constructed a number of buildings in the area and owned an apartment building in Allentown. As it turned out, Aaron's star might have burned a little too brightly.

Harry M. Goodman, who at the age of 37 became one of the original board members, in an interview published by Brith Sholom many years later, said Aaron was "a major force in the Center. Most of us couldn't believe the size, scope, or enormity of the project as it went up before our eyes. We were amazed and thought, *Nobody could even have dreamt of this.*" (*Brith Sholom Ad Journal, 1976*)

Aaron Potruch did, and he had been the one to insist that the congregation adopt the community center model for their synagogue. However, the Great Depression became a real problem for most of the Center's members. According to Henry Schiff, customers stayed home and shops closed. Aaron Potruch had purchased, some even believe built, a large home on the North Side at the corner of 8th and Prospect avenues just before Depression hard times struck him full force. His home was beautiful—while it lasted.

"We would visit them at their house," Robert said. But, apparently finding himself in financial difficulty, Aaron left town and returned to Brooklyn "to find a place for himself in business." He did not succeed there, and Aaron died in Brooklyn.

As for Aaron's sons, Robert said, "Max married a girl named Bertha and lived in Allentown in a beautiful house. Freddie went to college at Cornell to be a lawyer, and the others disappeared."

On a tip, I contacted Judy Murman, the administrator of Congregation Keneseth Israel, the Reform synagogue in Allentown, in hopes of learning more. "People called her Bertie, and they were members here until they died," Judy said. "Max died around 1970, and Bertie died probably in the 1990s. The problem is the people who could tell you more are all gone."

"That's the problem," I agreed. "Did you ever hear Bertie refer to her father-in-law?"

"No," Judy replied. "She only talked about her husband— and with utmost admiration. They had no children."

A later owner of the house at 8th and Prospect actively researched the name, even calling the few Potruches across the United States. None of them believed themselves related to Aaron.

On the face of it, Aaron left very little behind, just a few buildings and no descendants to speak of. However, he was the force behind the building of the Brith Sholom Community Center. At fundraisers, Aaron gave the largest donations and the best speeches. He experienced failure at times, but it was risk with a reason: Aaron cared about the Center, about building a community. In Aaron Potruch, the community found its guiding star. It was a perfect *shidduch*

(Yiddish for match, usually a marriage). He brought the daring and the financial savvy, and the community brought the cultural sustenance and the people.

In one of Aaron's speeches, after referring to "evildoers at the gates" (presumably recalling the pogroms in his native Russia), Aaron asked, "What is this Jewish Community Center that is now being built? Why do we want this building? Is it to show the community what our money can purchase? Is it merely a structure, a monument? No, it is the concrete symbol of Jewish idealism. It is a place where we can teach our young men and women, our boys and girls, the sacred heritage that is ours. When we are questioned, 'What have you done for your city and your nation?' we can proudly point to our young men and women and say, 'Here is our contribution—honest, loyal, and devoted citizens of our city.' These young people will carry forward our great ideals."

That was Aaron's reason for building the Center: that his generation's children might belong in the society around them more than those immigrant parents ever could. The children were his true cornerstone.

A Consistent Community Center Couple: Charles and Lena Schiff

Lovely Lena Berkowitz was born in Philadelphia in 1888. By that time, across the ocean in Lithuania, Charles Schiff was already a 13-year-old on the verge of leaving home forever. As we sat around the dining room table in their son Henry Schiff's Bethlehem apartment, Henry recalled, "My father didn't come alone because he was young. He had an older brother and a younger brother with him. They had to get out because of the Russian army [conscription]. You'd get shot in the front or the back because you were Jewish. He didn't stop in New York because the Silberts were here in Bethlehem, and he came to them. Silbert had a little grocery store up on Wyandotte."

Perhaps because it was such a monumental voyage for three teen boys to have made (here, my mind goes to my own three children, but the idea is actually unimaginable), it then became easy to envision Charles starting a business and establishing a place for himself in Bethlehem's Jewish community. Yet Henry said, "My father never put himself in the limelight. If you look at the big picture [of the founding fathers], he isn't on there." Quietly working, quietly leading would be a truer portrait of Charles and Lena. The couple married in 1908.

"My mother was young when she married because they could not turn to their 20th birthday [unmarried], or they would be called old maids," Henry said. Lena had finished school and become a teacher in Philadelphia, but she gave it up when she got married. Of his father, Henry said, "He never spoke about the past, but he had a lot of education, a good Hebrew education. He spoke wonderful English; he educated himself."

Charles and Lena's first child was a boy, Isadore, born in 1910. Sylvia came along in 1916 and Henry in 1922. At Brith Sholom, Lena became very active in the community and was president of the Ladies Aid Society—"the forerunner of the Sisterhood," Henry said. He learned from his parents' examples. "Wherever my mother went, I went," he said. "She was very involved."

Henry continued, "By the time I got to the community center, I was starting Sunday school. A girl named Libby Stone was the kindergarten teacher. She wrote my name with a small 'h.' I was trying to correct her, or maybe I never said anything. Hebrew School—I hated it, disliked it. When it came to language, I was never a good student, as I proved right then and there."

I also went to public school. I don't remember that there were Jewish children at school. Most went to Webster or Central. I went to Madison." Asked about antisemitism,

Henry said, "Oh yes. If a child got mad, he might say, 'You killed my God.' I couldn't run from it, and I was never a fighter. I would ignore it, afraid of getting involved with a fighter."

However, there was always a social group at the community center. Plus, Henry said, "Even at age 12, I was active [helping] in the office with Gert Makagon [the office manager]."

The Depression was hard for the Schiff family.

"My father had a small store on Third selling work clothes to men from the Steel, anything he could," Henry said. "He was 'finished' with the Depression. The Moravian Church would lend money very easily, so Jewish men would buy [property] on a shoestring. They would do it by just assuming the loan and paying the interest. There were people occupying the property. If the new owner couldn't pay [the loan], the property was taken. You wouldn't throw [the tenants] out. You just lost the privilege of managing the properties."

"My mother had to be the breadwinner," Henry continued. "She opened a dress shop in a prominent location, 95 West Broad Street" on the North Side, but in those days the customer base was impoverished. "People would come in and buy dresses with relief checks. My mother's social life stopped existing. She liked to play bridge at the Center, but things were changing. After she closed the shop, she got a job for the WPA teaching women how to make CCC uniforms [for young men in the New Deal's Civilian Conservation Corps]."

"Finally, my brother graduated from pharmacy school in Philadelphia," Henry said. "He came home and worked for Young's Drug Store."

Henry went to Broughal School, located across the street diagonally from the Center, and from there to Bethlehem High School. "What is now Liberty," he said. "My sister was already there. She had graduated from Temple University before her 20th birthday and started to teach in August of 1937, when she had just turned 21. She taught commercial subjects—shorthand, typing, and bookkeeping. They paid about $1,000.

"I graduated in 1940 from high school," Henry recalled. "There was not that much money, and I wasn't a great student. My senior year, I had pursued drafting as a vocation. Eventually, I ended up going to Bethlehem Steel. I applied in 1941, and out of the many applicants was lucky enough to get into the structural drawing room, as a trainee. In '43, I was drafted. I didn't volunteer. I was in the military until February of 1946.

"I went overseas to the European Theater. France was practically already taken…. I ended up in combat when they had gotten to the Maginot and Siegfried Line. We lay there for a long time on the German side, about six months. Eventually you had to get through it. The Battle of the Bulge did come. We were very lucky. The Germans broke through south of us. We were too fresh on the line for them to be able to break through where we were. South of us was Patton. We were in the US First Army, up close to the British who were north of us. Eventually we pushed off through Germany. When we got to the Rhine River, one bridge was still intact. As engineers we were doing mine work and flare work to protect the fronts. We would do our work at night…"

Henry said that when he and other soldiers came back after the war, "As young men, we were looking for activity. I would have been 24 years old that April. We would go to the community center where a Jewish organization called Abergad had dances. That stood for Allentown-Bethlehem-Easton-Reading. For the young men who wanted to go out socially, the community center was complete. There was the social floor and the sports."

Other towns had their Jewish spaces, too. In Easton, it was at the YMHA, and the Allentown Community Center was at 6th and Chew streets. At that time, there was an increase in interchange between the cities.

Getting Married, Building a Life: Henry and Isabel Schiff

World War II had broadened horizons and uprooted some in the United States. Henry's sister, Sylvia, left Bethlehem altogether when she married. The migration went the other way, too.

"I met Isabel Kaplan going to Abergad at the end of '46," Henry said. "She was an Easton girl, and I met her at the Easton YMHA."

Isabel had graduated from Easton Hospital's Nursing Program. She had been working in the Cadet Nurse Corp for two years.

"I was one of the first critical care nurses when that originally came out," Isabel chimed in from her seat next to Henry at their dining room table. She continued with nursing, making a career out of it. They married in 1948. They had two sons, Gary and Jeffrey, and shared how proud they were of their grandchildren.

At one point, Henry took out the photo of Isabel that he carried in his wallet, a snapshot from when the couple first met. In it, Isabel, with light, lush, wavy hair, poses in a bathing suit— easily rivaling movie stars of the day and unrivaled for Henry's heart.

~

"I was never the type of person that pushed myself into leadership positions, but I was in the office [at the Center] all the time," Henry said. Sooner or later, most who are active in the community got tapped for more responsible roles. "In the '50s, I was head of Men's Club. I was the Secretary and the Treasurer of the Board in the 1960s."

Henry remembered how welcoming the Center was to other Bethlehem organizations. "Most organizations that wanted to use the pool were able to do it," Henry said. "I can remember the Girl Scouts, the Boy Scouts, and others no matter what faith, used that swimming pool—and the gym."

In addition to what the Center gave the city, when pressed, Henry reflected on what he and Isabel personally contributed to Brith Sholom, which included "being members, being active. Isabel taught Sunday school," he said. "We haven't missed a plaque!" In other words, they contributed whenever a sponsorship opportunity arose.

"On Saturday mornings, we had 60 kids in junior congregation with a President and Vice President [elected from among them]," Isabel said. There were far fewer adults on Saturday mornings because "the merchants were all open on Saturdays." As a result, Isabel said, "The kids ran their own services." Looking at the photos in one of the synagogue's ad journals, Isabel pointed to one of their sons, happy and eager in a lineup of young basketball players at the Center.

The Center's offices had been on an upper floor, but by the late 1940s, Henry said, "There was an opening like a bank window, and you would be talking to someone in the window."

Otherwise, Isabel said, "People would come in, and they wouldn't know who was downstairs." It became increasingly problematic that the sanctuary was on the top floor of the Center, up several flights of stairs.

In the early 1960s, the congregation undertook a remodeling. They moved the exterior top forward to hide the elevator shaft, Henry said. People would then enter on what came to be called the ground floor instead of the basement. Above the new main entrance in the space that used to be a porch, rooms were added, and the giant set of Ten Commandments tablets replicas were installed on the front of the building. This did away with the central steps and the wide-open area that had been edged with that low wall, which was a good thing.

"It was a dangerous porch, if you know what I mean," Henry said.

~

Even as the Center's building was updated, its financial struggles continued. The Jewish population of Bethlehem wasn't growing, and those who remained were migrating to the North Side.

"We were with Rabbi Frankel through a lot of hard times, then he moved on," Henry said. "Do you know what he said? 'There aren't enough producing women in Bethlehem' to see a future here. I think he was looking for greener pastures."

And so it went for Henry and Isabel's sons.

"Our children did not stay in this area," Isabel said. "So many young did not stay here."

However, it wasn't all *simchas* and slivovitz (Yiddish for happy occasions and toasts with strong drink). "In the '50s and '60s, when we were raising our children, we got hurt a little there and drew back," Henry said.

Despite having pulled back from the community center, Henry and Isabel continued to be an important part of the congregation for many decades. In 2012, the congregation honored them on the pages of that year's ad journal. Both were regulars at weekly and holiday services for much of their time in Bethlehem.

Henry was 91 at the time of the second of our two interviews, which occurred as the couple looked forward to a wedding anniversary for which most of their family would return to Bethlehem. Isabel said their children wanted them to "move closer." However, after being so linked to their community in Bethlehem for this long, Isabel said that such a move "won't be anytime soon, I can tell you that."

A Teacher and So Much More: Abraham Weissman

A graduate electrical engineer who had worked in Schenectady, New York, at General Electric ...

96

Mr. Weissman built radios, in the early days of this invention ... [He] was also an accomplished violinist, directed a religious school orchestra, played expert chess, and taught many of us to play the game when we were youngsters. [Mr. Weissman] introduced into our community the Chassidic melodies we are still using in our daily and Sabbath prayers. (*Brith Sholom Ad Journal, 1963*)

~

Immigrant parents and the children of the 1910s called it *cheder* (the "ch" is pronounced as a guttural h). All the rest called it "Hebrew School." Starting in the afternoons, immediately after secular school, Hebrew School in Bethlehem was held at the Brith Sholom Community Center. For the job of leading the Hebrew School, the Center hired Abraham Weissman. He came to Bethlehem with his wife and five daughters. His youngest, Edith, was just a little older than Henry Schiff.

"That man was the greatest man that ever lived in my days," said Henry Schiff, who attended Hebrew School from 1927 to 1935. "It was the Depression, and we didn't have a rabbi. This man was everything to us. He not only operated the Community Center, he did everything for us."

Abraham's approach to teaching seemed revolutionary at the time. He didn't use harshness or physical discipline. "He was charming and had a good sense of humor, and he never raised his voice. He was a good teacher. He was a good guy all around," said Robert Kroope, one of Abraham's first pupils. Hebrew School was held five days per week after public school. "We didn't think anything of it," Robert added. "You just went." No question, no complaining.

Abraham kept the building open during hard times. He went "hat in hand" to the Jewish shopkeepers to collect money. During the Depression, Abraham assumed the Center duties of executive director, dues collector, religious school principal, and more (*Brith Sholom Ad Journal, 1963*).

Mr. Weissman, circa 1930

"He was being paid, don't get me wrong, but God knows how little!" Henry said.

The little Jewish community hobbled along. "Often, if dues were slow in coming or monies were going out too fast, he would go without his own salary for weeks," according to the ad journal article. Abraham was instrumental in the religious services during the Depression, although with no pretense at being the rabbi.

At a Jewish service, you don't have to have a rabbi or cantor, unless you want someone to speak, Henry explained. "Mr. Weissman was the greatest person in the establishing of the Community Center, the managing of it, and taking care of what needed to be done. If the swimming pool was broken, he was capable. He would go down to the boiler room and see what could be done.... I was even in plays that he put on. He didn't have to put on plays! That to me was an amazement. It's hard for me to explain his capabilities. Without him, we would not have been able to stay alive as a community."

However, in the 1930s and 1940s, Hebrew School meant something in particular. Henry put it like this: "Mr. Weissman's time was spent getting us to learn Hebrew, if you know what I mean: Not learning to *write* Hebrew or *interpret* Hebrew, only the reading of [the letters and words without an emphasis on the meaning of the words]." It was a tradeoff, and there were tradeoffs happening everywhere in those days.

Bethlehem native Gordon Goldberg, who attended Hebrew School in the 1940s recalled, "For my bar mitzvah, Mr. Weissman was my teacher. He really enjoyed me; I say that tongue-in-cheek. I lived on the North Side, so I would have to walk or run or go by trolley or take a bicycle to get there. It was different then.... We did a lot of walking. So for Hebrew School, I preferred to play. I invariably ended up coming after they were halfway through. I did not endear myself to him; it wasn't my thing."

Abraham apparently thought Gordon was learning-challenged, but Gordon said, "I just wasn't interested. They would recite the prayers. One time, they were doing the *kiddush* (Hebrew for blessing or sanctifying) for Passover. He expected everyone to be able to memorize it and go up there and recite it. Despite good grades in public school, I was considered the dummy of the Hebrew class, but I was also very competitive and did not like to be regarded as stupid. I raised my hand to volunteer. He looked at me and asked, 'DO YOU WANT TO DO IT?' I did the minimal for my bar mitzvah. I was not into it. Plus, because my parents had to start all over in their 30s following illness and changing fortunes, they were just too busy to go to services every week."

Other things were changing, including the Jewish population shifting to the newer homes on the North Side, near where Gordon already lived. By the 1940s, Ira Lehrich said, Hebrew School was reduced to three times per week instead of five. After going to Calypso Elementary School on the North Side during the day, the Lehrich brothers, who lived on Prospect Avenue, "would run down to South Bethlehem to go to Hebrew School—over the Hill-to-Hill Bridge."

Also, by then mothers like Isabel Schiff were teaching Hebrew School. Irving Kaplan's mother, F. Shirley Kaplan, taught at the Hebrew School from 1946 to 1966. What's more, new standards were being set.

"She was fluent in Hebrew and Yiddish," Irving said of his mother. "She was my teacher at Hebrew School for two years. I remember many years decorating the *sukkah* (Hebrew, a tent-like booth set up for celebration of the week-long harvest festival) with cranberries and popcorn (decorations) and all the yellow bees used to come out."

In 1953, an illness of Abraham's progressed to the point that he needed to retire, and a "magnificent farewell banquet was held in his honor" (*Brith Sholom Ad Journal, 1963*). In

March 1955, Abraham Weissman died. At the funeral, many of Abraham's former pupils served as pallbearers.

Ultimately, what Abraham did for the Center had at least as much to do with keeping it going as teaching in its school.

"He was our leader," Henry Schiff recalled. "There was so much to do, but it was never enough."

~

Esther in her hat, Aaron the entrepreneur, Henry pointing to an individual photo of his mother in a montage, Mr. Weissman who brought unheard of teaching methods. All these years later, what stood out in these stories about those who banded together to build and populate the Center is how very much this community was a collection of strong individuals. Together they created a complex community.

The Little Shul: Congregation Agudath Achim

Congregation Agudath Achim, fondly known as the Little *Shul* (Yiddish for synagogue), stood for many years on the South Side's Webster Street. It was an Orthodox synagogue, yet by many measures, it was hardly distinct from the city's only other synagogue a few blocks away, Brith Sholom, which was Conservative.

Instead of cleaving to one synagogue and "never stepping foot in the other," as a popular Jewish joke posits, the Bethlehem Jewish community needed and actively supported both. While outsiders might point to differences in the roles of women or whether men and women sat together (Conservative) or separate (Orthodox) in the two congregations, astute observers from within instead note the overlaps between the two. The existence of a second congregation in Bethlehem offered members of this Jewish community choices, more places to belong, and additional layers of connection among people.

As Edith Blinderman said, "On Yom Kippur [a very long fast day mostly taken up with religious services], we would take a walk down to the Orthodox synagogue and go up into the balcony and talk to the other women, then go back to Brith Sholom. That's the way it should be!"

On the other hand, Irving Kaplan attended Yom Kippur services at the Little Shul. "On holidays, Brith Sholom started at 8 in the morning. We went out of Agudas Achim (the final -th in Agudath is sometimes pronounced as an -s) before Yizkor (a service of remembrance, which typically those with parents still living step out of). We would walk down to Brith Sholom to help fill some of their seats."

Irving Kaplan traced the existence of Agudath Achim to 1924, though some say it started as early as 1920. Irving recalled less interaction on a regular Sabbath. "At Agudas Achim, they ended services early so they could go to work, so I never went to services on Shabbos there because I was at junior congregation at Brith Sholom. That started maybe at 10:00 and then we went into the main service sometimes or walked down to my *bubbie's* (grandmother's) apartment for lunch, and my *zayde* (grandfather, who was a member of Agudath Achim) would be in the store."

In contrast, attending services on Friday night for the start of the Sabbath, which goes from sundown to sundown, was the preferred way for Brith Sholomers to be able to open their shops on Saturdays. Though religiously prohibited from working on the Sabbath, the need to stay in business and provide for their families overrode the proscription from working. Again—effectively, not that different from one another.

So, rather than religious differences, it seems there must have been a different reason that a community apparently too small to support two congregations kept both going anyway. To search out the reason why, it was necessary to look for clues in the stories.

Where I Belong: A Rabbi and His Family Arrive From Bob Trotner

I have only one picture of my grandfather. My mom kept this picture in her dresser drawer. Once in a while, she took it out and showed me and my brother. The only thing is: My grandfather had this harried, worried look on his face. He was always worrying. In the picture, he is gray-haired, with his hair short and combed forward, and a cut beard. He cut his beard with scissors, so it was stubby. He had deep-set hazel eyes and was always super-slim.

My mom said all he ate was soup, and then meat on Shabbos, to save money. As rabbi, he got $500 a year plus the house. They were starving, so poor that when he would see a cigarette butt in the street, he would pick it up and smoke it. He had a smoking habit and couldn't afford it with five kids. He wasn't proud, and he wasn't ashamed. He was born in 1884 and came to America in 1923 with the entire family except for my mother, who hadn't been born yet. My grandfather's family name was Nachumowitz, but when he went into New York, it got shortened to Mowitz. He came from Kovna Gubernia in Lithuania.

There had been two pogroms. I'm assuming he had the foresight to see there was a potential for disaster. They came to Bethlehem [where] my grandfather served as a rabbi in Europe. All the people at Agudas Achim came from the same part of Lithuania between 1910 and 1920.

So they were joining their landsmen?

Yes! Mr. Miller was the president. He had a German name, but with all the moving around, his father had actually come from Lithuania. He brought my grandfather over.

~

When I was 10, 11, 12, 13 years old, I went to my uncle's clothing store. He called it "Victory" after the World War II Victory Gardens, and his name was Victor. This was the husband of my Aunt Florence—in Yiddish Froomka. During the Depression, she was a clerk in some clothing store, and he went in for buttons. She would always say to him, "Tell that story one more time! One more time!" Victor would say, "I went in for buttons and that's how I fell in love and started dating."

They dated even though she was Orthodox and dating wasn't generally allowed?

Yes, my grandfather was very tolerant. And he knew more ways to keep a synagogue together ... Benny Kaplan, the son of Abraham Kaplan, and also Harry Friedman, who used to be V.P. in the '60s—he worked at the Steel, he was a master woodworker, and when we moved the synagogue to the North Side in the '60s, he did a lot—well, both men fell in love with gentiles. This was a big deal. But my grandfather said, "No problem, I'll convert them." Now, you're not supposed to convert just for marriage. These women became so Orthodox! Their husbands didn't care so much, but they —Mrs. Friedman and Mrs. Kaplan—were the perfect Jews and kept the line going. They were active in Sisterhood and kept kosher kitchens of the type that could be trusted to bring food into the synagogue [where the kitchen was very strictly kosher].

Between the synagogues, the rabbis used to talk an awful lot. They were only about six blocks apart. In 1921, the *shul* had moved to 421 Webster Street, two doors up from the South Side Public Library. It was a twin, and they broke through the walls. On the first floor were all these chairs, and upstairs a balcony for the women to sit [separate from the men]. There was a social room. The Sisterhood was very active with lots of social events. It was informal in those days—lox and bagels, beet soup, nothing complicated.

In about 1945, my grandfather got a letter from a yeshiva for Lithuanians in Cleveland, saying he was picked to be one of the rabbi-scholars there. He ignored it and said, "This is where I belong." He came from a great lineage but was always modest.

"We're Talking Thousands": From Irving Kaplan

My father's bar mitzvah was in 1937 with Rabbi Mowitz. Mr. [Herman] Friedman always read the Torah, until he couldn't read it any longer, then the Rabbi read it.

My grandfather wouldn't lift a finger at home, but he would open Agudath Achim on Webster Street early and sweep it out. Those were businessmen.

The businessmen went to minyan *(weekday morning service) everyday?*

They had an early minyan, maybe at 6:30. It varied because of the opening times and on Mondays and Thursdays would start 15 minutes earlier.

Because of the Torah reading? (Done only on these two weekday mornings)

Yes. And the little *shul* used to auction off ark openings and aliyahs. This was on the Holiday. They did it early in one day, or maybe erev Rosh Hashanah.

How did it happen?

I don't know. Just auctioned it off.

Like, "who'll give me 200?"

I think we're talking about thousands. It would be maybe $200 for ark openings, $300 for *aliyahs*. So I might get the honor even though this other person won the bid. It happened one time, and I went back and sat down by my *zayde*, and he nudged me, "Go over and shake his hand, you have to shake his hand..." So I did. You would have a whole crowd cycling through shaking the hand of the highest bidder. Everyone who got an honor did...they were...they were grateful.

Because the person was supporting the shul.[4]

Yeah. There were four families who could really support it, and all the rest paid minimal. So this is how they raised money.

Was this during the days of Rabbi Mowitz?

After Mowitz. It was the mid-50s, and after '59 when I was a bar mitzvah.

Later the shul had a joint *minyan* with Brith Sholom for a while. In the 1970s, they rotated back and forth between the two locations.

The Trouble with Labels: From Rabbi Allen Juda

When my family moved here, we lived on the other side (the North Side). We walked to the Conservative shul, Brith Sholom. Walking labeled me as Orthodox [which prohibits driving on the Sabbath] in congregants' eyes.

In January of 1975, my grandfather died, and I mourned him very much. It was just a few months before I was ordained, before I got married. It was very difficult. Being in mourning, I grew a beard. So I had this long beard, and my head was covered. [He wears a yarmulke throughout every day.] ... As always, theology and philosophy didn't matter —not my involvement with Camp Ramah [a Conservative Jewish summer camp], growing up in a Conservative synagogue, or going to a Conservative synagogue for Hebrew School and to JTS [Jewish Theological Seminary, also Conservative]. All that didn't matter to the people here. If I had my head covered, walked to synagogue on Shabbat, and had a beard—I was Orthodox!

---

[4] Synagogues and their clergy are supported almost entirely by their own members; dues are paid but these are usually inadequate to meet all the communal needs. From keeping the lights on to special projects, additional donations are considered essential.

We lived in the Towers at the top of Spring Street. Other members of the community lived there, too. We would walk to synagogue across the Hill-to-Hill Bridge, which was a treat on a windy, cold day. When we were coming off the Hill-to-Hill Bridge, we used to take the curve down to Third Street, go a little bit, and walk up the hill to Brodhead [where Brith Sholom was located].

We would usually see the car with three or four Agudas Achim guys driving right by us! [That is, even though it was Shabbat and they were Orthodox.] They would wave. They started at 7 a.m. and tried to finish by 9 a.m. because Martin Schwalb owned the Hub. He was also a big seller of Israel bonds, a great guy. Despite all that, he wanted to have that Hub open by 9 a.m., so because of one person, they would finish by then. We were with the Conservative synagogue; they were with the Orthodox synagogue. We were walking; they were driving!

Also, because it was so difficult to make a minyan (an assembly of 10 people, and in particular for the Orthodox, 10 men), for the weekday service at either synagogue and because Agudath Achim was home to an expert Torah reader or two, the "minyannaires" from Brith Sholom would go over to Agudath Achim for these semi-weekly occasions. Although once the last Torah reader died, we switched minyan to Brith Sholom because then I was the Torah reader.

~

Given all that back-and-forth and the absence of clearcut differences in practices between the two congregations, I like to think that there was something more to this story. Although it might not have been the *intention* when building the two synagogues, the two institutions did offer a way around the limited dating options for the young people of each, like two tribes that could inter-marry. After all, I had heard the complaint from a Jewish man who had grown up in a small Pennsylvania town that the Jewish families in the little towns were all so close that "the girls I knew were like sisters to me." As a result, there was no one he felt he could date!

Likewise, a woman said, "You didn't want to date anyone who grew up with you, though nobody ever talked much about it."

Instead, out of necessity, Rabbi Mowitz sent his daughter, Bob's mother, to the dances at Brith Sholom, where they were experiencing dating dilemmas of their own. She found her husband there. Lil Schwalb married Morris Mindlin, who though his family was involved with both synagogues appears from his sister Jean's comments to have been more present at Brith Sholom. According to Bob Trotner, Ruth Friedman, whose father was Agudath Achim-founding member Herman Friedman, married "attorney Sigmon, who was a big *macher* (Yiddish for influential person; from the German *machen*, to make, do) at Brith Sholom." As mentioned, Bob's aunt Florence Mowitz married Victor Genel, who had been with Brith Sholom from the time of his arrival.

At the very least, having two synagogues made for a more complex, interesting social life. Back then, people were not in the habit of driving over to nearby Allentown or Easton, which were home to several synagogues. Karen Bader recalled her surprise upon arriving in Bethlehem and meeting people in the city "who had never been out of Bethlehem."

There needed to be shared spaces for a sense of belonging to develop, including belonging as part of a couple. I learned that the more spaces, the more opportunities. Community requires layer upon layer of connection. Once a feeling of belonging takes root, community can grow. Then there is room for compassion—that give and take that allows for both rules and exceptions, as seen in these pages. Psychologist M. Scott Peck writes about this sort of emotional malleability occurring in Christian communities as well. Instead of "one or the other" it can be "both/and."

~

It was 2011, about the time in my family's story that we held what we call our "Civil War seder." When my oldest son, Jacob, was about 12 years old, he developed a great interest in the Civil War. As a family, we liked to occasionally drive to Washington, D.C., and visit the Lincoln Memorial. So that year we went to D.C.'s Ford's Theatre for a reenactment of the great drama that had unfolded there long ago. We listened to a talk by the "detective" who had investigated the assassination of Abraham Lincoln. The actor responded to audience questions exactly as though he were there 150 years before. We're related to the 16th president through my mother's side of the family (some of my great-greats included the Hanks family), which only added to Jacob's fascination.

On the trip to D.C., we stopped at Gettysburg on the way. This was the scene of one of the most well-known Civil War battles and later the site of Lincoln's best known speech. Jacob wore a little navy blue jacket that we had made together. The jacket had brass buttons and looked a lot like the homemade Civil War uniforms seen in vintage photos. His accessories were a canteen and homemade "hard tack." (Think salty, dried, terrible-tasting biscuits!) But he had left that jacket off for a stop at a hat shop, where he explained to the proprietor what he needed.

"Are you North or South?" she asked.

"North!" And so Jacob acquired a cap to match his jacket, which he proudly wore to tour the historic grounds and also at our family Passover seder that spring.

I remember Jacob perched in his chair next to my husband, who was leading the seder. This was Jacob finding his way to connect to *both* his early American family roots *and* his Jewish heritage. Like Robert Kroope enjoying breakfasts with friends at his parents' table, Jacob was processing who he is right there at our dinner table.

~

On the other hand, it was a difficult time for me. My mother's health was failing, so I went to visit my parents in the Midwest. Late at night while they slept, I would attempt time and again to write Robert's story, the one that became the "Lox and Eggs" story. Before that trip, I had happily shown a friend the transcript-like writeup of my visit with Robert, which I found fascinating. My friend had gently shaken her head and said, "It's not good storytelling. Not yet."

Even worse, with half of the United States once again turning against the other half due to social and economic differences, visits to my hometown sometimes left me feeling like a stranger. I didn't seem to belong there anymore.

This wasn't so simple as the North/South choice that Jacob could so readily answer. The both/and of his identity that he so smoothly arrived at felt elusive to me—and to our nation. Differences at the ideological level and eventually the identity level were growing more marked in our society.

However, in those years, we were just beginning to observe, with the two parties in Congress largely unable to work together, that being on one side could mean those who didn't agree could be considered incomprehensible, even morally wrong.

Being "in" too often seemingly means that someone else has to be made to feel like an outsider.

Then I thought about my mom's life story and got inspired. Born during the Great Depression of the 1930s, as a child she wore homemade clothes re-made from hand-me-downs to her mother. Despite being an intelligent person, she nearly missed out on going to high school in part because her parents needed someone to take care of her toddler sister while they worked. With some help from her brother, my mom earned her diploma anyway. Yet she missed out on the nursing training she wanted so badly because the family needed her to begin earning right away.

My mom went to work as a telephone operator, but she also educated herself through reading. Eventually, she fulfilled her life's wish that her children would all love to read. She would even play a card game called "Authors" with us, and I found myself drawn to that idea. Being an author—imagine that. And what did Mom love to read? Biographies of the stars.

Chapter 5
"Morning Star, O Cheering Sight[5]"
Fitting In, Standing Out, Finding Belonging

One of my neighbors, John Angelucci, recalled of his Jewish classmates in the 1920s, "Fun was being made of them, but the Jewish boys were very smart, very nice guys."

I asked John, son of Italian immigrants, "What sort of 'fun'?"

"It was sort of like snickering. For me, I did very little of that. They were nice to me. As far as adults, I don't recall any adults being abusive to the Jewish people. The Jewish people have so much going for them. It's a shame there's so much turmoil. They don't get a peaceful homeland. Jewish people are really taken up with education and want their children to learn everything they could ... They always had their nose in a book, they were gonna make something of themselves."

John recalled that outside of school, down on the South Side streets, "it was the League of Nations.... We had all kinds—Hungarian, a Black family, Pennsylvania Dutch, German."

"And you all played together?" I asked.

"Yeah, if they weren't arguing ... but it wasn't like it is today!"

---

[5] A Moravian song traditionally sung on Christmas Eve. "A young person from the congregation is invited to lead the singing, which features a call and response." (Source: Moravian Church)

Brith Sholom boys, circa 1960, probably at day camp.

Five Standouts

At some time, nearly everyone needs to look for ways to belong with other people and John was no exception but we'll get to that. The stories that follow, about five Jewish boys growing up in various decades in Bethlehem, show their struggles when it came to fitting into the world around them.

None of It Was Glorious: From Bob Born, born in the 1920s

From Brooklyn, we came to the area on my ninth birthday: September 29, 1933. We first moved to Allentown, where my father had gone ahead and rented a home. After he got his feet wet and decided where we would be, we moved to Bethlehem. I went to Nitschmann Junior High School [on the North Side], and it wasn't fun. I think I had a fight once every two weeks.

On what grounds?

113

They used to pick up all kinds of nicknames based on the fact that I was Jewish.

Do you remember any particular incident?

You mean the time I got my nose busted?

You could tell me about something more glorious if you want.

None of it was glorious.

Being Small: From Jerry Hausman, born in the 1930s

There was a certain amount of antisemitism. You got called a "dirty Jew." Being small, I got the hell away. I didn't wear a yarmulke; we weren't Orthodox. I was born in the '30s, and we have five generations in my family here. I was raised in Bethlehem. We all lived on the South Side—all of the Jewish families—around the Center. My father had a tavern, and we lived on Itaska Street, then Carlton, and then in Fountain Hill (the borough adjacent to South Bethlehem). I went to public school. We lived on Tombler Street, and there was a house for the Rabbi in Fountain Hill, too. We walked or took a trolley car to Hebrew School.

A Deniability: From Ira Lehrich, born in the 1930s

I never went out of my way to say I was Jewish. It was like a deniability. I wanted to be a white Christian. We were living in an area with very few Jews. I learned this from my father: He felt it would be detrimental to his business [Ross Common Water] to say he was Jewish. People knew, but he would keep quiet about it.

I saw some antisemitism; yes, I did. There were certain clubs that wouldn't invite Jews to join. It was not advertised. But it was good for me in the sense of learning to live with other people. You learn to tolerate people who are stupid. This was good before going into the army. Some people who are hippies with long hair are nice people. It doesn't mean that different is bad.

A Separate Issue: From Gordon Goldberg, born in the 1930s

I went to Neisser Elementary School; it's no longer there. It was the oldest brick school in Bethlehem. It was on Wall Street closer to Center Street on the North Side. I was probably the only Jew in the school. I experienced antisemitism now and then. A kid might call me "Christ-killer" or something like that that they picked up from their parents or church. One teacher always picked on me and slapped me around. After the fact, I reflected on it and realized it was probably antisemitism.

The Class System Was Easy to Recognize: From Henry Lehrich (Ira's brother), born in the 1930s

I tried to hide being Jewish. I went to Moravian Prep [on the North Side of Bethlehem] for kindergarten and first grade. Then I went to Calypso Elementary until sixth grade and Nitschmann through ninth, then Liberty through high school. I did not feel any antisemitism at Calypso or Nitschmann. In high school, it wasn't overt. The class system was easy to recognize. I recognized and accepted it. Outwardly, it didn't bother me. The big class division was the North and West sides in one group, the South Side in the other. Even as a West Sider, I looked down on the South Siders.

We went to Brith Sholom as kids. I hated it, although I do have one good memory of Hebrew School. I can still picture myself on the third floor in the Sunday school in 1948, when Israel declared their independence. Our teacher, Roland Siegel's mother, said, "This is a day you'll always remember." I thought, *She's full of* ... At the time, it had no impact. I did not enjoy going to Hebrew School, did not enjoy being Jewish. My bar mitzvah was in 1950, and I did not go back. I did not get confirmed. My parents were not activists, and I guess it rubbed off on me. Be a good person, don't make waves. They were not Zionists in any way, maybe later.

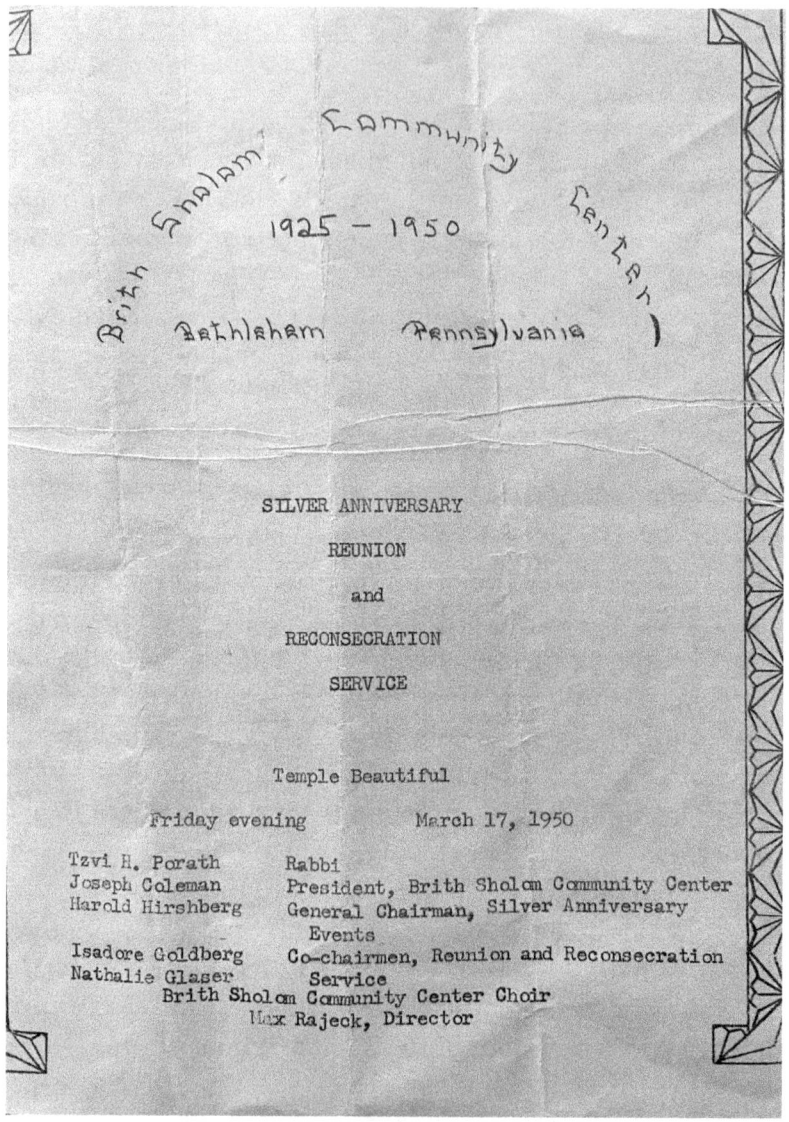

Brith Sholom Community Center

1925 — 1950

Bethlehem   Pennsylvania

SILVER ANNIVERSARY

REUNION

and

RECONSECRATION

SERVICE

Temple Beautiful

Friday evening   March 17, 1950

Tzvi H. Porath	Rabbi
Joseph Coleman	President, Brith Sholom Community Center
Harold Hirshberg	General Chairman, Silver Anniversary Events
Isadore Goldberg	Co-chairmen, Reunion and Reconsecration
Nathalie Glaser	Service

Brith Sholom Community Center Choir
Max Rajeck, Director

In March of 1950, 13-year-old Henry Lehrich got to give his "bar mitzvah address" to a full house on what was also the 25th Anniversary of Brith Sholom. Courtesy of Henry Lehrich.

Prayer	
Ma Tovu	Maz Rajeck and Choir
Sabbath Services	Pp. 11-25
Kiddush	Henry Lehrich
Mogen Ovos	Miss Bernice Blinderman Miss Norma Rajeck
Bar Mitzva Address	Henry Lehrich
Remarks	Rabbi Porath

RECONSECRATION PRAYERS

CONFIRMANTS' RECONSECRATION PRAYER

O God, with grateful hearts, we, who have been confirmed in the holy Synagogue of the Brith Sholom Community Center, come before Thee on this sacred evening of Reconsecration, to thank Thee for the love and tender care which Thou hast extended to us, from our earliest childhood to this hour. Under the rays of Thy goodness we have grown in strength of body and of mind.

May this service of Reconsecration strengthen us in the faith of Israel. May the influence of this hour ever remain with us, and help us to be loyal to the faith of our fathers, to the cause of right and truth. Help us, so to live, that we may find grace in the eyes of man, and reflect honor upon this holy institution which has given us our training. As Thou hast helped us to this day, so, we pray Thee, O God, mayest Thou help us in all the coming years of our life.

Amen.

My father was an *American* to his dying day. Thank goodness, our children all married Jews. The turning point for me was when we went to Israel in 1972. We were married 10 years already, very active [at a Reform congregation in Allentown]. When I returned from Israel, I felt proud of being Jewish. Before that, I tried to hide it.

~

Despite the early challenges, all five boys went on from these beginnings to find ways to be *both* uniquely themselves *and* part of a larger social fabric. Their teen years held challenges; as they grew to adulthood it was their unique personalities as well as the people around them—friends, teachers, family—who made the difference. What follow are more of their stories.

Understood: From Henry Lehrich

In my high school class [of perhaps hundreds], there were three Jewish guys and three Jewish girls. My friends were all Christian. I was active in AZA [the Jewish youth group], involved with that in high school. We had basketball and a lot of things at the Center. Marty Sonnenfeld was our coach. We played Pottstown, Hazleton, Allentown, and Easton. These were my Jewish friends, but my close friends were Christian.

My parents never said, "Don't date non-Jews," but it was understood. We were pretty assimilated, not religious at home and not keeping kosher.

A Caring Coach: From Gordon Goldberg

I was a good athlete, big for my age. I was as tall as I am now, maybe taller since I probably got shorter lately. The junior high school basketball coach wanted me to play varsity with the ninth graders. One day as I was going out, I was surrounded by three ninth graders who made it clear to me they didn't want a Jew on the basketball team. They were ready to beat me up. Fortunately, the science teacher, a big man, came out and chased them away. I quit the basketball team, just didn't show up to practice, and never said anything to anyone, not even my parents.

The coach couldn't understand why I quit. Later, he was taking tickets for a football game, and he asked, "Are you coming out for the basketball team?"

I said, "Yes, I am." Because the threat was no longer there, you see. Those guys were a bunch of hoods. Hoodlums. They probably all ended up in jail. But the coach sort of demoted me. Instead of having me practice with my friends, he made me practice with the kids who clearly wouldn't be making the team. It was his way of letting me know he wasn't happy. But I was talented, and he wanted me on the team. I soon got injured, and that was the end of my basketball career.

A Place to Be Accepted: From Jerry Hausman

After World War II, my brothers and I started Metro Products. My brothers had been in the service and when they came back, they opened it. I graduated from Fountain Hill High School and went to Muhlenberg College. I ended up in the Korean War ... left Bethlehem for four years and when I came back in '54 or '55, I went into the business.

Bowling Together: From Irving Kaplan, born in the 1940s

Some of the things we did at the Center: I can remember dance classes as a teen. And we had the Quad Cities set up by the shuls—Reading, Allentown, Bethlehem, and Easton. Then there was AZA [the boys' youth group] and BBG [the girls; youth group]. It's combined into BBYO [Bnai Brith Youth Organization] now. On our own, we played football, basketball ... it was all Jewish.

This was the '50s and '60s; you couldn't mix then. After Sunday school [at the Center], there was swimming and we'd play basketball. The pool table was the Men's Club's pride and joy. For a long time, they wouldn't let us use it. There were 32 men who bowled in the Old Steelworker's Club. One time, they were down a couple of men and they brought in me and another [teen], Mitch Fink. Until then, they'd all been "Mister" to me. That's when I started calling them by their first names.

Making Connections: From Bob Born

I went to Liberty High. One of the people I remember with tremendous fondness was Abe Weissman. He was the *melamed* (Hebrew for teacher) for my bar mitzvah ... Another was Harry Dandle. He was the [Liberty High School] teacher of Problems of American Democracy—Civics! And he gave all kinds of homework. He was the advisor for the "High Y Club" connected with the YMCA. I was the only Jewish kid in the club.

I got such a charge out of Harry Dandle. Previously, he had been a minister. It was from him I learned what Christians are all about. It resulted, after years had gone by and from his influence and that of Abe Weissman and particularly my father, in my becoming the National Chair at the ADL [Anti-Defamation League, which has Jewish roots] for Inter-faith Activities. I helped start the Institute for Jewish-Christian Understanding at Muhlenberg College and was quite delighted when at their first dinner they honored me.

~

Those five boys found their way to the manhood—the personhood—that they did, not only despite the adversity they faced, but in some ways *because* of it, though perhaps the same could be said of nearly anyone, Jewish or not. Back to John, my Italian-American neighbor, his was a long and difficult path due to having been orphaned early and needing to rely on his older siblings.

"I went to Liberty High School for two years before I quit. I was a big boy. One day, a fella said to me, 'Why don't you play football, John?' Well, when the bodies came *crunch!* together, I didn't know what to do. I played because my friend had asked me! He asked because of how I was built. The 12th grade had their own team. There was a fella [I remember], a good player. Well, there was a soda parlor near the high school. We all went in there at noon time in gangs. One time, I had just bought a pie—a big pie, like that *(he holds out his hands to show the measure)* if you can believe it—for 10 cents. Well, this fella grabbed it. If he had just given it back, it would have been all right. But he ate it completely. I said, 'What are you doing? That's my lunch!' He was a big guy, a popular guy. I was pleading with him."

"Years passed, and didn't I meet up with him. He said to me, 'I remember when I took that pie off you. I'm sorry.' How do you like that? And I accepted his apology. He was a big shot back then. When he ate it, he didn't care. Did I wish he would apologize? Anticipate meeting him? No! He had 15 years that it bothered him. I walked away thinking, *He had his just due, all those years that he thought about it.*"

But back then John's journey was just beginning. "I joined DeMolay's (a social club); I didn't have that much, but I did try to dress spiffy for it. There was a dance and I went up there. There was a mother, a guardian, at the door. I wore a coat that had a belt, we called it a Clark Gable. She wouldn't let me in! She said, 'You're not dressed.' That taught me a lesson. Some have it, some don't. I was on the side that didn't. I wasn't expecting everyone to know it. I wasn't expecting to have it thrown in my face."

"At 18, one of the first good things in my life happened," John said. "I got a job as a machinist apprentice with Bethlehem Steel. If that job hadn't come along, I don't know what would have happened to me." John apprenticed for four years and became a journeyman at the Steel, before surprising many around him by leaving the Steel to become a truck driver.

"I was trying to find that thing that would be out there for me," he recalled. And: "I was in the [military] service for a while, for a year and a half. They sent me to photographer school. If you don't go after something you want, you miss out. You have to keep your eyes and ears open; if something is attractive, go after it. That's how I went to photography school. I worked for five different companies until I landed a job at General Electric. Then I was in heaven, truly."

John and the five Jewish boys each needed to find their own way to belonging, as everyone does. And they did—at different times in their lives and in very many ways, while retaining their individuality.

Non-denominational Christian psychologist M. Scott Peck found that this is what community requires. Peck wrote that, compared to other kinds of groups, true community includes people of various demographics and stages of development, like a salad. "Community does not solve the problem of pluralism by obliterating diversity." (Source: Peck, page 234) Thriving happens in communities when individuals discover and stay connected to what makes them unique.

Brith Sholom kids and possibly neighborhood kids on the playground, mid-century.

That Star: Morris Mindlin

A shining, standout moment happened for Nevin Mindlin in the mid-1950s when his second-grade teacher noticed he could not see the blackboard. Nevin's mother, Lil (nee Schwalb), took him to the eye doctor near the North Side's Broad and Main streets.

Nevin recalled, "After I got my new glasses, as we walked up the hill, heading south on Main, I remarked to my mother, 'Wow, I never saw that star before.'"

Yet then and now, *that star* towers above South Mountain, shines with the light of hundreds of bulbs, and is visible up to 20 miles away. Growing up in Bethlehem, Nevin would have had to have known *that star* was there on the South Mountain, even if he couldn't see it well. But in Bethlehem, there are lots of 26-point Moravian stars illuminating porches, stores, and streets. People can be stars, too, and Nevin was close to one such: his father, Morris Mindlin.

Morris was born in Bethlehem. He spoke Yiddish as a child, and he didn't learn English until he got to public school. Morris's father, Abraham, was a painter. During the Great Depression, he also owned a hotel near the old train station under the Hill-to-Hill Bridge, and Morris had recalled waiting on tables as a kid there.

By the time Morris reached high school, he was salutatorian. He would have been valedictorian, but because he refused to sing Christmas carols, his grade in music was lowered, and he slipped to second place.

Morris's sister, Jean Mindlin Deutch, described Morris as "a hard act to follow" for another brother who was more physical and less academic than Morris. But coming along after Morris could be helpful, too. Jean remembered, "I was allowed in the debating club because my name was Mindlin; that is, because of Morris. Like him, I was very active in the synagogue. However, unlike Morris, there was no Hebrew School for me. My parents didn't believe girls needed extra education. My father could read Hebrew; my mother could not." Likewise, there was no college for Jean. (She said, "I wanted so much to go to college. I wanted to be a school teacher, but it wasn't meant to be. My parents couldn't see a girl going.")

Morris graduated with honors from Lehigh University in 1938 and from Pittsburgh Law School in 1941. He joined the Army later that year.

Jean recalled the day that Morris's path and many others' took an unexpected detour. Jean was about 17, helping out at her family's business. She was allowed to drive her father's truck and had gone over to Allentown one Sunday to watch a basketball game between the Center's team and the Allentown Jewish Community Center at 6th and Chew streets. It was December 7, 1941. Jean recalled what happened as she sat in the bleachers that morning: "We got word over the radio: War was declared. Morris was already in the service and was home on leave. That made a big difference to me. We went home immediately afterward, knowing he would have to go.

What did you do at home?

Nothing. Just listened to the radio.

How long before Morris left?

Very soon, as I recall.

~

"My dad went to Europe as a field artillery officer," Nevin explained. "His group was going right across France into Germany, right behind the infantry lines. Then he went into military government because he was a lawyer, down in Bavaria, I think."

Morris reached the rank of captain. Once he returned from the war, he went into law practice with Jackson Sigmon—that's Mark Sigmon's father, Nevin said. They flipped a coin to determine who would have the choice of front office or first name in the business. "My father chose first name and back office," Nevin said. "From there, he moved into public utility law and later held a position as a law judge with public utilities."

After Morris's return to Bethlehem, he had immersed himself in communal life, both for greater Bethlehem and its Jewish community where he took an active role in fundraising, among other roles. With his wife, Lil Mindlin, he would volunteer at the hospital on Christmas Day.

~

"Morris Mindlin was essential in the community," said Lew Schor, a friend and fellow Brith Sholom congregant. "He knew everyone and involved everyone, all of the community…. He was a true pillar of the Jewish community *and* of the general community. Everybody was friends with Morris. He's the only one I remember who could sit there in synagogue and really argue with the rabbi during the sermon. And you know what? He was right! And I never heard a derogatory comment about him. He was brilliant, compassionate. He knew the Torah better than most rabbis because he was interested. Morris was the authority at Brith Sholom, even more so than the rabbi at times. You would look at Morris and never think of him as an unusual person, but sit down and talk with him for five minutes and—boy!— he knew a lot. He could joke or he could be as serious as could be."

Nevin Mindlin recalled, "My father's family was more tied to what became the Conservative synagogue, Brith Sholom. My mother's family was engaged and part of the leadership in the Orthodox synagogue, Agudath Achim. My parents sort of insisted that I go to services. Friday nights, we had the traditional meal as a family.

Your mother, Lil, lit the candles?

She lit the candles. I was not allowed to go to football games on Friday nights because "it was not what we did." It was, "You're Jewish and this is what we're doing." My father did not work on Saturday mornings. [At Brith Sholom,] it was a very traditional service. The old men used to rib each other about how they spoke Yiddish and what countries they came from. In America, it didn't mean as much.

Morris and Lil had two children; Naomi Mindlin was Nevin's sister. "My parents were both very busy politically, communally, and with the synagogue," Nevin recalled. "My father didn't spend a lot of time at home. He ate dinner there every night guaranteed; then Friday nights, Saturday services, and I remember road trips together, with my father driving. He was completely absorbed in career things. It's not like we played baseball together; we just didn't do that. As I got older, we had a different relationship. We could talk more; it was easier for him to relate."

Nevin continued, "I had occasion to work with my son. I ran for mayor of Harrisburg, and my son ran the campaign. It's a great experience to work with your son. It doesn't usually happen, even less so now than in the past. But I learned how to read law with my father. I learned the Socratic method. He taught me how to research: You establish the fact pattern ... describe the holding. We would debate it! He was hugely wonderful, once we got past childhood. His connections got me started. We would have lunch together when he came to town; we had a good adult-to-adult relationship.

"My wife described my parents as being very liberal. They let us do whatever it was that expressed ourselves. They said, 'We don't care what you do, but do it the best you are able to do it.' My mother didn't care if I would become a plumber. She said, 'As a matter of fact, they make very good money and you ought to think about it.' If anything, they didn't pay attention. My father never hit me; he cross-examined me. I would wish for the spanking to get it over with!

"One time, I decided I was going to run away. Murray Nathanson picked me up in his car. My mother should have known something was wrong because I told her we were going to the library. Instead, I called my cousin, Stan, one of Jean's sons, and told him that we were running away, be back in a couple of days, that they shouldn't worry. We spent all our money on a day in Washington, D.C. When I came back, it was a conversation with my parents about what we were doing, why, that there was no excuse, and that I would have to deal with the school myself.

"Murray, on the other hand, had the car taken away and was grounded. He said, 'What did they do to you?'

"I said, 'Nothing.'

"My parents felt it was more important to learn from experiences. They raised us as independent thinkers, and we wouldn't be that way if they weren't that way. My parents were great role models.

"My mother was in Hadassah, Sisterhood and with my aunt in doing Braille for the Blind Association. She was engaged 100 percent. My parents were involved in interfaith groups and in the 250th anniversary celebration of Bethlehem every which way you can be. We pretty much

Morris and Lil Mindlin, at Morris's graduation from law school in 1941.
Contributed photo.

came to an understanding that we would have to deal with [their commitments].

"My father could be everything he was because of my mother, and my mother was everything she was because of my father. She had a degree in music and was going to be a teacher, but they made an agreement and she became a stay-at-home mom. When I came home from school, she was there. When I needed her, she was there. They were equals in many, many ways. It wasn't a subservient relationship; she was a very modern woman. She had her own things that she did; she didn't live vicariously through him. She gave huge amounts of volunteer time. My parents had a lot of affectionate physicality ... and toe-to-toe arguments. She was as much a partner as he was. The two of them made a choice; my mother was right there beside him. There was nothing my mother ever wanted that she never got.

"My mother passed away at Passover in 2007, and my father, in 2009 on *erev* Christmas (Hebrew for eve)."

When asked about discrimination, Nevin said, "I was oblivious to it—other than a couple of times I was called names. When I grew up, Bible verses were read every morning at the start of class, and Wednesday afternoons, my elementary school [Christian] classmates would be excused early, during school time, to go to Bible school. What was troubling was that I had to sit in class until school was over, and then when the Christian kids went out to play, I had to go to Hebrew School. I could never understand why we could not do our religious studies advantageously at the same time."

He added, "My parents may have felt more separation and discrimination than I ever did. My mother noted on occasion that there were social clubs in Bethlehem to which we could not belong. As mentioned, my father was penalized in a music class for not singing Christmas songs."

Nevin said he was always aware that he was part of a different culture within a larger community. He reflected positively on that experience. "I grew up and lived in two worlds, a Jewish community and a public community, with relative ease. Being distinct has never been an issue. I feel blessed that I grew up in Bethlehem, able to live comfortably as a Jew and as an American."

~

Through the years, from Depression to wartime, then during a period of greater prosperity followed by the social change of the '60s, night after night, the star shone from Bethlehem's South Mountain. Nevin said, "The star was just part of the cultural environment in which we lived. I was always aware that I lived in a city that was very Christian in culture, one proudly named after a seminal Christian event."

Growing Up and Fitting in on Prospect Avenue

Back around the time of Morris Mindlin's birth in the late 1910s, Bethlehem Steel named a young man, Eugene Gifford Grace, as its president. This Protestant son of a sea captain-turned-shopkeeper graduated valedictorian from Lehigh University in 1899. He got a job at Bethlehem Steel as an electric crane operator. As Eugene worked his way up through the ranks, he married Marion Brown, the boss's daughter, and they settled in a house on Fourth Street in Bethlehem.

The South Side was becoming crowded with steelworker families. Developers put up row homes on any available land bordering the city center. This included building up what became known as the West Side of Bethlehem—north of the river and west of the original Moravian settlement.

After he was promoted to President, Eugene Grace moved his family to a mansion in the West Side on Prospect Avenue, which soon boasted the mansions of his top executives as well, between about 11th Avenue and 15th Avenue. But other families not affiliated with the Steel lived there as well, including some Jewish families.

Bethlehem had a viable, active Jewish community, Ira Lehrich said, and in Bethlehem, "Jewish people did not live in any one particular place, like the way in Allentown they [historically] lived around 17th Street. When I was a youngster, very few of my friends lived on the South Side. They lived in Fountain Hill, Center Street, and on the North Side in Edgeboro,[6] the Rosemont Section, the West Side. You could buy a house anywhere, and nobody bothered you. On the North Side, there were Jewish-owned drug stores like Milgreens, Dr. Glazier was on Broad Street, Sadie Berman had properties there, the Borns—there was a building vacant and the city of Bethlehem transported some of [the company Just Born's] stuff with their own trucks from New York. It became a tremendous factory."

"My parents originally lived on West Third Street in Bethlehem," said Henry Lehrich, and like many natives of this city, he pronounced it Beth-lem. "Dad was a wonderful guy, [he had been] a private in the army. After World War I, his mother had died so he came to live in Bethlehem with his Aunt Nan and Uncle Henry. Henry was in the beverage and liquor business, Wiesenberger Beverage, and my dad came out to work for him in the early 1920s and met my mother here. I had a good relationship with both of them. Dad was very quiet, unassuming, an absolute gentleman to the nth degree. I never heard a bad word from him. He was a meticulous businessman."

Henry continued, "He was never involved in any degree with the Jewish Community Center. He was brought up in the Reform tradition; his father was from Austria-Hungary.

---

[6] Rabbi Allen Juda shared that there was a neighborhood in Bethlehem with a covenant to exclude Jews." This was not uncommon at the time; often, covenants also excluded Catholics. He recalled members of Phillips family purchasing a home in the same neighborhood, however, "probably in the 1950s."

My father was born in this country in 1896. He never had a bar mitzvah. He didn't have much Jewish love or knowledge. He spent maybe a half an hour [observing] Yom Kippur. He was not a leader; he was a hard worker."

"As a kid, I used to love to go to work with my dad. He was a bottler of Nesbitt's Orange Soda. I used to pull out the cigarette butts from the returned bottles. He had a retail operation. One time especially, in 1955, the week before Christmas, the water in Bethlehem turned brown, and we were busy. Dad bottled spring water at Ross Common in the Poconos. We had five-gallon bottles to deliver to offices. After my uncle died, [my father operated] Ross Common Spring Water and Beverage Company, first on West Third Street, then on Walnut Street where the parking garage is."

"After Prohibition, he went into beer. My dad was not a bootlegger. Notice I said 'my dad was not'? Sam Wiesenberger, the brother of my great uncle, he *was* a bootlegger. They were an old family in Bethlehem from the late 1800s."

When Ira was born, the family moved to 1111 W. North Street, also on the West Side and from there to 7th and Prospect Avenue.

"We had a cluster of Jews around our neighborhood," Henry said. The house across the street was Morris Black's house. Sam and Edith Black lived there with their children, Robert and Ellen. I used to babysit. At 8th and Prospect, there was a house built in the 1920s. The Borns moved into it in the '40s. Across from the Borns was D.M. Goldberg. In the middle of the block were the Refowiches, Bill and Sylvia. They had a clothing store at 3rd and New. We were very close, used to walk up and down the block and visit. At Market and 7th or 8th was Joseph Coleman, one of the presidents of Coleman Furniture Store."

"There was a big closeness among the Jews that lived in town at that time," Henry said. "Antisemitism was always there; people looked at us as being Jewish. We were 'the Jews who lived at 7th and Prospect.'"

A horse stone or carriage block in front of the former Lehrich family home on Prospect Avenue in Bethlehem. The stone bears both the restored name of the original owner and ART LEHRICH, the father of the Lehrich brothers who grew up in this home. The family no longer owns the house. Photo by the author.

~

For me, it was like finding treasure to realize that, in a neighborhood of historic significance for its industrial leaders, there were some Jewish families and that this same neighborhood where I lived was meaningful to Jewish Bethlehem's past. Prior to the Lehrich family's residency there, Aaron Potruch, the Center's first president, had lived at 8th and Prospect. Years after the Lehrichs and other families had aged out of their homes, the Kay family moved to Prospect Avenue. When my family moved into the same neighborhood upon arriving in Bethlehem, the Kays were among the first to reach out and befriend us. We had unwittingly tapped into that "big closeness" among Jewish families scattered through the neighborhood, one rooted in this particular place.

A Newcomer's Welcome: Elsa Heilbronn

Ira Lehrich, the eldest son in a family of three boys, shared a story that shows how Bethlehem's Jewish families had enormous capacity to welcome and help newcomers belong. In about 1936, during the runup to World War II, "the rabbi at Brith Sholom announced that the Hebrew Immigrant Association had young people [who needed] to leave Germany and Europe and get accepted here," Ira recalled. "The parents could not leave Germany, but the children could. The idea was that later the parents would come over or the child would go back. [The plea was] for a home for a Jewish girl. She came and lived with the family."

"Elsa was brought up as a member of the family. We had to do a lot of work at our house—laundry, babysitting," Ira said. My mother had a chart for us with stars and was a little tough—very regimented, very difficult. [Plus,] Elsa walked to Liberty High School and back every day."

Lehrich family portrait, circa 1945. Top row, left to right, Ira, Arthur,
Elsa Heilbronn, Sylvia and Moe Perkin. Bottom row, Betty, Henry, Paul,
Grandma Fanny Perkin

Henry continued the story. "My sister, Elsa Heilbronn,
was confirmed at Brith Sholom. In the mid-'30s, Congress
passed a special law allowing about 1,000 children to be
brought to this country from Germany. They chose children
as the least intimidating, [being] those that wouldn't steal
jobs. They would be placed in homes in rural America where
they could be easily assimilated and not seen as a threat.
Parents sent their kids, recognizing the threat of Hitler. My
sister came in '36 at the age of 13. Her sister had come to
this country in '35. They came with the assumption that
their parents would come, too." They did not. Elsa's parents
and youngest sister died before they could escape Europe.

"After high school, Elsa went to Johns Hopkins Nursing
School," Henry said. "She had corresponded with her
parents until about '42. Their last letter to her said, 'We
are leaving for Poland.' [Poland was the site of a number
of concentration camps, including Auschwitz.] Elsa kept all
the letters and donated them to the Holocaust Museum. She

moved to Israel in '72. I considered her my sister, and I had a good relationship with her."

"You've Been Elected": Rabbi Tzvi Porath

Sometimes, rather than people having to work to fit in or try to stand out, they are chosen by a group to belong to that group. That's what happened for Rabbi Tzvi Porath.

"My father was a chaplain in the army [during World War II], then he went to Philadelphia and worked for B'nai Brith," said Rabbi Jonathan Porath. "His name was Tzvi, and he passed away [several] years ago. My mother, Esther, will be 96. The way she tells it, my father was invited to give a talk at [the Brith Sholom Jewish Community Center] in Bethlehem in '47 or '48 about his wartime experiences. At the end, there was a hubbub in the audience, some talking amongst themselves. Someone stood up and said, 'You have been elected rabbi of our synagogue.'"

"When my parents got married, they were not going to do a rabbinic career. Until Bethlehem. My mother has only wonderful, warm feelings about Bethlehem. And it was the beginning of a 50-year pulpit rabbi career."

Jonathan was four years old when the family moved to Bethlehem. "We lived on North Clewell Street in Fountain Hill, across from a cinder block police station, firehouse, and jail. The cemetery was up the hill. The neighbors behind us were Jewish [the Rosenbergs] and had a garden. They had a truck and would give my father and me a ride to the synagogue on Friday afternoons. Of course, we walked home on the Sabbath [which starts at sundown on Friday]. And I remember the people: Alice Phillips, whose son was David. The Lehrichs, who had a soda business. Mr. Weissman taught Hebrew School. I started earlier because I was the rabbi's son, and began studying Torah there. I started public school in Bethlehem. I remember Main Street and walking along with my father. He would stop in all the shops; there were so many Jewish shops along there. I remember the pool and the basketball court downstairs at the Center. It was across the street and down the hill from Lehigh. We would go to the Lookout Point. It was a lovely childhood."

Fitting in By Knowing People: Betsy Glazier

The day I met with Betsy to learn more about her story, she fluttered around her apartment like a songbird, not content at first to stay still. Finally, she went into the bedroom and brought out a newspaper clipping. More at ease once she had the newspaper in her hand, she sat with me at her kitchen table.

Decades before, Betsy became a central figure in Bethlehem society, but for another reason from those of Morris Mindlin or Rabbi Porath. As a result, talking with her gave me a different glimpse into Bethlehem Jewish lives. The clipping Betsy shared with me came from the *Bethlehem Globe-Times* (the two newspapers had merged). The clipping was undated and described the closing of her father-in-law, Morris Glazier's, furniture store some decades before: "Glazier remembers well the early marketplace of Third Street —the informal credit that was always honored, shopping housewives with their money knotted in handkerchiefs, and trolley cars."

Betsy flitted between subjects, mentioning her own father's work and referring me to other potential interviewees. I could tell our conversation was difficult for her, being the person interviewed rather than the other way around. Reporting was in her blood.

"My father was a journalist, author, and folklorist," Betsy said. From another room, she retrieved framed articles about each of her parents. When I asked their names, she pointed to one of the frames. Below a photo, the label read "George Korson."

To get on in life, Betsy said, "you have to know people." She credited help from other people as the key to her whole writing career. It might have been the key to much more than that as well. Betsy's father had become editor of the *Red Cross Courier* in Washington, D.C.. At a convention, George ran into an old friend from the *Allentown Chronicle*, where he had also worked. Fred Ritter, who had since become the managing editor of the *Bethlehem Globe-Times*. Fred told George, "Our women's editor is going into the service. Send your daughter up for an interview."

In the early 1950s, Betsy came to town by herself, lodging at the Hotel Bethlehem. "I was so scared, I put a chair against the door," she recalled. She got the job as editor of the *Globe-Times*' Women's Page. "We printed every women's meeting, the wedding announcements, the church groups. You wanted to get your picture in there. It was a social thing. One time, I did a story on a 'Mother of Twins' club."

The women on this page were "of a certain class," Betsy said—white, married women who did not need to go to work. "Everyone wanted me to be their friend. I was invited to speak about how to get your group publicity."

Betsy smiled and leaned toward me. "So what does a young Jewish girl do to meet people when she's just moved to a new place? I joined the synagogue. Rabbi Tzvi Porath invited me to lunch at the Hotel Bethlehem. So he goes home and tells his wife, Esther, about me. And you know how we women are: She wanted to be a matchmaker."

According to Esther Porath, there were three eligible Jewish bachelors in town. "The first one, my husband's cousin, had mononucleosis so he was out of play," Betsy said. "The second one I went out with, but he wasn't my cup of tea. Meanwhile, I had a romance going with the night editor of the paper, an Italian, a real good-looking guy. I would go home from work and take a nap, then go back to the office.

"Well, I rented a room from a family. The third guy called me there, and that was my husband. He told me he fixes 'choppers.' I thought, 'Ooo, helicopters,'" Betsy said, squeezing her shoulders up and batting her long eyelashes over a sweet smile. "But he was a dentist."

Betsy and Harold Glazier had their first date at Walps's, "specializing in Pennsylvania Dutch meals." Though no longer there, the restaurant was located on the former Route 22, now Union Boulevard, at Airport Road. Postcard courtesy of Bethlehem Area Public Library.

For their first date, the couple went to a restaurant called Walp's on Union Boulevard and Airport Road. "We shared a chocolate pudding. Isn't that funny?" Betsy said. "I don't know why we shared." Harold Glazier was from a wonderful family, she added. He was born in Bethlehem, one of five children, and went to public school on the South Side. His parents had the furniture store, and his father, Morris, was on the original board of trustees of the Brith Sholom Community Center.

Harold and his two brothers all went to Bucknell University in Lewisburg, Pennsylvania. Brother Bernard went to law school and brother Nat got a master's degree in business administration; both went back into the furniture business before expanding into a toy store and a carpet store on the North Side. When Teddy's Toy Town opened and knocked out the toy store, Betsy said that business became a card shop. A few doors up was Milgreen's, a large 5 & 10 cent store owned by Harold's sister's husband, Milton Greenberg.

Betsy Glazier wrote plays for congregants to act out at the Center. She's shown here as one of the cast for her 1964 "Anniversary Waltz." Front (l to r): Art Larky, Marcia Weinberg, Lucille Newman, Art Schachter. Back (l to r): Beth Neuman, Ralene Cook, Marty Sonnenfeld, Zelda Levin, Linda Kreeger, Betsy Glazier, Sue Robinson, Stuart Brown, Bunny Glickman, Bea Schachter, Murray Glickman, Paul Lehrich, Stuart Goldberg.

Today, the shops are all closed. And the people? "All gone," Betsy said. "Harold was the youngest and the last to die. The others all went before him." He died in 2005 at the age of 84. Betsy said she missed Harold, but she did not dwell on it, preferring to tell this story: "He started on West Broad Street, between the family carpet store and the toy store, across from the Boyd movie theatre. His last office was at 701 West Union Boulevard where he rented from Ed and Arnie Cook, [Jewish] orthodontists."

Things went along well from the start, except "there was a newspaper guild in Allentown," Betsy said. "They knew my father and that his daughter was working at the *Globe-Times* in Bethlehem. So they got in touch with me, and I met them at my in-laws' house—I was engaged at the time. They wanted me to organize, and that's how they would do it. So there were about six of us, and between one thing and another, the newspaper got rid of us. They couldn't do this today, but they said they were firing me because I married. So when the *Globe-Times* people went on strike, I brought them coffee in the street."

That didn't sit well with everyone.

"The managing editor, Fred, the one who hired me, saw my husband at the Pure Food [a lunch restaurant] and said to him, 'You're a professional man in town, and I don't think it's appropriate for your wife to be involved with these people.' Well, it didn't come to anything anyway." Betsy's voice trailed off. I pressed her, asking whether she would have continued to support the movement, had it not died out, even if her husband had pressured her to stay away from them.

"I probably would have," Betsy said. "I was independent at the time."

Harold's business thrived such that he was able to refer patients to other dentists, many of them just starting out. "Whoever contacted him," Betsy recalled, "he would send them patients."

The family first lived in a two-room apartment next to the Hotel Bethlehem downtown and later on Eaton Avenue, on the North Side, with their three children. "I was very restless," Betsy said. She did a lot of volunteer work, and once she could "get away," went to a homemaker service that helped mostly older people and included a Visiting Nurses Association that paid Betsy to help with their billing. Later, she went into social work.

Betsy has a daughter and two sons. "They're all in the helping professions," she said. "My daughter, Nancy, is a high school guidance counselor in Irvine, California. Steve is a child psychologist in Melrose Park and the father of triplets.

Dan has a J.D. and M.S.W. from Washington University and is head of Legal Services of Eastern Missouri."

Betsy got out a framed article from the time Dan received an Unsung Hero Award. The article was from the *Jewish Lights* newspaper of St. Louis. Betsy was quiet by this time, calm. She pushed the framed article closer, urging me to read all about it.

Betsy also understood my gradual progress as a writer, discerning more easily than I could what it all meant. After all, she had been through some of the same career steps. Betsy, of course, saved all my *Bethlehem Press* clippings.

~

The more Bethlehemites I spoke with, the more connection I saw between what I was doing and what the New Deal era researchers had done—Zora Neale Hurston, as mentioned, and documentary photographer Dorothea Lange, whose work I had long admired. Hurston in particular wrote of editing "the huge mass of material" she had and getting it "arranged in some sequence." (Source: Hurston, 1942, page 251) Spending time with Betsy helped me see the meaning and dignity in what I was doing. After all, she, too, was one of this community of women, chronicling lives, unbounded by time.

Chapter 6
"O Come Ye to Bethlehem"
Arriving Survivors

As a young soldier during World War II, Gus Levin shipped out to Italy, leaving the only home he had ever known. He was a friend of Betsy and Harold Glazier, and Betsy had encouraged me to call him. Gus was one of more than 145 young Bethlehem-born Jewish men who enlisted, along with most of the other young men of this city.

After the war, Gus traveled through Italy, delivering payments from the US government to Italian families whose sons had died while enlisted in the US military. Gus eventually returned home. The story of a vast number of Europe's Jewish men, women, and children ended very differently.

Gus and Zelda Levin at their Bethlehem apartment, February 17, 2011

In Gus's Bethlehem apartment some 70 years later, he said of the fate of European Jews, "It wasn't until we got home that we knew." He shook his head in silent reflection. Perhaps that's because except for the soldiers who liberated the concentration camps and could witness the magnitude, many soldiers overseas were unaware how bad things were for so many people who one man declared did not belong— both mirroring and backed by his masses of true believers.

Six million Jewish people were murdered. Some after being arrested, told to report to train stations and sent to gas chambers. Others were marched into forests en masse and told to dig their own grave. An additional five million non-Jewish Europeans suffered the same fate—including Poles, homosexuals, Romas, political dissidents, and more. Eleven million people total. A small fraction of the targeted individuals survived, either in hiding or despite the horrendous conditions in slave labor camps, until they were liberated by Allied troops.

Even the arrival in the United States of European Holocaust survivors in the 1950s at first did little to shed light on what had happened to them. They were referred to by many Americans as "DPs" (Displaced Persons), a term that had a stigma attached. Yet these survivors had been through a world torn apart, and in some ways, they could never break out of the resulting terrible landscape of the mind. They had had little choice in what had befallen them and now the few choices they did have would need to suffice.

Several of the survivors who came to Bethlehem took on—or perhaps more accurately, were given—significant roles by the Jewish community, both for who they were as people and for what they had been through. Neither the survivors nor the community in Bethlehem wasted any time weaving them into the fabric of life.

German forces invaded and occupied Hungary beginning on March 19, 1944. Tanks rolled into Budapest, and a pro-German government was installed. Mass deportation of the Jewish population, the last intact Jewish population in occupied Europe at the time, to German slave labor and death camps in Poland began. From May 15 to July 9, 1944, Hungarian gendarmerie officials, under the guidance of German SS officials, deported around 440,000 Jews from Hungary.
(Source: United States Holocaust Memorial Museum)
Photo courtesy of Jewish News Syndicate.

"The Man," Bill Weisz: From Rabbi Allen Juda

Bill Weisz was a Holocaust survivor from Hungary. His wife and two daughters were murdered by the Nazis. He survived by working in a slave labor camp. When he came here, he married Ann Gandel. Her father was Reverend Abraham Gandel, one of two very significant early personalities. He was a *shochet* (one who is able to ensure meat is kosher) and a *mohel* (one who performs the Jewish rite of circumcision).

Bill and Ann lived on the South Side, and they were very traditional. They walked to *shul* (Yiddish for synagogue) on Shabbos and *yom tovs* (holy days). He was head of daily *minyan* (10 people, referring to the minimum number required for the morning prayer service). Bill had a list near the phone in the hallway at the Center, which he would use to call businessmen or people up at Lehigh. This was the "on call" list for when there weren't enough to make a *minyan*. He rarely missed anything. He was very kind, remarkable when you think of what he had been through. He had always been in good health.

I didn't always go to *minyan* when it was at AA [Agudath Achim] on Linwood Avenue. One day, those brilliant guys noticed Bill wasn't getting up at the times for the prayers. He had had a stroke; they waited until the end of *minyan* and drove him to the hospital. This was a few days before the Yom Kippur. I think Harry Friedman drove him.

I was literally getting ready to go upstairs for *Kol Nidre* (the evening service at the start of Yom Kippur) when I got the call that Bill had died. I had to go up and tell everyone. It was just a ... a communal mourning.

Bill got along very peacefully with everyone, except for one person, Joe Spitz, of all people. Joe was also from Hungary. His wife and two daughters were also murdered by the Nazis, and he also survived in a work camp. He also came here and married someone from Bethlehem. Neither of these two couples had children because they were too old. Bill was clearly "the man." Once Bill died, Joe became "the man." People embraced him, or maybe he came around more then.

Laszlo

"His name was Laszlo," said Laszlo's son, Sam, who requested that his last name not be used. "In English, Les. Leslie." Laszlo grew up in Hungary, the son of a successful Jewish family that owned an estate. In early adulthood, this is where he lived and labored. This well-liked family employed between 13 and 30 people, depending on the season, together tending vineyards and bottling wine and seltzer. As with other landowning men of that time and place, Laszlo's father, Samuel, was considered an official, a sort of judge. Laszlo himself was a leader among men, lively and strong, with plenty who called themselves his friend. But during World War II, the Nazis took control of Hungary and imprisoned the Jewish men in forced labor camps, including Laszlo and his three brothers, two of whom were later killed by fascists. The camp Laszlo was in was called Sarospatak and that's where he first met Joe Spitz, with whom he would later cross paths in Bethlehem.

"My dad was very resourceful," Sam said. "He was able to sneak out because he was needed at home ... He was still keeping the place going."

One day not long after Laszlo managed to get home, the Jewish population was notified of a mandatory move to the ghetto, a segregated and walled-off area of the nearby town. He had a newly-married sister living in this section already and there they all went.

"My dad figured out how to get out of there," Sam said. However, Laszlo had a dilemma. His parents, sisters, and grandparents were still in the ghetto.

Then his mother, Rose, sent him a message that they were about to be moved, saying, "You're going to have to come with us."

Here Sam paused, trying to make sense of what happened next. "My father was about 30 years old ..." Understanding has proven elusive, but Sam forged on: "So okay, he gave the keys to the estate's workers. He said, 'I don't know if I'm ever coming back; if that happens, this is all yours.' They were like family. He snuck back into the ghetto, found his family, and boarded a train with them ... to Auschwitz."

In the "selections" that followed deportation by boxcar, Laszlo and his older brother Louis were assigned to slave labor. Their parents, grandparents, sisters, and all the rest of the extended family were then murdered.

147

Laszlo spent one month in Auschwitz before being transferred to a sub-camp, Kittlitztreben. It was during this time that he met another person with whom he would also again cross paths, ever so briefly, years later in Bethlehem. That man was a *kapo* (prisoner-supervisor) who abused the prisoners.

Sam did not grow up knowing this story. "It was not talked about," he said. "No one talked about the Holocaust until the mid- to late-'70s.... I knew there were secrets. If something about Nazis or the war came on the television, my mom changed the station, or else my dad would scream at night in his sleep. He was prone to fits of violence."

Sam did not realize until adulthood that there was such a category as "children of Holocaust survivors." He eventually met a therapist who was the wife of a rabbi. She asked Sam, "Do you ever feel like the Nazis control your life?" That was a cathartic moment for Sam, who said, "It always struck me that this hateful group of people, so far away, so long ago, have so much effect on what I do every day."

Sam might not know all of the details of what his father endured in the camps, but he has lived his whole life with the effects—and for our conversation, he didn't dwell on them. "Skip to the end," he said of the war, as if his narrative were a movie. "The Russians were coming. My dad suspected something when the SS came in and said, 'Everyone out!' and 'March!'"

SS stood for Schutzstaffel. From the beginning of the Nazi regime, Adoph Hitler tasked the SS with the removal and eventual murder of political and so-called racial enemies of his regime. The SS was specifically intent on murdering all of Europe's Jews.

Sam continued, "My father and nine friends were in the hospital barracks; he had an injured back. He refused to go—risked being shot—but the SS were in a great hurry. My dad said to the others with him, 'We're staying. We know what's here, but we don't know what's out there.'"

When only these 10 remained, they broke into the SS quarters. "There was food on the stove, clothes hanging on hooks. Some of the men couldn't walk, but there was a bottle of morphine. Someone poured the morphine on sugar cubes, and that's how the rest of them got up.

"So here they are, walking down the road in the SS uniforms and, to make matters worse, my dad has this little Hitler mustache, and the Russian soldiers who look like Cossacks come. So there's this big Cossack-looking guy on a horse with a gun pointing at my dad. My dad lifts his cap and shows his head is shaved with just a stripe down the middle of his head that all the inmates got. The man on the horse leaned forward and asked, *'Bistu a Yid?'* (Yiddish for are you Jewish?) The guy was a Jew!"

Then the Soviet army decided to send Laszlo and the nine frail survivors he led to the battlefront, but Laszlo orchestrated the group's escape. He was in such poor condition by the time he returned to his hometown that the mayor, who had sided with the Nazis, giggled in derision upon seeing him.

However, Laszlo was generally a feared man—and not only because of his powerful connections. Sam said, "He was volatile and not a person to be messed with."

By that time, his family home had been taken over by someone with no right to be there, the family's belongings parceled out. Laszlo was determined to get them back. While there were those who had reason to fear Laszlo's return, others were glad to see him.

Sam continued, "As my father was walking, one of the [estate] workers saw him and ran up. He said, 'We need to make sure this doesn't happen to you again.' He outfitted Laszlo with a machine gun and two bandoliers of bullets that Laszlo wore over his chest, like Pancho Villa."

Thus armed, Laszlo approached his home. "Here's my dad coming and the man living there is scared," Sam said. 'I want you out of here by 3:00,' my dad said." *Sam leans forward and gives me a piercing look.* "'And I want it clean!'"

So Laszlo resumed his work on the family estate and was still there when the Communists came in '49. "They took the farm and communized it," Sam said. "[The Communists] tried to kill the Roman Catholic priest. My dad was friends with him, and when he got word they were going to try and kill this friend, my dad stood guard at the door with a pitchfork and said, 'You'll have to take me first.' He had a reputation! He got a commendation for saving that priest, and he always carried it with him.

"Throughout this time, Laszlo worked with the underground in a loose network smuggling Jews out of Europe, from Hungary to Austria. The authorities suspected him and eventually arrested him along with his connection. They held them each for about a month and tortured them, but neither gave up the other.

"The next thing was that my dad was going to be killed by them. There was a guy that my grandmother had babysat, an official who came to see my dad. He said, 'They're coming to kill you. You don't know me, I wasn't here, but I'm leaving the door open. Don't go home.'

"Always oppositional, my dad went home. He put together a group and got out of Hungary. One of those in the group was three years old, and my dad carried him on his shoulders because he was too little to run fast enough.

"Years later, I went with my dad to a wedding, and there's this American soldier, and he saw my dad and started crying. My dad hadn't known the man was going to be there, but he was the kid he had saved."

Laszlo made it to a DP (Displaced Persons) camp in Austria. Sam recalled, "He had an uncle, Max Hausman, here in Bethlehem, who is Jerry Hausman's father. Max said, 'Come to the US.'"

So Laszlo made his way to Bethlehem. On arriving, Sam said, "The two Adams girls came over from South

Young Sam with his parents, Laszlo and Ruth, on Third Street, South Bethlehem, circa 1959. Contributed photo.

Bethlehem, and they were fluent in Hungarian. One was tall and one was very small. My dad liked them both. He asked, 'Which one isn't married?'"

~

When I asked Sam whether small meant petite, he replied, "That's my Aunt Mildred." Laszlo married Ruth Adams, the taller sister, after a one-month engagement. He had been in so many places and lost so much, but finally, in Bethlehem, he helped weave himself into the community. He worked briefly at Just Born, the candy company started by Sam Born and Jack and Ira Shaffer, then got a job in a garment factory on the South Side, where Aunt Mildred worked.

On Laszlo's first day of work at the factory, a worker brought over a load of garments and dumped them in front of Laszlo. The two men looked at each other. Laszlo's eyes widened, then narrowed. The worker paled. He was the *kapo* from the concentration camp; he went out for lunch that day and never came back.

In Bethlehem, Laszlo came across Joe Spitz, whom he had also met in the labor camp. Joe had been through his own nightmare, and the two would spend time together in Joe's store. In these ways, Laszlo and others were able to build new lives together in Bethlehem.

Sam was born and grew up in this city, seemingly completely removed from the scenes Laszlo had witnessed and survived. Sam learned about his father's past when the family went to Hungary in 1976, but he realized something else as well. "Word got around that [my father] was there," Sam said. "People were hiding from him! People were terrified he was going to wreak havoc.... I guess my mom had always made excuses for his behavior, that he had 'been through a lot,' but I realized he'd always been a violent guy! This lack of self-control: It's the way he always was, and it was how he survived."

The Name-Changer

In 1934, before Rosalie Rosenbaum gave birth to her only child, she extracted a promise from her husband, Isak: Under no condition would the child be named Sophie. Her mother-in-law, who had died two years earlier, had been named Sophie. Rosalie detested the name.

Rosalie was admitted into a Viennese sanatorium for the birth. (It was the early 1930s, and hospitals were not commonly used for childbirth.) When Rosalie came to afterward, she discovered that her daughter had nevertheless been given the name Sophie.

Did Rosalie keep quiet about it? Let it roll off her back? "She talked about it all the time," said her daughter. Rosalie was a firebrand, and it served her—and her husband and daughter—very well.

In 1898, the Rosenbaum family had opened a chain of dry goods and pharmaceutical stores in Vienna. Isak and Rosalie lived in an apartment one block from the Danube River. They spoke Austrian German and had a comfortable life. Then came November 9 and 10, 1938, *Kristallnacht* (or in English, the Night of Broken Glass), a pogrom in which Nazi storm troopers and local citizens wreaked havoc on Jewish businesses and persons. They committed violent acts against Jews across Germany and Austria and arrested some 30,000 Jewish men, including Isak. He was sent to "jail" at Dachau concentration camp.

In those early days, the prisoners were allowed to correspond. Isak sent Rosalie several postcards and letters in an effort to arrange an exodus. Their daughter said of the prison system, "When it was shown that someone could leave the country, they would be released from the concentration camp. The United States quota for that nationality was full. Isak could not gain admission to the United States.... He could go to Argentina, to Shanghai, or to Palestine."

The earliest available was Palestine, so Rosalie purchased a ticket for Isak and submitted the paperwork to arrange safe passage with the government. Isak was released on January 3, 1939.

Isak left the country immediately. He entered Haifa, Palestine, in June of 1939. His wife and daughter remained in Vienna, but Rosalie had a plan. On July 9, 1939, she packed a small suitcase for five-year-old Sophie and placed a treasured teddy bear in the child's arms. Rosalie then put her young daughter on a Kindertransport bound for London. The Refugee Children's Movement in Europe had organized the rescue and how it would be done. The documentary *Into the Arms of Strangers: Stories of the Kindertransport* narrated by Judi Dench shares more.

Kindertransports were trains and ships that carried unaccompanied Jewish children under age 17 away from the worsening situation to foster homes in England, with the stated intention that the children would return to their parents after conditions improved. Between December 1, 1938, and September 1, 1939, the British rescued approximately 10,000 such children, placing them in Jewish and non-Jewish family and group homes in Britain. Private citizens or organizations had to guarantee funds for each child's care.

Some of the children were babies, who were carried by other children. Their parents foresaw that the only way to save their children was to send them away with no knowledge of where they would end up, with whom, or if they would ever see their children again. For her part, Sophie held fast to her teddy. She wore a cardboard sign on a string around her neck, bearing her name and her number, 8672. In Manchester, England, Sophie was placed with a Jewish couple that had been hoping for five years to have a baby. "All I remember is that they wanted to keep me," she recalled. "They said, 'If everything doesn't work out, we'll adopt you.'"

Sophie arrived in their home knowing no English. "You had to be a fast learner," she said, and she was. Her new home felt comfortable, and Sophie started school. However, within the year, the German air raids became so bad that the little girl was again sent away with other children, this time to live in the country. "The family I was with, it was wonderful that they took me in," she said, "but they worked me." This time, Sophie lived on a farm where she was given chores, took care of chickens, and washed dishes standing on a stool at the sink, until eventually she was sent back to Manchester.

"Then my mother arranged that the furniture and household goods be sent to the United States," she recalled. "When that happened, she emigrated there herself. She arrived in the United States on March 28, 1940."

Rosalie lived and worked in Philadelphia, and she sent for Sophie, who arrived in the United States on September 10, 1940. Both Rosalie and Sophie's entry into the country were sponsored by Isak's first cousin, Benjamin H. Sobelman.

On March 26, 1943, one month after Sophie's ninth birthday, Isak boarded a ship at Port Said, Egypt, bound for the United States to rejoin his family. He reached Ellis Island on July 11 of that year, and the family was reunited.

His daughter said, "The Holocaust was a horrendous experience. Isak wanted to divest himself of reminders. He legally changed his name from Isak Jean Rosenbaum to John I. Roberts. Jean, a perfectly acceptable man's name in Europe, is a feminine name in America. Jean became John. My mother, all of the relatives, and all of our friends called him John. I never heard the name Isak. Isak Jean Rosenbaum disappeared, and John I. Roberts was born: a new name, a new life, a new country."

"I was called Sophie until junior high. We were changing names [on the citizenship papers], and my mother said, 'It's time.' She [still] detested the name. So I disappeared also."

Or did she?

"A teacher had suggested I adopt a middle name." As a result, her citizenship papers read Sophie Karen Roberts. From then on, she went by Karen. The family had left behind several countries, the Holocaust, and now, their names, but they were together. They lived in Philadelphia, then moved to New York. After high school graduation, Karen enrolled in New York's City College, now City University, and majored in chemistry.

"Most of the people in the department were Jewish," Sophie said. She met Morris Bader at a departmental party. "Morris was the bouncer. He was a college wrestler. He was strong and he was tall and muscular. He asked one of his friends to take care of me and not let anybody give me a problem; by this, he meant no one should be talking to me. I had a 'reserved' sign.

"He walked me back to the apartment where I was living with my parents. When he left me, I remember walking him back to the subway, which was five blocks, and then he walked me back." They married in 1962. For a time, Morris worked for Marietta College in Ohio. "We wanted to get closer to family, which was in New York, so we came to Bethlehem," Karen said. Moravian College hired Morris, and they moved to town in 1962.

All of their children were born in Bethlehem: William, Joel, David, and Debra. "In our mind, it was 'Deborah,' after my grandmother, but the nurses wrote it like this, and we said, 'What the heck?'" Karen recalled lightheartedly. Could this be the daughter of Rosalie? Of course; it makes perfect sense: While Rosalie needed to be strong and go against the tide to save the family, her daughter needed to be a fast learner, malleable, even willing to disappear if need be.

My first discussion with Karen of any significance happened at a *kiddish* (lunch after Sabbath services) when I asked her if we could meet for an interview, but the timing wasn't right.

"My son called me to come and take care of his six children," Karen said, and not just for an evening—for two weeks. "And they have this dog big enough to eat everything off the table, and there's a little dog. She's diabetic, and you have to give her shots." While this setup sounded to me like the makings of a zany movie, Karen just smiled and went on to lovingly describe her grandchildren. "I enjoy them," she said. "They just know they have to get in the flow of how Grandma does things."

At the time, I wondered how Karen could be so free of stress contemplating this situation. Now I see it's all about being willing to lose the baggage. (Her childhood suitcase is long gone.) Give away the teddy bear. ("It's in a museum. I can visit it anytime I want.") Change the name. Survive.

When asked how changing her name affected her life, Karen shook her head and said, "Not at all." That's because she kept what was truly important. Of the family's escape from Europe, Karen said, "We didn't talk about any of this. This was never a subject of conversation. I was not allowed to talk German to my parents; they spoke it to one another. I became a fluent understander."

Here is some of what Karen Bader understands: She has a good family. She had a wonderful, understanding husband, now departed. Morris was protective of his wife and children, "as if herding his sheep," she said. Of their modest means while raising a family, she said, "We had enough for our needs. Life was good."

Karen Bader, then and now. Photo by author.

~

These unique individuals, these *survivors,* at the very least cooperated to fit themselves into the Bethlehem community. At the same time, it was imperative to themselves and the community that they maintain their uniqueness. Their distinctive and in some ways quirky mix of adaptiveness and inflexibility resonated with and influenced the community to become what it is today.

Bill, Joe, and Laszlo all passed on before I had the chance to meet them. Two of the four people described here had no descendants, yet they left a legacy. They are remembered for the aspects of their stories and their personalities that made it difficult to get along with others. One was recalled with apparent fondness as "the most unforgiving person" the speaker had ever met. If there could be a silver lining in their stories it is that they survived—such grit! Let that be a lesson to us all.

In Bethlehem, those around the survivors didn't wait but rather reached out proactively to welcome, invite, or otherwise integrate them into the community: by marriage (like the Lenape with the early fur traders!), with jobs, recruiting them to volunteer, and via friendship.

That the community might reach out a hand came as a surprise to me despite the outreach to my family of Brith Sholom membership chair, Sandy Wruble. Strange as it now seems to me, I had always envisioned belonging as an internal and individual—solitary!—process, one that requires effort, desire, and most of all courage. And so it may, but in these stories, it was not the effort of the one that brought about belonging, but of the many.

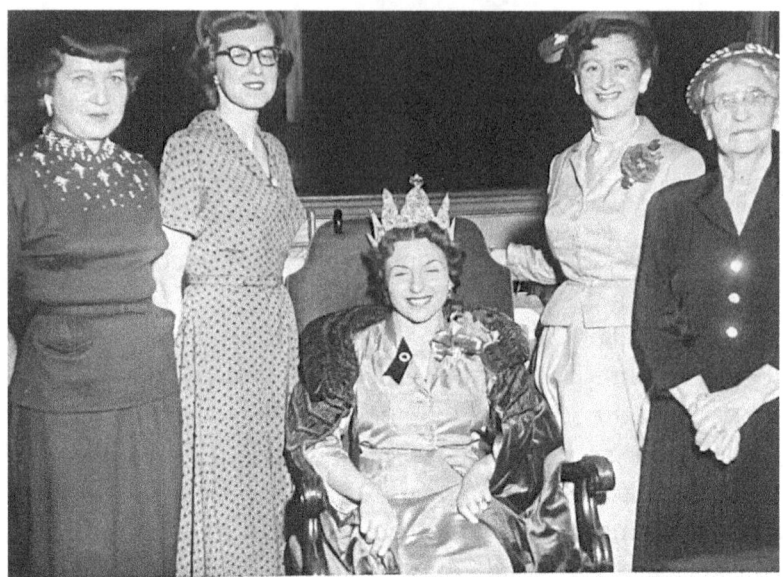

This March 10, 1954 Hadassah Luncheon photo appears to be in celebration of its new president. We can't be sure of her first name because the photo label uses the convention of the day (l to r): Mrs. Victor Genel, Mrs. Henry Schiff, Mrs. Harry Goldberg, Mrs. Sam Black, Mrs. O. W. Brisker. Three of these women appear in the stories shared here: Florence Genel, Isabel Schiff, and Cecilia Brisker, first president of the Bethlehem chapter of Hadassah. And after a little research – the person of honor here is believed to be Jeanette Goldberg.

Chapter 7
"Like a Diamond in the Sky"
Women of the Jewish Community

Until I began this project, the faces of the early Jewish community of Bethlehem as far as I could see were all men—the first Brith Sholom Community Center Board members. Their photos can be found in the Brith Sholom library as the first Board of Trustees, first president, vice president, secretary, and treasurer. Interestingly, no rabbi of those early days is memorialized. Some rabbis back then didn't want their photo displayed. They didn't appreciate the attention.

Instead, the people I met for this project were the so-called "ordinary people," quietly going about their work, the dependable stalwarts or the connectors among people: teachers, medical professionals, concerned neighbors, and friends. They are who this book is really about. There's more recognition nowadays that these are people whose stories we need to hear, the people we really need to see. Todd M. Edelman wrote about this in his book *Broadening Jewish History: Toward a Social History of Ordinary Jews*.

And, from the Bethlehem stories I heard, it was clear that the women of the community worked right alongside the men: whole families getting the Center up and running and keeping it functioning. Zelda and Gus Levin volunteering at the hospital on Christmas Day. The Podbereskys and others who ran brick-and-mortar businesses that provided livelihoods for many. People can sometimes be the communal version of bricks and mortar, building a life and a community. They dwell at the heart of every story.

The Women Were Highly Praised

A couple of years into my research, Barbara K. (she asked that her last name not be used) invited my family over for Friday night Shabbat dinner. As Barbara did every Friday night, she lit the Shabbat candles. She had prepared a feast: golden home-baked *challah* (a braided Shabbat and holiday bread), savory vegetable soup, juicy roasted chicken, crunchy salads, and sweet potato pie.

But Barbara didn't spend every Shabbat at home. She and her husband, Arnold, traveled all over the world. They had also lived in many locations, including Switzerland, because of Arnold's work as a physicist.

Barbara shared that, due to their 22 household moves, she did not develop many hobbies because she didn't want to move extra belongings from house to house. But there was one. On the evenings when Arnold was away for his work, Barbara occupied herself with the fine art of painting eggshells. Barbara showed me an array of creative, clever scenes and dioramas. The broken yet beautiful eggshells gave me a glimpse of joy and patience, tinged with something more difficult that, despite the delicacy of the medium, suggested resilience.

Around the dinner table, my family and I joined Barbara and Arnold as we all sang the traditional "Shalom Aleichem," that those who are travelling home would be protected by angels. Arnold then led the blessings. Turning the page to "A Woman of Valor," from the Book of Proverbs, chapter 31, he lifted his gaze to Barbara, who was seated at the opposite end of the table, and began, *"Eishet chayil mi yimtza ..."* (Hebrew for "A good wife, who can find?") Arnold read slowly and with meaning:

For she is far more precious than jewels.

The heart of her husband trusts her completely

And he has no lack of gain ...

The strong bond between our host and hostess was palpable. Arnold continued to read, concluding:

Grace is deceitful and beauty is vain,
But a woman who reveres the Lord is to be praised.
Give her of the fruit of her hands,
And let her works praise her in the gates.

~

Nearly every man I interviewed for this project spoke in the most glowing terms of at least one woman in his life—mother, sister, wife, daughter. They praised these women because of their lifetimes of thoughtfulness and good works, intelligence and example, influencing those around them for the better. Present or now gone, in the works of a lifetime, these women's impact often extended beyond family to the Jewish community and to the general community of city or valley.

What stood out in the stories of nearly every woman I interviewed was that most had experienced some traumatic personal events, yet they showed neither self-praise nor self-pity. During my research, I was struggling with the responsibilities of family *and* a part-time job. I sometimes felt apart from the Jewish women I met in Bethlehem, more for my own perceived lack of resilience than for any differences in age or situation. I wondered whether I could ever truly belong among them—seemingly meeting the ups and downs of life with equanimity.

One spring, the women of Brith Sholom's loosely organized Sisterhood, of which I was a member, approached me to give the *d'var Torah* (Hebrew for the talk about Torah, the sermon) during the annual Sisterhood Shabbat service. The particular Torah reading that week was one known as "Naso,"[7] about a census of the Jewish people. The *haftarah*

---

[7] Each Torah portion has a name that indicates (in Hebrew) what it is about.

(Hebrew name for the supplemental reading) that followed covered the announcement and birth of Samson. In it, an angel appears and speaks to a woman whose name is not given, telling her that she will soon have the child she longs for. This woman is described only as "the wife of Manoach." When the man and woman offer a sacrifice in thanksgiving for their expected child, the flame leaps high and both throw themselves to the ground, with the man saying they would surely die.

I liked that the woman then stands up and says to her husband, "If the Lord were pleased to kill us, the Lord would not have received a burnt offering and a meal-offering at our hands, nor shown us all these things, nor would the Lord at this time have told such things as these."

So yes, I agreed. It would be my pleasure to give the *d'var Torah*! I noted that when the baby is born, it's the woman who names him Samson (Judges 13). The question I explored in my remarks: Why is the woman's name not given?

I believe that in her we find the cultural power of Jewish women and that this is why she is not named. She is Every Jewish Woman, certainly very much like the ones I met in Bethlehem and every bit as capable as I aspired to be.

As was the practice prior to the 1970s, this circa 1925 Advisory Board of the Brith Sholom Sisterhood is labeled using their husbands' first initials with their shared last names. The only available additional descriptors mostly compound that practice of defining women based on their relationships to others but it will be done, for the sake of helping the reader put names to faces. In the foreground on low stools: "Mesdames" H.M. Goodman (that is, wife of original board member Harry M.) and H. Lanin. Front (l to r): Mesdames L. Klein, I. Goodman, F. Stone (hubby Frank was another original board member), W. Bornstein (wearing the author's favorite outfit of the bunch), I. Signer, S. Stoumen, C.O. Schiff (Lena, a name we know! Also mother of Henry). Back (l to r): Mesdames J. D. Fraivillig, A. Dornblatt, S. Kessler, J. Kessler, J.G. Beilin (Esther Hirshberg's mother), A. Potruch (that is, the wife of Aaron).

On This They Agree: Natalie Merkin

One day, I spoke with Zelda (Z) Levin and her husband, Gus (G).

G: I can remember when I was in first grade, the teacher stood me up on the windowsill, and we looked down into the street, and I saw my mother and sister coming home in a taxi.

Did you wonder where they were coming from?

G. Oh, I knew! *(I later deduced they must have been coming from the hospital after his sister, Natalie's, birth.)* Natalie married a boy named Norm Merkin. She had gone to Temple University and majored in biology. She did blood work at Easton Hospital and then became a science teacher at Northeast Middle School.

Z: Everyone loved her. She did a lot for Hadassah and the Sisterhood. She wrote poetry. She wrote a play for Hadassah. They [performed] it at the national Hadassah meeting in New York. It was Edith Blinderman and her daughter, Ann, who played the guitar with the group, Marsha Weinberg, Anne Fink, and Natalie.

G: They did a wonderful write-up of my sister in the *Globe-Times* when she died years later. I'll show you.

And Gus did! He had kept that clipping close at hand and his sister close in his heart.

A Very Persistent Person, Betty Perkin Lehrich: From Henry Lehrich

My mother was Betty Perkin. Her father came here in 1901 and was a jeweler, a member of Sons of Israel [the Orthodox synagogue] in Allentown. Mom was confirmed at KI [the Reform congregation of Keneseth Israel in Allentown]. In Bethlehem, we were members of Brith Sholom. The year I was a bar mitzvah, the 25th anniversary of Brith Sholom was the same weekend. That Saturday, the place was jammed, filled with people. [The sanctuary is said to have held 600 people.] I remember Mom catered the whole lunch.

She was a special person, a real doer—at home raising us, involved in all the activities like every woman in those days ... at the Center, Friends of Music, teaching full time when I was in 10th grade. She taught elementary—second and third grade—in Easton, at Palmer Township, then in Allentown at the Ritter School. She loved it. She was a wonderful person, very ... persistent, almost to the sense it was something annoying.

Later, she was involved in a program [eventually joined by] Rabbi Juda at the State Hospital. They went once a month to visit the Jewish—not inmates but—residents. In her 80s! She went with her walker. She was a good person, a wonderful manager.

In the early war years, she had a Hungarian friend in town—Mrs. Singer, the mother of Bob Singer, and she [had been] a lawyer in Europe and her husband worked at SureFit—and they had benefit concerts to raise money to send packages to Hungary.

A Rose Among Thistles: Cecilia Coleman Brisker

The following is an excerpt from a tribute to Cecilia Coleman Brisker that ran in the Brith Sholom Ad Journal, 1976. *The tribute quotes a report Cecilia wrote in her volunteer work with the Ladies' Aid Society, a forerunner of the Brith Sholom Sisterhood, which apparently went out into city neighborhoods to assist those in need, regardless of religion.*

The report we have on hand has no date. It concerns six cases of children who were either orphans or living in difficult circumstances. Here is Cecilia's clear, pointed prose describing the problem and current progress of one of the children.

"Case No. 3. Joseph, a boy of 15 years, I found in a very deplorable environment living with parents who themselves were the objects of charity. The boy was suffering from an incipient case of tuberculosis. I took him to the local State

Clinic ... The clothes necessary for this case I gathered from the Third Street merchants, who responded graciously. ... After a period of two months ... Joseph was discharged as cured, and my last report as to him was to the effect he was employed in an honorable position."

Cecilia closed this report of 45 years ago (around 1931) with a quote from Abraham Lincoln, "I planted a rose where only thistles grew before."

Those who received the bounty of Cecilia's good works were many. But the greatest benefit was to those of us who were fortunate to work with her and learn from her.

~

Born in 1883, Cecilia Coleman Brisker passed away at the age of 91 on July 18, 1974. Cecilia was also the first president of the Bethlehem chapter of Hadassah.

Found up on the Hill: Hani Silberstein

I read this on the headstone of Hani Silberstein, who died in 1941 and is buried in the Fountain Hill cemetery; to me it showed how our own families whom we love can also at times be unceasing in their demands for "more."

"Our mother, she worked for us, looked after us, loved us, forgave us, then died and left us."

She Had Hazel Eyes, Ida: From Bob Trotner

My grandmother was Rivka. I don't think I knew her maiden name. On her gravestone, which was written by my grandfather, it said "fifth generation from Israel Salanter," the famous Israel *mussar* scholar (concerned with a particular ethical approach) who was a prodigy at the age of five. When the rabbi was away, Rabbi Salanter substituted and quizzed prospective bridegrooms on their knowledge of the Torah. That was my mother's mother's family.

EDWARD SILBERSTEIN.

Edward S. Silberstein, a student at Bethlehem Prep, died Sunday afternoon after a four months' illness at the home of his mother, Mrs. Hani Silberstein, 644 North Front Street. The deceased was interested in charity work. He is survived by his mother and the following brothers and sisters: Mrs. Samuel Levy, Allentown; Mrs. Max Manles, Philadelphia; Mrs. I. Silberstein and Jacob, South Bethlehem; Mrs. Wm. Frey, Trenton, N. J.; Mrs. A. Cohen, Allentown; Louis, at home. Funeral Tuesday morning.

This clipping from the *Allentown Leader* for May 28, 1917 hints at how much Hani Silberstein went through in life before she left.

My mom was born in 1924. The other children were Benny, Harry, a girl Channah—or Anne—who died at birth, Frieda, and Florence. They had Yiddish names, too. My mother was Ida, called Itka in Yiddish. She was very pretty. I saw her high school picture and back then she was blonde. She had hazel eyes, a very special person.

My grandfather (Rabbi Abraham Mowitz) wanted my mother to get married before he died. Even though men and women aren't supposed to dance together [in their Orthodox tradition], my grandfather said to my mother, "The most important thing is for you to find a husband and have a family, and the best way for you to do that is to go to the dances at Brith Sholom." He was a different kind of guy, my grandfather. He knew when to give and when not to give. My mom and dad met at a dance at Brith Sholom. They got married in June or July of 1950.

Later that year, a week or two before Rosh Hashanah, my grandfather was at the cemetery, and he had a heart attack. [The congregation president,] Mr. Miller who was with him drove him to St. Luke's Hospital, but my grandfather signed himself out because, he said, "They don't have kosher food."

He had been sick for a while. Before marrying, my mom had been a typist at the Steel, but she also nursed her parents, first her mother and then her father. A few weeks later, my grandfather was at the cemetery again for a funeral. Again he clutched his chest, then he fell over and died.

My mother pronounced her Vs like Ws. I thought it was funny when she would tell me to watch the "Tee-Wee." Otherwise, her English was perfect. The only time I heard Yiddish in the house was when my father left for work at 10:00 in the morning. After that, my mother and aunt sat around talking in Yiddish—probably trying to figure out how to pay the bills. Everyone was sort of poor after the war.

My father wasn't religious, but said "fine" to whatever my mother wanted to do in the house or with the kitchen. He hired a worker to finish the attic [to rent out]. This was at 1910 Bayard in Bethlehem, where we lived from 1950 to 1962. The first [renter] living there with us was a man, an engineer. My mother must have been scared to death. She was always nervous, always scared—a shy person. She never said anything [about it], but she never liked having a man walk in there when her husband was not in the house.

When my brother and I were seven, my parents got a divorce. Dad had moved out, and Mom said, "We need to rent out the house on Bayard, and I need to get a job." She went to see Willie Rosenberg. He was a fixer. All the people went to him. She was trained in accounting. He got her a job working for the Treasurer's Office in the City of Bethlehem for $2,500 a year. Then in 1962, we moved downtown above the Victory shop, owned by my uncle Victor Genel, husband of my Aunt Florence (Froomka).

One time after High Holy Day Services, my mom walked us up to Lookout Point on the South Side. She had brought us chicken to eat even though it was Yom Kippur (a day of complete fasting) because we were young, about eight by then [so still allowed to eat on the fast day]. She was brunette by that time. She was beautiful. But we listened to her because of the kind of person she was. She commanded respect in the way of love.

The Matchmaker: From Judy Aronson

Judy Aronson has a gentle smile and an aura of being able both to dream and to accomplish. It's a powerful combination, one that inspires others. Judy brings people together.

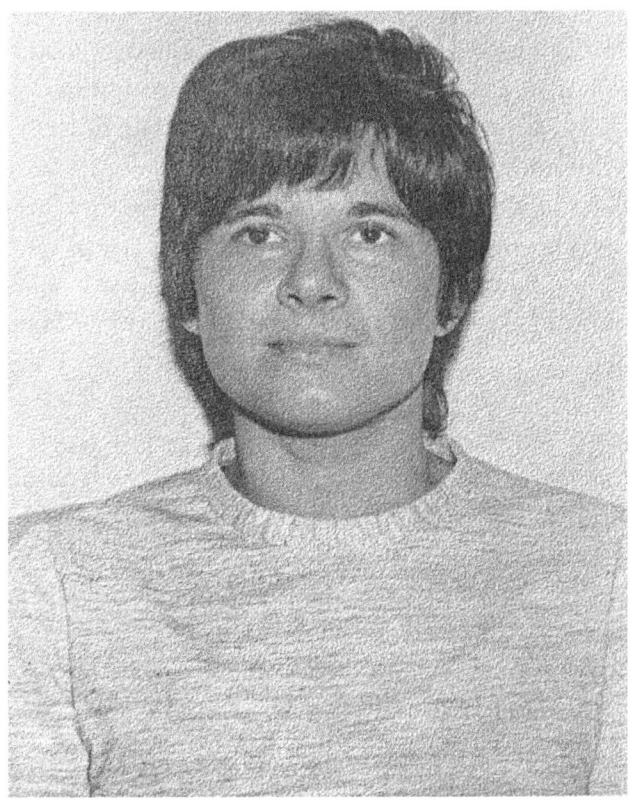

Judy Aronson, circa 1971

I felt when we came here that Jewish life was different from Worcester [Massachusetts], where I grew up and where it was more a matter of "keeping up with the Joneses." There were many more organizations that gave you a certain status in Worcester. It may or may not have changed tremendously since then, which was 1965.

I thought the Jewish community in Bethlehem was very gracious and open and not at all materialistic. Just as an example, when we got a new couch, I was almost embarrassed. Instead of rejoicing that we could afford it, I felt we were showing how materialistic we were. We only got it because we needed it. It might have been the entire [Jewish and non-Jewish] community in Bethlehem that we got those vibes from.

The two communities I know are the Jewish community and the University [Lehigh, where Judy's husband, Richard, taught]. My feelings about people come from those two.

My father was a Reform rabbi, so the congregation we joined was [a Reform one, in Easton] because my father was good friends with the rabbi. We went to services there, and our children were educated there.

Our girls were born in '62, '64, and '66. They were bat mitzvahs, and two were confirmed there. They went to Bethlehem public schools. In the summers, they went to Camptown for Easton and Bethlehem children. It was in Williams Township, a beautiful place. The Jewish community of Easton had bought the property. There was a beautiful pool.... It was called The Grove in the early '70s.

My father would say, "Rabbis come and go. It's the community that stays and should be cohesive." That's meaningful. When many of our friends took an active role at Brith Sholom, where we had been social [associate] members, it was time to switch over. Our girls were already educated.

The first thing that happened [when I arrived in Bethlehem in the 1960s] was I met Renee Schwartz because her husband was a colleague of my husband. She was regional president of Hadassah, and the first thing she said was that I must join Hadassah. I had been involved with it in Worcester, and I had thought upon leaving there, "Oh good, now I can give up Hadassah." But the flavor of the Hadassah meetings was so different here. Women wore hats, maybe gloves. I had at that time what I called "meeting dresses," this was coordinated clothing nicer than what I usually wore. I always wore a dress and heels to meetings. At these meetings, a luncheon was served to 60 or 70 Jewish women from only Bethlehem! [The community was much bigger then.] If you were a Jewish woman, you went to Hadassah. Easton's Hadassah was even more demanding. They had a formal ball!

One funny story that sums up the way it was: Gail Hyman was president. She was a very glamorous, beautiful woman of 30 or 32—quite young, with kids. One day, we were having a meeting, and she appeared in a pantsuit. Immediately, there were whispers, "it was wrong," "disrespectful," and so on. I looked at her and said to those near me, "It's okay because she's wearing a hat." *(Judy laughs, as if in wonder at her younger self.)*

Early on, I was involved in creating lunches for 60 women for under $100. These were very, very elegant. It was to socialize and to learn. We met once a month without fail.

Once, we put on a show. It was "Fiddlin' for the Loot," a takeoff on "Fiddler on the Roof." It was Edith Blinderman, Marsha Weinberg, Ann Fink, and Natalie Merkin who wrote it, plus Ann Beth Blinderman [Edith's daughter].... The first time I saw Ann was when she was playing guitar. She was a beautiful young teen, and I said to myself what a wonderful girl she must be—this adorable teen willing to be involved with her mother and her mother's friends. They went all over the Eastern United States, got paid, and earned their Life Memberships [to Hadassah].

"Fiddlin' for the Loot." Front (l to r): Marcia Weinberg, Ann Beth Blinderman, Natalie Merkin. Back (l to r): Renee Schwartz, Ann Fink, Edith Blinderman, circa 1970. Although Renee was not a member of the cast, she was a Hadassah president of the Bethlehem chapter and also of the Pennsylvania organization and a friend of the cast members.

Ann Beth Blinderman caught my eye. It wasn't until [my daughter], Miriam, was at Camptown that I noticed her again. She was a counselor. She went on the bus and looked out for Miriam, who back then, had long, long blonde hair. [My daughter] Annie wanted to go, too, though she was only three. Ann Beth was so good to my girls.

One New Year's Eve, my brother Jonathan, who is 10 years younger than I am, was coming to visit. He was a junior at Brown; Ann Beth was a sophomore at Pitt. We fixed them up. They came with us to a party, feeling very out of place. They were a different generation from us, which is probably all the more reason they hit it off. (Jonathan and Ann married!)

They are such a wonderful couple. They live in Framingham, [Massachusetts]. Ann is a high school librarian and probably the only one who left who yearns to come back.

Finding Leah Black

I couldn't help but feel a bond with the people I met for this project and even some I never got to meet.

My first "introduction" to Leah Black, daughter-in-law of early settler Morris Black, was when my 80-something-year-old friend Betty Diamond described the time when, as a young mother of two, she first met Leah. They were both in the ladies' room of the Center, and Leah asked Betty, "Do you enjoy your children? Because I enjoyed mine."

Immediately, I liked Leah Black.

The second time I heard of her, she was involved with the national MIA (Missing in Action) group, hoping to gain the release of the youngest of her three sons, who was taken prisoner of war when the helicopter in which he was a medic went down in Vietnam during the US war with that country. She was relentless.

I heard of Leah a third time. It was in the early 1970s when the Schiff family set off for Israel and Leah handed them a small piece of paper with a prayer written on it. They were to place the prayer in the Western Wall, said to be the gateway to heaven through which all prayers go. By then, Leah's son Neil had been imprisoned for seven and a half years in the infamous prison camp known as the Hanoi Hilton. By then I understood Leah to be a person of hope.

The Schiffs placed Leah's prayer in the Wall. Soon after, Leah's son arrived in the United States on a planeload of POWs whose release had been gained through a grueling international negotiation process.

These were only glimpses. Leah remained obscured from my view because she died in the 1980s, well before my arrival in Bethlehem. Back on a dark, rainy night when I visited Leah's middle son, Ron, and his wife, Linda, they told me Leah came from the Chicago area, that she was born in 1910. She had met her husband, Ben, while he was in law school at the University of Wisconsin. Leah came home with him to

Bethlehem and lived her entire adult life here. Yet none of this was enough to make her seem to me like a three-dimensional person.

On a cool October day in 2015, I took my middle son to school at 7:30 in the morning, then chaperoned the band as they marched around the neighborhood across 8th Avenue from Nitschmann Middle School, playing patriotic tunes. The fife in particular made the moment feel timeless.

After the school bell rang, I drove to the home of Alan Black, Leah's oldest son.

"What's he play?" Alan good-naturedly asked when I explained where I had come from. "Clarinet?! Me, too—at Liberty High School. I remember needing to get over to the high school at 7:30 in the morning, too, and I'd always be running late."

Alan's wife, Donna, interjected, "'The late Mister Black,' his director called him."

A slight smile crossed Alan's face, his eyes constantly on the middle distance due to the stroke that had taken his eyesight. He continued, "Many times my mother would drive me even though we only lived two blocks away."

So Leah had a soft heart, I thought.

Alan continued, "As boys, most of our activities were not with her. She had her luncheons and card games, and she was President of the Sisterhood. I just saw our father as my idol. He was the guy I aspired to."

Like his father, Alan became a lawyer, and his legal practice in Allentown thrived. Well into his career, Alan was elected Judge of the Court of Common Pleas for Lehigh County, selected as President of that court, and then by his colleagues as senior judge. Today, his name is on a plaque among those of other prominent graduates in Liberty High School's front hall. Alan and Donna raised two children, Martin and Sara, and they have two grandchildren.

By the time we met, Alan was "off the clock," retired because of his vision loss. Yet when I asked him again to

Mrs. Benjamin Black

ho is serving with Dr. L. C. Ziegler, as co-chairman of the 15th
nnual Charity Ball of the Brith Sholom Community Center, which

Leah Black, circa mid 1930s

recall something about Leah, he paused for a long time, quite obviously considering the scenes that he could still see in his mind's eye. "We loved her a lot," he said at last.

He added, only somewhat light-heartedly, in reference to her discipline methods, "I remember her pinch." Although apparently, their father did his share of disciplining, too.

Donna said of Leah, "She was devoted to her children, devoted to her community."

My curiosity was so great that I realized that, even though this project began with the stated goal of discovering the past, another goal all along had been to find out how to keep our Jewish community going, so it will be there for my children "when they want it," as Edith Blinderman described one important purpose for Jewish institutions and communities.

Most of the mothers of adult children who contributed to this project see their children only infrequently because those children have moved away. "There was nothing for them here," as Isabel Schiff put it. Although two of Leah's three sons stayed in the Lehigh Valley, that generation is of retirement age and staying seems to have become less likely with each succeeding generation. The two who stayed remain members of Congregation Brith Sholom. Alan was active with a synagogue in Allentown, yet he still supported Brith Sholom because, he said, "I want it to continue."

These words touched my heart. They mirrored, too, the words of Joe Spitz, the survivor of slave labor camps, who wrote of the need for "keeping the fire alive."

Though I had yet to ask some of my research questions, I realized why this project and this community mattered—for me as much as for Alan, the Schiffs, the Blindermans, and all of the other parents I had met who seemed to treat me more like a daughter than a stranger, even on first meeting. That October morning as we were standing at the front door saying our goodbyes, Alan reached out, moved by the shared emotions around the memories we'd been talking over. He grasped my

Mod Clothes, Hair Styles 'Quite a Shock' to Sgt. Black

WASHINGTON (AP) — The biggest shock to Air Force Sgt. Arthur Black on his return from 7½ years as a prisoner of war was flare-legged pants, loud colors and long hair.

"He looked at his brothers' clothes," Black's mother said. "He looked up and down at them and kept saying, 'I can't believe it, I can't believe it.'"

Black, 28, who was released from captivity in North Vietnam earlier this week and flown to nearby Andrews Air Force Base, bid, for medical checks and debriefing early Thursday, went on a shopping trip with his brothers, Alan, 24, and Ronald, 30. He found the latest men's fashions something of a shock.

"His brothers were surprised at him," said his father, Benjamin F. Black of Bethlehem. "His tastes were very, very conservative.

"Before he went away, he had always dressed in the latest fashion. But the flare-bottomed trousers and loud colors were quite a shock to him."

Mrs. Black said that after much persuasion, her returning son finally selected a new wardrobe in the current styles, including a pair of balloon flared slacks.

But the elder Black said his son still has some qualms about

sideburns and mustaches on his brothers.

"He couldn't get over that for a while," the father said.

The parents said one of the first things Sgt. Black did at the reunion at the base's Malcolm Grow Medical Center was to offer a champagne toast to President Nixon.

"He said, 'I want to make a toast to my commander in chief for bringing me home to you,'" Mrs. Black said.

The champagne had been sent to the hospital by an old friend in anticipation of the sergeant's homecoming, they said. Black's father said the family talked little about the war or Sgt. Black's imprisonment except that the helicopter crewman said he had been aware toward the end of his captivity of antiwar activities in this country.

However, Black said, his son felt he was "in the service of his country and proud of what he was doing."

"We think what we did was proper," the father said of the war and its settlement. "I have wholehearted support for what our administration accomplished, and I don't think they

could have done any more."

Officials at Andrews announced that two more freed POWs would be arriving at the base hospital Friday night. They were identified as Col. Fred Cherry of Suffolk, Va., and Maj. Norman A. MacDaniel of Fayetteville, N.C., both of the Air Force.

Navy Cdr. James S. Bell of Cumberland, Md., also was scheduled for the flight but will be transferred to nearby Bethesda Naval Hospital.

Also going to Bethesda were four civilians who had been held prisoner: Norman John Brookens of Chambersburg; Franklin County; John J. Fritz, Jr. of Williamstown, N.J.; Douglas K. Ramsey of Boulder City, Nev.; and Richard W. Utecht of Fayetteville.

Arriving at Andrews but continuing on to other hospitals were: Navy Capt. Walter E. Wilber of Millerton, Tioga County; Marine Capt. James P. Walsh Jr. of Winsted, Conn.; Air Force Capt. Edward A. Brudo of Quincy, Mass.; and Air Force SM. Sgt. Arthur Cormier of Bay Shore, N.Y.

Wilber was destined for a hospital in Philadelphia and Walsh for one in St. Albans, N.Y. Brudo and Cormier were going to Westover Air Base in Springfield, Mass.

ICE SKATING AT ALBETH

JUG MILK 49¢ ½ GALLON
Windmill Dairies

Mr. and Mrs. Benjamin Black tell newsmen their POW son found mod clothes shocking.
THE MORNING CALL, Allentown, Pa., Sat., February 17, 1973 5

The *Morning Call* covered Sgt. Arthur Neil Black's return from the North Vietnamese prisoner of war camp dubbed the "Hanoi Hilton." He'd been imprisoned for seven horrific years after the rescue helicopter, on which he was a medic, went down over Vietnam. In the February 17, 1973, interview, Leah Black quoted her by-then 28-year-old son as making a celebratory toast to his commander in chief "for bringing me home to you"—his family. If you look closely, Leah can be seen in the middle of the top photo, among her sons.

hand, raised, and kissed it. I, too, felt words were somehow not enough.

The Wonderful Role of Women in the Kaplan Mishpacha (Family)

It started with a diamond ring and a broken engagement.

"My mother's mother was Fannie," said Bethlehem native Irving Kaplan. "She was engaged to someone in Latvia, but he fooled around, philandering while he was engaged. She broke it off but refused to give back the diamond ring. She cashed it in for passage to America."

Fannie came to America and years later brought over her cousin Lilly and her brother Reuben. Fannie was a seamstress in Brooklyn, where she also raised a family, including Irving's mother, Florence, who went by the name Shirley.

Of his father's father, Irving said, "The only paper he ever read was *The Forward* [at the time, a national Yiddish language daily newspaper]." His name was Nathan Kaplan, and he was born in Latvia in 1884. In 1903, he immigrated to America. "That was just before he turned 19 because at 19 they were conscripted into the Russian army," Irving explained. A conscript had to stay in the army for 25 years— if they survived the conditions.

In New York, Nathan met and married Anna, also from Latvia. "He spoke English here, could read and write it." The family moved to Palmerton, which is about 20 miles from Bethlehem, part of the hilly coal country, where Nathan worked as a tailor. In 1924, Anna and Nathan welcomed baby Herman, who later became Irving's father.

"Even when they lived in Palmerton, they came down to Bethlehem to Agudath Achim for the High Holy Days," Irving continued. "They stayed with the Millers. The Little Shul was started in the back of Miller's Furniture Store. Not the five brothers, but the old man. My father remembers doing this for at least five years, but it could have been longer, from before he can remember."

At the age of 62, Nathan moved to Bethlehem with some of the family. "[My grandfather] had the shop to go to," Irving recalled, "but didn't really do so much business. Really what helped them was my Aunt Augusta, who never married. Out of high school, she worked in a tie factory in Slatington when they lived in Palmerton. [Then] she worked 31 years at Sears Roebuck in Bethlehem. She did everything. She ended up in credit. First on Third Street, and then they moved to 44 W. Broad—you know the glass building? In '71 or '72 she retired. She didn't drive. She lived on Third with her parents for a while and moved to High Street, and lived on Market—at Market and Main."

Where his paternal grandfather exerted a great influence on Irving was in the area of religion. "He did the [Passover] Seder from memory," recalled Irving. "I didn't realize it when I was young, then when I got older I wondered how he did that." Irving realized, eventually: "That's all they learned. Hebrew School was their only school. It was all they learned in a rural Latvian farming community."

Irving was named after his maternal grandfather, who had died at the age of 38 when Irving's mother, Shirley, was just 14 years old. "He died trying to save someone who was drowning," Irving said, "and he drowned."

"My mother didn't want to talk about it much," Irving said. "Because of that, she became a Red Cross Water Safety Instructor when she came here. We lived in Hellertown for a while, she taught at the Willow Park Pool in Hellertown and also at a pool in Bethlehem. She taught, and so did I and so did my brother, because of her father drowning."

He explained how his parents met: "Sol Fink was my father's best friend; he used to go to New York with him. My father was at Sol's aunt's house, and my mother was there. That's how they met. My father went into the war in '43. He was a staff sergeant in Europe. All they would tell my mother was that he was wounded. A month went by ... He was shot in the leg at the Battle of the Bulge. He was laid up a month in the hospital. When he was shot, they had to cut his boot off of him, and he wore a size 13. He was laid up waiting for another pair of boots. He was supposed to go over to Asia, but they dropped the bomb. My father came out of the war, and nine and a half months later I was born."

After his military service, Herman went to work for Ben Fink at Fink Supply Company. Irving said, "They used to go to the railroad at Allentown, over Seidersville Road, and pick up sacks of grain, big sacks of 100 pounds. In winter, hey almost drove off the back road, with the ice there."

Of his parents, Irving recalled, "My mother was the religious one. My father was not that religious." In that, Irving became like his mother and his paternal grandfather. "My earliest memory of shul is of sitting on a blanket with my brother while services were going on."

Like Henry Schiff and Henry Lehrich, Irving was linked to the Jewish community because of his mother's involvement. "My mother taught for 20 years," Irving said. "She was fluent in Hebrew and Yiddish. She taught from the late '40s to the '60s. She was my teacher at Hebrew School for two years. On our own, we played football, basketball ... it was all Jewish."

"There were three families who took off from school for the holidays of Pesach and Shavuot. My mother used to believe that if you're sick you take a day off, and if you're not sick you thank God and take off for the holiday," he said. "One year it fell out on a final exam that was one-fifth of the grade if you missed it. I was in Northeast Junior High School. My mother said it's 'not proper.' She went to the principal and to the superintendent. They changed the policy.

"When I was in my teens, my mother would go to Pezzner Brothers, a slaughterhouse in Wilkes-Barre, to get meat," Irving said. "She would serve rack of lamb for Pesach (Passover) sometimes. There's no longer a kosher butcher there. When I was 16, I used to go up and get the meat. We soaked and salted it using the laundry tub."

"From November '65 to October '69 I was in the Navy; '65 was the buildup year. I went to boot camp on November 30th of that year, the A-training school, which was radar school for gun mounts. I took an Air Force hop to California, missed my flight, and went through the Philippines to get to Hawaii where my ship was.

"Before that, my *bubbe* (Yiddish for grandma) was killed by a truck in '63," he said. "A truck backed up over her. It took my grandfather hard. He lived until '69. I was away when he died.

"When my grandfather died, they asked me whether I wanted to go back. We were patrolling off Taiwan. I said no; I had my *tallis* (Hebrew for prayer shawl) and went out on my own and said the prayers. I was the only Jew on the ship out of 200 ... It was a small ship. It used to coast at three knots between Alaska and Russia before Vietnam; they didn't [use] satellites then, see? In the Navy, I didn't eat pork products, but you have to eat. I skipped those meals with pork, but outside of the Navy, kept kosher and still do.

"I knew my wife already, or knew *of* her because she was friends with my sister. My sister was three years younger than me so I wouldn't have anything to do with her friends, but I knew who she was. I came out of the service in October '69 and went to her house. My mother would have me get meat for a bunch of families so I took it over to her house. Her name was Lynne Rita Blinderman. She did a lot of volunteering, a lot. She was a pianist and could play 10,000 songs from memory and knew the words to 5,000. We sat and talked, and within a month or so, we were married."

Irving worked for Lehigh County in the Crisis Intervention Unit (the mental health emergency service) for 26 years, and as Director for 20 of those. After retiring, he traveled with Lynne until she died three years later at the age of 56. I asked what came next after a loss like that. Irving's answer: "Now I volunteer *(at the time he led the Brith Sholom Ritual Committee)*. I have a lot of nephews and nieces. I travel a lot."

Postscript: Irving eventually found additional happiness some years later in marriage to a wonderful newcomer to Brith Sholom, Casey Goldblat.

"You Get Up and Walk": From Ann Goldberg

My belief is that if a child is lucky enough to have a home, to be safe and well fed, a lot is possible. My convictions came from seeing things that I didn't want to have happen.

My twin sister and I were born in St. Louis. Our father was from Rovno, Poland, which is now part of Ukraine. He wanted to go to engineering school and did at Washington University [in St. Louis], where he met my mother. My father's mother then came here to "see the twins." She left Poland in August 1939.

What a good time to leave Poland! Germany invaded that country on September 1, 1939.

Not really because she left her daughter there. I grew up hearing that my father's younger sister Manya "died in the war." Manya and 23,000 other Jews—women, men, and babies—were taken to a ravine and shot.

~

As an adult, Ann made her way to Philadelphia and from there to Nigeria where she and her husband taught in the 1960s. Their first child was born there.

Like most normal young women, I went to the maternity hospital there to have my baby. It was an open-air place, and I remember the bougainvillea flowers over the walls. They said, "If you want to have this baby, Ann, you get up and walk." So I did.

When my next child was born, in '63 in Columbus, Ohio, I insisted on natural childbirth. They warned me, "You're taking a risk," and "it's uncivilized," but because I had done it before, I knew I could.

Mel got his Ph.D. in Columbus. He was very devoted to his parents [who lived in the Lehigh Valley] and found a job with Bethlehem Steel Research Labs.

My third child was born in Allentown. I had to argue and convince my obstetrician [to allow me have natural childbirth]. I remember it was both Easter and Purim (a Jewish holiday commemorating Queen Esther, a Jewish woman, saving her people). I sat up in the recovery room, and all the women around me were sleeping. They brought lunch—a robin's egg blue Easter egg!

Later, I went to [the University of Pennsylvania] one day a week and finished a master's degree as a reading specialist. Meanwhile, Mel worked about three years at Research. He came up with a new idea for coating on tubing, but they weren't interested, so he went out on his own. With some help, he bought Eastern Chrome Plating. He was good at metallurgy, but he wasn't such a businessman. So in '70-'71, I went to work for the Easton School District. I wasn't so great a teacher and became a bookkeeper for Mel.

Finally in '75, I knew I had to get a job. I went to work with the Bethlehem Area School District full-time as a reading specialist. I had a wonderful principal where I worked at Fountain Hill (the borough adjacent to the South Side).

Mel and I chose to live in Bethlehem. It was not far from the research labs, which were on the mountaintop. We liked the idea of Bethlehem being less fancy, less materialistic compared to other places we knew. We met many close friends there. I never denied my Jewishness, and the wonderful way the Israelis [the couple's friends in Nigeria] treated us made me feel so linked.

We had gone to a Reform synagogue in Columbus. When we came here, I contacted the rabbi, who put me in touch with Marsha Weinberg. She told me how lovely the community was and that we'd be happy here. We joined Brith Sholom right away, in October of '65 .

Most of the people on Montgomery Street [on the North Side, where we lived] were steelworker families. By and large, there was no antisemitism. One neighbor had four children, who played with mine. Later, she said to me that she had never met a Jew and she had thought that all Jews had horns. Another neighbor was a devout Catholic who wanted to come to our house for Passover and Hanukkah celebrations. I was tutoring children at that time, so I would have the children come to my house or I would go to their house. There was a man at Lehigh who would recommend people to me.

As part of B'nai Brith Women (a social and civic Jewish organization), I did "Dolls for Democracy." So there was Gandhi, Helen Keller, Marie Curie ... They were wooden dolls with the appropriate dress. The goal was that B'nai Brith members would go into the schools. I remember going into Ruth Radin's [public school] classroom. The schools welcomed us; it was storytelling about those famous people. This was in an age when we didn't have videos. There's nothing like face-to-face.

Of course, we went to the Brith Sholom Community Center on the South Side. That building was remarkable. I'm sure my kids were misbehaving, but they loved to go. There were about 12 children of Ken's age, 10 or 12 of Adele's age, and eight or nine of Elena's age. Now I understand there are fewer. It was very nice.

I don't want to emphasize prejudice, but when Ken was 12, he came home from [public school] upset. When the teacher had turned her back, some boys drew swastikas on the board. I was outraged. I went to the teacher; she was cordial. I was working in the school system, but not at that school. She said, "Well, boys will be boys, Ann. He has to learn to defend himself."

I'm not proud of this, but I didn't go to the principal. What we did was enroll Ken in karate school. And in seventh grade, he did run into plenty of tough boys and was able to take care of himself. I don't credit that teacher, though. Her behavior was deplorable, with no interest in what it meant or how painful it was.

Then Mel was diagnosed with leukemia. Today, the kind of leukemia Mel had would be curable. He was 45. Mel spent his last six weeks at Penn. The teachers had gone out on strike at that time, which was a boon to me. I was able to go and stay nearby at Father Divine, which was an African-American institution. It was $15 a night, with men and women sleeping on separate floors.

After Mel died, Penn was offering a supervisor's certificate. When you lose your husband, your social support is eroded, and I needed that focus. I would go down once a week for a class. My friends were so good to me. Ken was 21, Adele 19, and Elena was 15. It would mean an increase in income. The two older children were at Penn.

In '93, there was an opening in Language Arts for the school district. I became the head of the new English as a Second Language program. Since the '70s, children had been taught in Spanish and eased into English. This was done at Marvine Elementary, and they were gradually transferred to their home school. The superintendent felt it wasn't working. He got a team together and got the board to switch. It was a huge trauma. I was on a committee to design a new program. I believe in teaching in English with plenty of Spanish-speaking teachers. There were sit-ins, sometimes police at the meetings.

I was told, "You're going to have to be the head of a large number of bilingual teachers from all over the country." The teachers who had been teaching coursework in Spanish weren't fired, but now they were ESL. Some were very angry. I met with them, and they knew I cared about the kids and that the kids were learning. It was very painful the first year. The woman at the state was so angry that she pulled all our money. Thanks to No Child Left Behind, we got a huge, beneficial grant that was very wisely used. We were able to find good bilingual people.

The second major accomplishment was Reading Recovery, a program very near and dear to my heart. As a result of this method, children who were in the lowest 20 percent of first grade, after 12 to 20 weeks achieved average or better in reading. Some of these children would otherwise have been doomed for years to remedial schooling. The other benefit is that teachers learned for the first time how to teach struggling children how to learn.

The third accomplishment was the School-to-Work program. In the English Acquisition Program (ESL), we were worried about a particular group of unmotivated high school students, mostly Spanish-speaking but others as well including students from India. They were absent a lot.... I investigated a program in Boston that was putting struggling high school students to work in hospitals. I became convinced that this is what we should do here. Thanks to school district officials who knew people at St. Luke's Hospital, these ESL students spent half their time in special classes about health issues—so their science classes were linked to health, and English had to do with medical terminology.

~

About seven or eight years after Mel died, I decided to keep kosher. It was a way of showing how grateful I was that we all survived and that the children were all right. And in a way, it brought me together with my husband (Herb Gilles, see Chapter 2).

I wish I was more knowledgeable about Judaism. My son married a Jewish woman, and my two daughters married non-Jewish men. One son-in-law is a Chinese-American, and the other was raised a Muslim. Yet they are all raising their children Jewish. Jewish values are meaningful and powerful.

Judaism is very much a part of my life; perhaps I got that from my father. Even as a child, I had strong opinions. When kids feel okay, it gives them a kind of power. I encouraged my children to be who they really were, that who they were was accepted and valued.

I identify with *tikkun olam* (the Jewish value of "repair the world"). I want to leave the world a better place.

~

I reached out to Ann when author Edgar Allan Poe's strange stories proved too much for my youngest child in his 6th grade English class at Nitschmann Middle School. I asked, How do I speak to the teacher about this in a way she'll understand? (I never did crack that code.) And I asked, How do I make sure my son's English class isn't accompanied by nightmares? (That one we found an answer to!) As a mom, there was a lot I didn't know, and I couldn't ask my own mom because she was facing health challenges. Ann was easy to relate to, and she helped me get through it, not without a few scrapes.

~

Now is the time for me to share about my return to the workforce and the job I found back in 2012 (see Chapter 1). I had just learned from the producer that there were people with credits a mile long wanting to work in his studio and had easily accepted that I was not qualified. When I got home that day, upon changing into my comfy clothes, I reached out to the Managing Director at *Hakol* (Hebrew for the voice), a monthly regional Jewish newspaper, headquartered in Allentown. I'd recently submitted a couple of history-focused articles such as "Women of Valor: A History of Jewish Women in the Lehigh Valley." The publication lacked an editor, and it was nearly press time. I offered to help edit.

Although my intention was to build my editing skills and professional network, within a few days, I was asked to apply for the position.

My interview was on the holiday of Purim. I got the part-time job, which I held for three years. Because the newspaper was understaffed, in addition to editing the 36- to 48-page newspaper, I also wrote four or five stories per month. Along with the recurring deadlines, this was a lot of pressure for a mom of three school-age children. I admit that I didn't always bear it well. I found myself getting angry easily.

"Mom," my middle son, at age 11, said, "maybe this isn't such a good thing for you."

Yet I was writing for a living! Learning about advertising and layouts! Going out into the region's Jewish community on behalf of my employer—the Jewish Federation of the Lehigh Valley! Wanting to be successful, in addition to working when the boys were in school, I worked many Sunday mornings. During the week, there were just so many distractions.

But there were peaceful times, too. One day, I reached out to Sam, a lifelong member and communal leader at Brith Sholom about this project. Maybe we had met before, but I think neither of us were quite sure how long (or short) that first conversation would be. I had two of my sons with me, and we all met at the nearby Rose Garden Park on 8th Avenue. That was where I heard the story of Laszlo. It was beautiful sunny weather, and I thought, *If only more days could be like this one.* I couldn't sustain the positivity, however. After occasional bursts of creativity like that one, I would once again put away the stories, which were taking the shape of a manuscript, often leaving them dormant for months or more, as I was busy raising my children and getting the newspaper to press.

More Than They Wanted to Know: From Laura Bochner

I went to fifth grade in Hanover Township *(adjacent to Bethlehem, the time period was the late 1990s/early 2000s)*. I was one of very few Jews in my school and could probably count the number of Jews on one hand. Always, I was the token Jew or ambassador. My friends didn't know any other Jews. So when they had questions, they would ask me, and I would tell them everything they wanted to know.

But I felt uncomfortable. I didn't want to be the voice for Judaism, the one they all came to. I didn't want to misrepresent my people. I thought of the whole situation as a burden. I wasn't unhappy to be Jewish, but a little nervous that I was the only one my friends talked to. I was happy to be Jewish, wasn't embarrassed, just a little uncomfortable that I was one of only a small number—for reasons of stereotyping.

As I got older, I grew out of it. I'd say things like, "There are many types of Jews. It's a heterogeneous culture, religion, and people." I didn't want them to peg me as the "typical Jew." I'd say, "Some Jews do this; others do that. Some keep kosher. Some don't. Some go to services every day. Some don't." I started to talk about Jewish customs and present a wider picture of what being Jewish is. As I got older, I told them more than they wanted to know.

~

If you've thought about getting married someday, how important is it to you that you marry someone Jewish?

Not very long ago, I would have said it's not very important. Recently, I changed my mind. I care about preserving the tradition in my own life and in the lives of my future children. They would be Jewish because I am Jewish, but it's important that my potential spouse either be Jewish or willing to convert so there wouldn't be tension over that point.

I want to say that my mom has influenced me a lot. I can attribute a lot of my current stance to her. When I was growing up, she signed me up for nature camp; we would go for walks on preserves, we were always hiking. She took me to Hebrew School; we went to synagogue; we had involvement.

I went through a falling-out period in college. I didn't do much with Hillel [the Jewish college students' organization]. I just went to a couple of Hillel dinners, but they were open to the whole campus, and a lot of people, including non-Jews, went because of the free food. During my senior year and this year [the one following graduation from college], I started to reconnect.

What brought that about?

The primary agent was my mom's breast cancer diagnosis, and also my trip to Israel. A big factor would be my mom's interest in [Judaism]; she's been pursuing it more, she had a bat mitzvah, and [has become] more active with the community. I wanted to support my mother in all the ways she needed support—transportation, emotionally, and spiritually.

At the beginning [of her year-long bat mitzvah study], I shrugged that off and didn't pay much attention. Then I realized I should support my mom in what she wants. It's important to my mother so it should be important to me, too.

Emma and the Frankels

It was autumn of 2013, and the annual Hadassah fundraising concert had just ended. Bethlehem native Ann Klein, visiting her mother and sister-in-law from Massachusetts, posed for a photo, one hand resting lightly against her shoulder. On her finger, a ring caught the light.

"This was Emma's ring," she said. Emma Frankel was Ann's maternal great-aunt, and among the first women to work at the Steel.

Ann Klein wears her great-aunt Emma's ring,
October 2013. Photo by the author.

She was *the* first, said Ann's mother, Edith (Podberesky) Blinderman. Emma was the sister of Edith's mother. "She started as the secretary to Charles Schwab, who was the founder of Bethlehem Steel, right after high school, and she retired 40 years later from an executive position in accounting," Edith said.

"She was born in 1902," Edith continued. "I don't know how come they hired her. She had no 'in.' She must have had high recommendations from high school. It was very precarious. She felt she was walking on eggs because she was Jewish. They did hire other Jewish people, not a lot, but at the time she was the only woman. Later there were other women. She was very attentive, very particular about her job. She typed up reports for big meetings."

At the Lookout on South Mountain, circa 1930 (l to r): Emma Frankel,
Esther Pisarev, Anna Frankel.
Contributed photo.

Edith continued, "My aunt lived with two brothers, Louis and Jake. It was two bachelor brothers and their 'spinster' sister. Louis was a bookkeeper for [the Steel], and Jake did some kind of millwork. He wasn't white collar. They lived on East Union Boulevard in a two-bedroom house. In addition to working full-time, Emma did much of the cooking, cleaning, and laundry. They had hired help as well because men didn't lift a finger in those days."

Ann said, "Had Emma lived today and been able to take advantage of what's available to women, she would have gotten her MBA and become an executive.... I wish she had that chance." Ann viewed herself as carrying out at least some of what Emma might have done.

Ann also spoke of her grandmother, Emma's sister. Her name was Anna (Frankel) Podberesky, and she died of a brain tumor at the age of 46. (See "The Borders Were Always Changing," Chapter 3.)

"Her absence has been a very important part of my life," Ann said of Anna, who owned and operated a shop on the South Side called Podber's. "The things about my grandmother that I heard.... I'd be walking with my mom, and people would say, 'You're Edith Podberesky, aren't you?' And they would talk about my grandmother. She was beautiful and incredibly charitable. She sold shoes, clothes, and nightgowns. It was that kind of store. Apparently, during the Depression, she would make sure people got what they needed. She would give them things.

"The family lived above the store; there was never enough wealth to move up and out. She was very sustaining to people in the neighborhood. I'm named for both my grandmothers; my other one was Bessie, so as a child I was Ann Beth. As an adult, I chose to be called Ann, but people who know me from childhood call me Ann Beth. It is very sweet to hear."

In connection with her own vocation, Ann pointed out that Anna and Emma came from a large family and that their brother, Sam Frankel, "kept a 'notebook.'" She explained: "Sam was the oldest of the Frankel siblings. His son, Mel, wishes his intelligent father had been able to go to college, but as the oldest boy, he had family obligations that prevented it. He was a bookkeeper, and was employed for many years at the Bureau of Unemployment; he also did freelance bookkeeping for other companies. His true passion, however, was collecting information on Jews and Jewish life. He archived articles, photos, news clippings, notes, and other material in a series of scrapbooks. I believe his aim was to create a Jewish encyclopedia. Like Emma, he had that analytic, detail-oriented brain. Mel told me that Sam read five newspapers every day in order to judge for himself, among various biases, what was true. I regret not being able to spend more time with him as an adult, and I wish he had lived to access the wealth of online resources we have today. I can imagine him spending time adding information to Wikipedia."

Just like Sam did, so, too, a librarian gathers and organizes information and that is Ann's profession, although she said that what she likes about information today is that it's electronic and "can grow and change as time goes on." Of Sam, she recalled, "He was tall; an interesting man ... My sister [also] became an accountant. There's a 'Frankel Mentality'—the detailed, analytical minds. They didn't have a sense of humor; the funny gene came from the other side of my mother's family."

So, there is Emma's ring on Ann's finger. There is Ann's vocation, so similar to that of one of her great-uncles. There is her beautiful smile and warm manner, reminiscent of her grandmother and yet with something special all her own. The smile seemed to ask, "Who's to say earlier editions can't be improved upon?"

~

At the end of 2013, my mother passed away. I found myself at a low point, where even religious ritual didn't offer the comfort it otherwise might have: My mother was Catholic. In this situation, the Jewish prayers and sitting *shiva* (Hebrew for seven, referring to seven days of formalized mourning by the immediate family) didn't seem to apply. Neither did Catholic prayers.

But for that first, long month that followed, I found a common denominator: January has 31 days, and there are 31 Proverbs. I decided to read and reflect on one Proverb each day. I shared this plan with my dad, and he decided to do the same.

At times, my dad and I talked over the day's proverb on our daily phone calls that strengthened our heart connection and more than anything, helped us get through that time.

On what would have been my parents' 49th wedding anniversary, January 30, 2014, we read Proverbs 30. (It's the one that comes right before "the Woman of Valor" that Arnold had read to Barbara.) In Proverbs 30, we found the words my father had been searching for to inscribe on my mother's gravestone, which I hoped it would be a long time yet before the two of them would share: That God's Word is true and that God is a shield to those who turn to God.

Chapter 8
"Adeste, Fideles"
Honor, Fidelity, Commitment of the Men, and More about the Community

In the course of gathering stories, I heard so many incredible stories of fathers and, beyond that, so many people giving so much, in so many ways to those around them. They provided and gave, struggled and cooperated, all with purpose. What follows are their stories, starting with some whose names have already appeared on these pages.

The Canal Paths Were His Stomping Grounds: From Gordon Goldberg

My father was born in 1903 and went to Broughal on the South Side. It was an elementary school then. He dropped out of school after the sixth grade, which wouldn't have been all that unusual. It could have been later, but I know my dad did not graduate from high school.

He was big for his age and was able to get a job for Bethlehem Steel. During the first World War, what they called the Great War, he was a machinist.

My parents were Harry and Esther Molly Goldberg. They married in 1927. At the time I was born, my parents had a house on Elizabeth Avenue (40 W. Elizabeth). It's still there, near Moravian College. It was a twin.

My father and mother had a difficult time. They had a grocery store across the street from Liberty [High School, on the North Side] .... In 1940, they lost the grocery store and their house. I could never understand it [when] there were so many programs to help people.... My father said he got very bad legal advice.

What also happened is my father lost his vision; he was considered legally blind by 1930. He fell out of a tree as a child and got a skull fracture. It made it almost impossible to find employment. He started over in real estate. My mother was his eyes. She did all the driving. They had rental units in several buildings; she did all the renting and kept all the books.

My father got his real estate license, his salesman's license and broker's license, all after he was legally blind. They had an office at 501 Market Street—the Goundie House (a historic building on Main Street built in 1810 by a Moravian businessman). I go in there now and remember.

I had a real estate license too and worked there. *(Note: Gordon also earned a PhD in history, a subject which he taught, including for 35 years at Kutztown University.)* We used to study with him. He was resistant to Braille because he never fully reconciled to being legally blind. He could read a headline from a newspaper. He and my mother would go to movies and sit in the second row, or he would sit right next to the TV screen.

We would print out or tape things for him. He would sit and listen. It was very difficult for him. He also experienced antisemitism as a real estate broker, among the other brokers. [But] he knew how to leverage real estate; he knew how to finance things. He was very astute. My mother was a remarkable person, and my father was remarkable too. He could have written a book.

~

The neighborhood where we lived was contiguous to the Moravian area. I ran through all those buildings. Where Moravian Academy is now was the library. I loved to read, and it was so accessible to me. I would go up there all the time.

The canal paths were my old stomping grounds. I did everything my mother told me not to do there. I went ice skating on the canal and once fell through the ice. I went home sopping wet. We used to swim in it, which wasn't such a good thing to do because it was terribly polluted. We played on the railroad tracks.

The New Street Bridge was a toll bridge, then there was the Minsi Trail Bridge, though that didn't have trolley tracks. On the New Street Bridge, sometimes in hot weather, a spark from the trolley would set the bridge on fire. Then the tollgate keeper would run out and put sand on it. We used to think it was terribly funny. To cross the bridge in a car cost a nickel, and pedestrians paid a penny. We would go down below the tollbooth and under the bridge because we knew sometimes when the money was tossed in the basket, it would fall down below. We would find coins and sometimes came away with big money because a nickel would buy a Coke or a bag of candy. I [also] sold bundled newspapers.

I tried out for the glee club at Liberty High School, which was very difficult to get into, very selective. I don't know if they were impressed with my voice, but there was a card and when I looked at the card, it said, "Goldberg—yes." In other words, my junior high school teacher had recommended me.

One time, a teacher tried to incorporate me into her church choir. It was Easter time, and I felt very uncomfortable. I finally told her, "My parents want me to drop out." I used that as my excuse.

I love the Christmas carols—"O Little Town of Bethlehem" or "O Come all Ye Faithful," Handel's "Messiah"—but they have a very distinct meaning for Christians. We used to sing Vespers at Liberty High School as a precursor to Christmas. The question of whether this was appropriate for a public school is a separate issue. You have to separate the artistic out. It has nothing to do with your Judaism.

When I went to high school, there were a handful of Jews in my high school class, maybe five, six, seven, if that many. My buddies were all Gentiles. There were things that friends were invited to that I wasn't invited to. Maybe a parent would be a member of the DAR (Daughters of the American Revolution) and invite kids to a party. It raised questions in my mind. When you're a kid, you're hurt by it. You look for reasons.

[Yet] I don't think Bethlehem was ever as affluent as Allentown; it was never as stratified socially but that's one of the endearing things about it.

Having been a company town owned lock, stock and barrel by Bethlehem Steel, that prevented it becoming diversified economically. At one time, Bethlehem Steel employed 30,000 and not just from Bethlehem, but from all over. These were good paying jobs.

I knew people who had the primary goal of graduating high school and going right into Bethlehem Steel and living the good life. It was hot, dangerous work. If they spent their career there for 30 to 35 years, they could live well thereafter.

I lived [in Bethlehem] until I got married in 1963, about 30 years, but my family still lived in Bethlehem. My wife, Rose Lee, and I were at a synagogue in Allentown for maybe 20 years, until we left and came to Brith Sholom. Before that, there was nothing keeping us in Bethlehem. All the young couples lived in Allentown, and to some extent that's still true today, but I'm in Bethlehem now more than I am in Allentown.

"He Was Not a Boss": From Bob Born

Pop worked a lot, 14-hour days at the [Just Born candy] factory. He would come home and listen to the war news, or we would play chess together. I was getting ready to graduate from Lehigh so I said, "Pop, I'm going to be leaving soon. What you're doing is not good. You need to get a hobby or something. When you were a kid, you played violin; why don't you start again?"

"No."

"You admire Churchill and what he does [which included painting]. Why not get an easel and paint kit?"

"No, no."

"Maybe go down to Sears and pick up a tool kit. You'll have projects that you work on."

"Don't bother me with this."

When I came home from Guam eventually [after serving in the military], the first thing my dad said was, "Come down to the cellar with me. Remember you suggested the tool kit?"

So we went down to the cellar. He pointed to the corner. I had to really look to see what he was pointing at because, basically, he had about every machine that Sears carried, to the point where he put up a structure in the yard to do nothing but house these machines.

~

I never had any intention whatsoever of being in the candy business. My desire [at that time] had been medical school. I was interested in biophysics. Dr. Bidwell at Lehigh, who happened to be Lutheran, said to me, "You can get your Ph.D. in biophysics and get a job in a hospital, but a Jewish boy in a hospital without an M.D. is nothing but a poop boy."

It happened that I was on the slowest ship of the Navy going home. I got there a month too late to start school ... What was I going to do, sit there? So I asked Pop for a job for the next 11 months. Fifty years later, I retired. We had a wonderful time together. He always gave guidance; he was not a "boss" per se. Each day when I came to work, I was looking around for something new to do. I went in to him one day and said, "I have an idea for another kind of candy."

He said, "Why don't you go out in the factory and make some?"

As I was going out the door, he said, "Oh, and make a small batch." *(Bob laughs.)* He knew it wouldn't be any good!

He died at 69; I'm a little older than that now. *(Bob was nearing 90 at the time.)* But I would still like to be as good as he was.

From Under the Table to on the Air: From Sam

People knew my dad (Laszlo from Chapter 6) was a Holocaust survivor, but it was peripheral. He didn't talk about it with anyone. It wasn't in the air; there was no media.

My parents were older than anyone else's parents, my dad spoke with a Hungarian accent, and I always felt completely alien from anyone else, anywhere. I had a couple of friends, usually others who felt equally marginalized. I would walk home from Calypso [Elementary School], which was half a block, and risk getting beat up. *(Sam, an actor, goes into the role, making his voice sharp)*: "HEY JEW! DIRTY JEW!"

Everyone knew I was Jewish, all the kids, all the teachers. Plus I was from the South Side, which was at least as big a deal. Coming out of Nitschmann (then a junior high school), there would be kids laying in wait in the park. *(Note that for the interview, we met at that same park, sitting on a park bench across the street from Nitschmann. Sam glanced around, as if seeing the scene replay.)*

One day, by those two pillars to the Rose Garden, there was a kid up there. I was walking toward him and thought, *There's gonna be trouble.* I got closer, and he hawked a big wad of spit. He spit right on my head. I said to myself, *I'm not even gonna blink.*

"HEY!" he yelled. "HEY!" I pretended I didn't notice—I wouldn't give him the satisfaction.

Then there was a teacher ... who the other kids in BBYO (the Jewish youth group) said was antisemitic but who I didn't have any problem with until one day I had this notebook that I would write poetry in and he said, "Those aren't allowed!" He confiscated it. I told the other Jewish kids, and they said, "He hates Jews." He never gave the notebook back. I guess he threw it away.

At high school, there were other Jewish kids, and I was in BBYO. We had a little network. It was very interesting socially [with at least four or five other Jewish kids]. I was best friends with Rabbi Wasser's son, David. We had the largest Hebrew School class ever, more than a dozen.

With the things that were happening publicly for you, was your home a refuge?

Not really. Reading was a refuge. BBYO was cool; we would do stuff in town. Scott Brown, the chapter president, was here; there was this whole BBYO/AZA world.

What about the bullies? Do you ever see them now?

One guy who went to my school I sometimes see; we say hi. Other than that, the real bullies, I sometimes see one of their last names in the newspaper, in the crime section.

The main thing I hadn't realized from the last time *(by then we were on our second interview)* was that I had a support group pre-made when I got to high school—older kids and my peer group. Being an only child, you don't get much of a reality check. I had two close friends who were not Jewish and then the rest of the kids from BBYO. I did get involved in the school newspaper. I had edited the chapter newspaper for BBYO, and the other kids said, "You're doing a real good job at this. Try coming over to the school newspaper." *He lists others Jewish students:* Scott Brown wrote for the Liberty [High School] paper. Elaine Deutch was the managing editor, Dan Glazier was the sports editor, Mark Diamond was the features editor. Sue Ungerleider was there ... We did have some non-Jews there *(said with a wry smile)*.

After high school, I wanted the least possible disruption to my life so I went to Moravian College. The good thing about that is the schools in the valley have a consortium, so I could register at Moravian and pay tuition there, but take classes at Lehigh University and Muhlenberg College.

At first, I majored in chemistry, but then I switched to communications/journalism. I worked at the *Bethlehem Globe-Times* for my first job in college. This was the early '70s when [colleges] were starting to say, "What can we do for you?" They encouraged you to design your own college experience, so I did.

I worked for the paper and for a cable company. I ran the camera, did behind-the-scenes work ... I worked for a radio station, which was exciting ... There was a magazine called *TV Time and Channel*, a competitor to *TV Guide*, and we outsold them in the areas we were in. It was on East Broad Street, in a little house. We had three typesetters ... They had a computer owned by Pentamation, and the magazine was a subsidiary of Pentamation.

In those days, if you had a computer, you made your money by selling time on the computer. People brought in their card stacks with payroll ... My boss noticed there was a small publishing business that [could be] in-house and [get] free time on the computer, so we put out a television listing guide with original copy. *(Sam worked long hours editing seven weekly cable guides for low pay.)*

So for about the past year before that, David Green, who was the cantor and administrator [at Brith Sholom] and a fabulous tenor, got me involved in the theater world because he thought I would be good. So when I quit the magazine, I decided to go into theater. I was in "Lenny," a show about Lenny Bruce, in Philadelphia, when an agent came to see me and said, "Come to New York."

First, I did a round-the-country tour for a couple of years doing an industrial show that went to the high schools. It was a one-man show, so I went around in a van on the West Coast. I had a ball. When I got back, the agent wouldn't take

205

my call. And that's just how it's been. Anytime I get a job and it ends, there's never a prospect until one comes along.

When I worked for the magazine after college, my boss was a World War II buff. You know, the kind of person who has to know every detail. He knew that my dad had survived the Holocaust, and he kept bugging me, "You call yourself a writer ..." And I kept telling him he never talked about it and I would never ask him, that he got nightmares when war stuff was on TV. Finally, [my boss] said, "I'll tell you what's gonna go down ... You have a week, and if you don't ask him, I'm coming over to ask him." So I got a tape recorder. We sat down and he started to talk. He didn't go into a lot of detail, and there were no personal comments. It was the first time I heard that he had a sister.

[Years later,] I got to New York and the woman, Sylvia Kauders, who played my mother in "Lenny" was playing the mother in "Torch Song Trilogy." I went to see the show, and it blew me away ... it was magic, sensational. The star in the play was in [for] three hours, three acts. It was about a gay guy coming out to his mother and dealing with being gay. This was way before AIDS. This play was the major thing, the thing everybody wanted to do. So I had dinner with Sylvia and Fisher Stevens. They held auditions for the touring company, there was a casting call, and I went because I wanted to meet the casting director, and ... they kept calling me back and gave me the part.

You got the lead?

Yes. I gave up my apartment, bought a backpack, and got a new agent. I had met him, so I called him and said, "Call them. You'll negotiate for me. The only thing is, I'm not going to work on Rosh Hashanah and Yom Kippur and 'Seder Night.'"

He called me back, "No, no, they're not negotiating. They called someone else."

"Wait! This is negotiating? I gave up my apartment! I got a new backpack!"

So I didn't get out of bed for a week. I talked to a friend who said, "You have to decide who you're going to be. Are you a Jew or an actor?"

I said, "At this point, I've already decided or it's been decided for me."

So it's been a recurring theme. There'll be nothing until just before the holidays, then I get a call.

It's like your ...

... Albatross. The only one who got it was when I had an Orthodox agent. So I've done theater—regional theater. The only thing is, when you do regional theater, it gets very difficult to get anything in New York. My agent wouldn't take me on a regular because he said I have too many limitations on working. If he saw on the list "Jew," he'd call.

What about you and your dad during this time?

We were never confidants or buddies. We had a good time. I loved him, and he loved me. When my mom was sick, he took care of her completely on his own. It was never supposed to be [that way]...

He got in a terrible accident when I was a kid. In fact, the state trooper called and told us he was dead. My mom was on the phone, and she fainted right on the floor. It's one of my early memories. He had a '57 Chevy with a horn around the steering wheel, and it cracked in the accident and pushed into his chest and pierced his heart. They got him to the hospital and realized he was alive.

In what ways are you like him?

The survivor instinct, the sense of justice—when you see an injustice, it's not right. I was involved with the antifluoridation movement. I didn't drink the water in Bethlehem until the '80s. I went and got our water from Allentown. It was my introduction to politics and "there's nothing you can do." I went to meetings of city council, and my comments were reported in the news. Dad told me I'd better give it up. His tomato plants were torn out ... He knew how this worked.

I'm not risk averse at all. I did stupid things, which I won't even begin to get into, and I paid the price for some. I went to [children of Holocaust survivors] support groups in New York. Some people were really, really damaged. Others, like myself, were functioning at a pretty good level. It made me think about my relationship with my dad and his relationship with everyone else. *(Sam described how perceived slights caused his father to shut himself off from most of his family members, including his mother-in-law, who was not allowed in his house.)* There was "The Day" that my father [finally] went to my grandparents' house. He went to their house and went in so my grandmother would be permitted to come to my bar mitzvah. He eventually distanced himself from everyone. He would perceive some slight. He didn't speak English completely fluently and sometimes didn't get the nuance, and if there was anything he didn't understand, he would assume it was directed against him. This included the rabbi and our cousin, Jerry Hausman, who [until that time] had been the only person who was acceptable. Until there was only my mom and me.

You were driving out from New York to Bethlehem to be the chazzan *at Brith Sholom (the one chanting the Shabbat and holiday services) for all those years?*

Every single week, if I wasn't working on a play, always, leading services exclusively since David Green left. [After my mom died,] I was the only person who was allowed in the house with my dad. He started calling me in New York. He only ever had one eye because of amblyopia, and [the good eye] was foggy with a cataract. He didn't want to have it worked on because if anything went wrong, that was the only one he had. He couldn't see the clock. He gave up driving and sold the car, which I was very grateful for because I thought I was going to have to get it away from him.

Winter came. His days had been regulated by gardening and TV. The shows started coming on again in the evening, and it was dark, so he would take his pills at the wrong time. I knew things were not going well with his medications.

So I had to leave for a show in D.C., and I gave the keys to the rabbi—"Just in case." I got to Washington, D.C., and called my dad up. It was 4:30 in the afternoon, and he had just had dinner, which was good. We talked and joked around until about 5:00, and I told him I loved him and hung up.

The next morning, I called and there was no answer. Now, this had been going on for years: He'd be out in the garden, and there I am panicking. So I waited until 6:00 at night and still couldn't reach him.

I called Doe Levan, who happened to be near the synagogue. "Would you mind going over and seeing if he's all right?"

She called back, "There's no answer, and the dog's barking like hell."

I called the rabbi, "Do you still have those keys?"

The coroner said my dad had been dead for about 24 hours. He was in the bedroom. He must have hung up the phone from our call and that was it. He got exactly what he wanted.

~

I have no regrets. If somebody had found him, they would have taken him away, put tubes into him, his worst nightmare. This was the best possible way within the limitations he had set for his life.

When the rabbi went into the house that night, he immediately called Jerry, who called me.

I asked, "Are you in the house?"

Jerry said, "Yep. And you know what that means."

My dad had died; that was the only way Jerry was getting past the front door.

How old was your dad?

Ninety-two-and-a-half.[8]
He lived a long time despite what he'd been through.
Bitterness will keep you alive. You just have to fight everything.

Giving "More Than Their Share"

> Rabbis have, over these years, inspired us ... But there always were men and women who have, from the beginning, given more than their share and, in some cases, devoted good portions of their lives to this congregation. There have been others who have served far beyond what is normally expected. These people ... have worked modestly, quietly, and faithfully without any wish for accolade [or] acclamation. (*Brith Sholom Ad Journal, 1963*).

The men whose stories are shown next each made a difference to so many others, yet their stories at first seemed hidden away except for a few clues: a blurb in the ad journal, a worn photo, small but fond remembrances mentioned not by just one but by many, or the work of a lifetime brought to light only with the right question. These community builders and influencers could so easily have gone unnoticed, as happens for so many—the "ordinary people" whose dedication and hard work seem nevertheless to keep the world turning.

Lou Makagon, From Brith Sholom Ad Journal, 1976, article by Harold Glazier

In 1934, during the heart of the worst depression in our country's history, a young man from the city of Pittsburgh began his job as Youth Director of our Center. Our Center Board ... certainly landed a gem when they hired Lou Makagon.

---

[8] This was March 29, 2006, outside this project's scope, but it felt important to cover the rest of Laszlo's story.

Mac was truly a great guy. He was not an athlete in the concept of today's super-star. Because he excelled in swimming, and every one of us was taught the fundamentals of this sport right in our own pool.... Lou was also a champion walkathon competitor. Not an exacting sport, it was, however, very grueling. Also, because he excelled at Arts and Crafts, it was natural in later life that he opened Mac's Hobby Hall.

... Above all this, Mac was a real person who instilled honor, fair play, and sportsmanship in all of us," Harold continued. "He also had a great love and affection for young people. This affection was mutual for we loved and respected [him also]. Speaking of love, during this period, we had a very competent secretary in our Center office. Her name happened to be Gertrude Goodman. Well, need I say more? Within a short time, we, that is all the kids at the Center, attended a wedding in our sanctuary. What a natural! Our secretary and our youth director became man and wife. I'll never forget that wedding.

Reverend Abraham Gandel, From **Brith Sholom Ad Journal, 1976,** *article by Harold Glazier (slightly edited)*

He was a humble person who performed his duties without fanfare, and with great sincerity ... a low-key person—low key that is, until one was faced with a religious question (or any questions concerning human nature) that required interpretation. You see, Rev. Gandel had that uncanny ability to make sense out of nonsense. He also had a great ability to make relevant to the times many interpretations which some of his colleagues would have answered more dogmatically.

He was extremely liberal but traditional. ... His Torah reading was always flawless and meaningful. Like his son-in-law, Bill Weisz [a Holocaust survivor, "The Man," Chapter 6], he remembered everyone's Hebrew name. Upon Rev. Gandel's passing, one might now conclude, "So ended a most pious and beneficial life." Physically, it did, but spiritually his legacy has been carried on by a wonderful daughter and son-in-law.

We often refer to the phrase, "The Lord giveth and the Lord taketh ..." I'm inclined to believe that when the soul of Rev. Gandel physically departed from this earth, William Weisz was purposely brought to Bethlehem by some immortal power to fill in the gap formerly held by his dear father-in-law."

Let's Put the Dentist in His Own Chair: From the **Brith Sholom Ad Journal, 2006,** *an article by Rabbi Allen Juda*

Dr. Harold Glazier was a man of great honesty and integrity. He was a modest and humble human being who shunned credit even though it was most deserved. Both in his professional and personal life, Harold engaged constantly in noble acts and often turned aside personal gain. ...

Harold was born in Bethlehem in August of 1921, the youngest of five children in the Morris and Rose (Kaplin) Glazier household. Harold always had an enormous commitment to extended family.

Harold attended Webster Elementary School, Broughal Middle School, and graduated from Liberty High School in 1939. Following in his older brothers' footsteps, Harold continued his formal education at Bucknell University and his informal education at Sammy—Sigma Alpha Mu.

Following his studies at the University of Pennsylvania School of Dentistry, Harold became a lieutenant junior grade in the Navy. After a short stay in Jacksonville, Florida, Harold served as a Naval dentist in French Morocco for two years. ... [Upon] his discharge in 1947, Harold returned to Bethlehem. After working for a short time with Dr. Cristol, and then recovering from a broken wrist that he earned

A life well-lived

New Years
Greeting
2006-5767

K or Z

Strength-Strength

Congregation Brith Sholom
1190 West Macada Road • Bethlehem, PA 18017
Tel: 610.866.8009 • Fax: 610.866.8000 • www.brithsholom.net

playing touch football at the [Center], Harold opened his dental practice....

Harold was an excellent dentist; there are even those who claim that Harold made going to the dentist fun. And his good heart far outpaced any good business sense. Harold undercharged everyone, and if someone had a financial problem, he didn't charge them at all. Harold may be the only medical professional in the 20th century to be accused by his patients of charging too little....

Harold's concern for people did not end with his retirement from dentistry in 1989. He was a wonderful, devoted volunteer at the Community Service Foundation, at the West Side Food Pantry, and as a tutor at the Fountain Hill Elementary School. But much of Harold's time, thought, energy, and passion were generously showered on the Jewish community and Brith Sholom. As a young man, Harold was the Chair of the 33rd Anniversary Ball ...

For many people, in and outside his family, Harold was a hero. He was a model and example of leading a meaningful life. Harold was a force for calmness and steadiness and giving people a feeling that everything would ultimately be okay ...

Postscript: And it was! All that volunteering may just be why Rabbi Tzvi Porath's wife, Esther, thought to introduce Harold to Betsy Korson when she arrived in town (see Chapter 5, "Fitting in By Knowing People").

In 1958, Harold Glazier (right) volunteered to chair the 33rd Anniversary March Ball at the Brith Sholom Community Center. Shown here with Morris Mindlin.

A Great Guy, Willie Rosenberg: From Rabbi Allen Juda

Willie Rosenberg was someone who would do anything for the shul. He ran the "wine room"—for *kiddish* (lunch after Saturday morning services), Passover, or anytime you wanted to buy kosher wine. Willie was also the Ritual Chair for many years. He was chief chef for the "Husbands Cook for Wives" dinner. He had a truck and would schlep stuff. He was a great guy if you needed anything.

He was someone who would sleep very comfortably during services, at the end by the balcony or sometimes even in front of the *bima* (the raised area where main service proceedings occur). He was a great guy if you needed anything.

"Have you heard?": From Steve Bergstein

Have you heard of Willie Rosenberg? He was the *gabbai* (one who ensures correct reading of the Hebrew from the Torah) forever, the salt of the earth, wonderful.

"Salt of the Earth," Julius Gross: From Steve Bergstein

Then also Julius Gross—he was a Steel worker, also salt of the earth. When they [showed Rabbi Juda] the old cemetery—it had been neglected—Julius, along with Willie Rosenberg, and Rabbi Juda, cleaned it out.

I said, "I wonder if my great-great-grandmother is buried there?" I went and looked for her and found her—Suzy Glasawitzki. I went to the library and found the *Globe-Times* announcement. I told Willie the story; I was very close to him. He said, "We have to go tell Julius." Julius sat there bawling.

A Sign on their Door: From Rabbi Allen Juda

For years, Julius Gross was *"the* man" at Agudath Achim. This was not in the sense of [leading] the service, but on their door was a sign if anything was needed to call him, and it gave his phone number. This was before cellphones!

Brith Sholom Board of Trustees, 1974-5: Front (l to r): Richard Herzon, Ralene Cook, Fae Gidaley, Jon Tenzer, Leah Schiff, Bruce Smackey. Back (l to r): Milt Goldfeder, William (Bill) Weisz, Jack Shaffer, Renee Schwartz, Marty Sonnenfeld, Rabbi Joel Chernikoff, Art Schachter, Nan Bauder, Willie Rosenberg.

The Bitter and the Sweet in the World of Sam Born: From Bob Born

During the war, Bethlehem Steel took all our people. That came first, but there was always a demand for candy. There was a demand for sugar, too. Pop came home angry one night; a couple of men had come in and he threw them out. There was a quota for sugar based on the usage the company had prior to the war, and Pop was always a straight shooter. These guys wanted to buy the sugar direct from him to make booze.

Another time, a man came in and said *(Bob adopts a Yiddish accent)*, "Mr. Born, you are missing an opportunity here. You should be making candy *kosher shel Pesach* (kosher for Passover, which sells for a higher price due to extra levels of care and supervision required)." My father told him, "I can't. My machines are made with carbon steel, and if I *kasher* (make fit

216

for use producing kosher food through a particular cleaning process) them with steam, they would get rusty. I can't buy new machines to use for just a week out of the year."

"What do you mean, new machines?" The man took some stickers out of his suitcase and said, "Just put the labels on the box." That man was another one who found himself thrown out.

~

One of Bob's big moments with Just Born happened in 1954—bringing Peeps Chicks marshmallow candies to Bethlehem and developing the machinery to produce them.

At the American Caramel Company in Lancaster, there was going to be a sheriff's sale, and we heard about it. I went down to Lancaster with our plant manager. In the back were about 80 women with these huge cake decorating bags, only they were huge, three feet long. They were squeezing the Peeps out of them onto wooden trays. The next day, somebody went through and sprinkled sugar on them. They were on brown craft paper that would then be turned upside down and sponged so the Peeps released and the bottoms would be sprinkled with sugar. They were then sent down to be packaged. The whole thing took about 27 hours.

~

Bob's son, Ross Born, later explained, "My father was the genius behind the engineering. He was the brains behind it, an engineer. That's what he studied at Lehigh University."

But Bob was modest, saying of himself and his team at the time, "We looked at it and figured we could do it mechanically ... so we made a machine that got the time down to seven minutes. That's the story of the Peeps."

Glimpsed Through Good Works: Jack Shaffer

Unwavering: From the **Brith Sholom Ad Journal, 1963**
"Strong, vibrant, unwavering" are words which can be used to describe Jack Shaffer. His personal persuasion, his

straightforward approach to problems, and his steadfast adherence to his many and varied assignments will be an example to all. When everyone but the most optimistic thought the task impossible, Jack Shaffer said, "We will do it." And it was done.

Presenter: From Gus Levin

When I was in the army, my mother, Selma,—they called her "Sal"—was the secretary for Hadassah and all those organizations. She worked at the Center. Jack Shaffer of Just Born was sort of in charge then [absent a rabbi in Bethlehem during World War II, the lay leadership needed to take the reins]. He was "the presenter," a sales person, a funny man, a nice person. So it used to be one person ran the office and had three or four people helping.

Donor: Excerpted from the **Brith Sholom Ad Journal, 1963**

In mid-1961 came the culmination of five years of meetings, discussions, and get-togethers when the congregation voted to proceed with the rebuilding and rededication of the Center. In August, we hired the firm of Heyl, Treby and Duncklee, Architects, to design the remodeling phase ... We also hired Bernard Karmetz, Philadelphia Fund Raiser and set a goal of $180,000. Jack Shaffer assumed the chairmanship of the campaign. Total pledged: $230,000!

Loved to Dance: From Various Sources

Over the years, there were many social events and dances at the Center. Several individuals recalled being at the dinner-dance celebrating the 50th anniversary on a May night in 1976. Everyone was having a great time, "but it was hot!" After one particularly fast number ended, Jack Shaffer exclaimed, "Let's get some air-conditioning in here!" (A cheer went up.)

Last Word: From Irving Kaplan

Jack Shaffer was such an important part of the shul. He really was.

A nighttime view of the updated and newly rededicated Brith Sholom Community Center, pictured here on the front of the *Brith Sholom Ad Journal, 1963*. The daytime scene is circa 1971. It was the tablets on the front of the building, likenesses of the 10 Commandment tablets Moses brought down from Mount Sinai, that first cued me in to the building's history.

Rising Above the South Side, Lehigh University

In the early 1900s, Tillie Mindlin, Jewish immigrant and mother of five, would rest from her work at the window of her little New Street apartment on the South Side and look at the students streaming down the hill from Lehigh University. She would raise her eyes to its stone walls and spires. She considered her hopes for her children, two of whom were girls and therefore not eligible to attend Lehigh, which at that time had all male students. Notwithstanding her plans that her boys be educated, the inevitable conclusion of her reverie would always be to say, not without longing, "My children will never go there."

Tillie had good reason for this conclusion. Through the 19th and into the early 20th century, college was mostly limited to the well-to-do. At the turn of the century, just 2 percent of the American population attended college, though this rose to 7 percent by 1930. Nevertheless, Lehigh University did not set itself apart from the town but instead was and continues to be integral to the city.

The main campus of the university, which was founded in 1865, is centered around several cathedral-like buildings original to the school that closely border the residential area that runs eastward toward the former Steelyards. Today, the university reaches over the hilltop known as "South Mountain," which forms the southern Bethlehem border. It is from this same hillside that the Bethlehem Star shines each night.

The Brith Sholom Community Center on the South Side stood across the street from Lehigh's northwest corner. Following the ground-breaking for the Center, the *Bethlehem Globe-Times* ran a front page story on Monday, March 31, 1924 reporting that Lehigh University President Reverend Russ Richards spoke from the podium for the occasion, saying in part: "Insofar as it is dedicated to the highest ideals

Lehigh University Packer Hall. Lehigh University Postcard Collection,
[LUPC LUPC0034], Special Collections, Linderman Library, Lehigh
University, Bethlehem, Pa.

and traditions of your ancestors and of American citizenship, [the Center] will be a powerful force for the advancement of civic and personal virtue, of clean, decent living, and of obedience to the law." (Source: Frey)

The Center had come to be during an anti-immigrant era in the United States, the 1920s. Just two months after this speech, Congress passed the highly restrictive Immigration Act of 1924, or Johnson–Reed Act, including the Asian Exclusion Act and National Origins Act—setting quotas favorable to Western, not Eastern, Europe—and creating the US Border Patrol. Presumably, for the general society, Brith Sholom Community Center meant law and order. The Jewish merchants might have had something else in mind. In addition to serving as a Jewish gathering place, the Center would support their children as they entered all facets of American life. It was the first tangible step toward realizing a host of dreams.

As it was for Tillie, Lehigh University was certainly in the physical sights of the Jewish merchants who lived and worked in Bethlehem. Also in the sights of many of these Jewish immigrants were college educations of some sort for their children. Education is an important Jewish value.

As Carol M. said, "My mother's parents came from Kiev and Riga. My grandfather went from shtetl to shtetl as a day teacher, teaching families in order to have a bed and food. He worked his way to a port. My *bubbe* remembered being hidden under floorboards while the pogroms were going on. They would not talk about it. My grandfather said, 'It was bad enough to have to live it.' My grandfather used knowledge to get out of Russia."

Carol said that she doesn't know for sure whether this idea of a potential threat is still a driving force among Jews in pursuing education today, but said, "It should be. Anything else could be taken away. Education doesn't necessarily equate to wealth or huge success, but it's something good to have." She echoed her grandfather, who had said, "Get all the higher education you can because it's the only thing they can't take away from you."

True to her own words, Carol holds a master's degree.

In Pursuit of an Education

It was remarkable to me that, of the more than a dozen Jewish men and women born in the 1910s through the 1930s whom I interviewed, most had attended college. Sociologist Marshall Sklare researched and wrote about Jewish life, publishing comparative statistics on educational attainment in 10 American cities in 1950 for the Jewish and total populations. US cities averaged more than twice the percentage of Jews having attended at least some college compared to the total population. In Gary, Indiana, 38.8 percent of the Jewish population had attended at least some college, but only 10.7 percent of the total population. In Camden, New Jersey, the numbers were 21.3 percent and 5.3 percent, respectively. (Source: Sklare)

Surely, these statistics depended on many factors, but one that mattered to some of the Bethlehem merchants was the drive to get their children out of the *shmata* (Yiddish for rags, or everyday clothing) business. A college education would make this possible. But college was expensive.

Tillie Mindlin's daughter, Jean Mindlin Deutch, said that, although her family was poor, her mother "could squeeze a nickel. She did without a lot of things to enable [her sons] to go to college."

However, an education like the one on offer at Lehigh, which was started as and is known for being an engineering school, would not be easy to obtain. Robert Kroope, who was born in Bethlehem in 1917, went further afield: "I went to Penn State ... It was expected, almost demanded, that we go to college and get an education if you wanted to get along." Robert's family did not restrict higher education to the boys: "Every one of my siblings went to college. Eugene went to Penn State, too. We were members of a fraternity. Hilda went to Moravian College."

At many of the nation's top universities, Jews were subject to quotas, as has been well documented, such as the cap of 15 percent at Harvard University in 1926. (Source: Karabel) That went on at least until the 1940s. But when I asked Robert about gaining admission to his college in the face of quotas, his good nature predominated. "It wasn't too hard," he said. "We had good grades, and they were able to admit us. We had A's and B's on the application sheet and they sent back, they verified it."

Some interviewees shared their opinions that Lehigh was no exception to the quota system, but I wondered about that because I had spoken with quite a number of Jewish men and women who attended Lehigh over the years, including prior to World War II, and with several professors who were Jewish. None mentioned quotas. However, Willard Ross Yates, for his history of Lehigh University, searched the minutes of faculty and board of trustees meetings and found a list in the April 15, 1929 board minutes of quotas for "alien and unassimilable races," including Jews, which were set at "50 each." (Source: Yates, page 242)

Then there was this story, from Bob Born. "It was in 1941, and I was getting ready to graduate from Liberty High. I had an appointment with the admissions officer at Lehigh. I went into his office to find that he had spread all over his desk papers describing my activities in high school. He greeted me with a big smile. 'Are there any other schools that you are thinking of?' he asked.

"'Yes,' I said. 'MIT [Massachusetts Institute of Technology].' And the next thing I knew, he was telling me why Lehigh would be better than MIT. I was amazed. I came in prepared to do a sales job on myself, but he was selling me on Lehigh! Then he asked, 'By the way, what kind of education do your parents have?'

"'My mother studied design engineering at Cooper Union,' I said, 'and my father is a graduate of Berdychiv.'

"Dead silence. Then, 'I'm not familiar with that school.'

"'At the time, it was the most outstanding rabbinical seminary in Eastern Europe.'

"'Well,' he said, 'don't put all your eggs in one basket. We have a quota on Jewish students.'"

Bob's response: "I was so burnt up with this character and what he was telling me that in spite of him I went to Lehigh. I got into MIT later when the Navy sent me there for graduate school for a while!"

~

It turns out that Jewish students gained admittance to Lehigh University in numbers great enough to have five Jewish fraternity houses (though a mere fraction of the total number of fraternities). Though unforeseen by Tillie Mindlin, her son Morris graduated from Lehigh University. Among the soldiers sent to Lehigh during World War II "to keep the university open" were Jews from surrounding states. Jean Mindlin married one of them, Bernard Deutch.

Society-wide, college became more attainable after the war. Universities grew, Lehigh among them. The school hired more teachers, including Jewish professors, many of whom, with their families, became active in the city's Jewish community beginning when they arrived, in the 1960s.

Bethlehem native Gordon Goldberg said, "I entered Lehigh right out of high school. The Korean War was on, and my parents felt it advisable to get started and finish before I might be drafted. I entered with the largest class of Jews up until that time. There were about 70 of us. The first Black student was in our class, also, the class of '55."

Society was changing, and it would continue to do so. Bob Born, who was told by the Lehigh admissions man of the quota added, "Years later, I'm sitting in Allentown. It's an executive meeting of the Jewish Federation [then of Allentown, now of the Lehigh Valley]. They tell us, 'Tonight we have a couple of guests.' They were the presidents of Lehigh University and of Muhlenberg College. They came in and what did they want? This was in about 1960. They wanted us to encourage more Jewish students!"

Today, Lehigh University is highly respected and has as its diversity statement: "Lehigh does not tolerate discrimination or harassment on the basis of race, sex, disability, religion, national origin or ethnicity, sexual orientation, or gender identity or expression." (Source: "Diversity, Inclusion, & Equity at Lehigh ")

Postscript: One of my sons graduated from Lehigh University with a bachelor's degree in mechanical engineering!

Murray H. Goodman Stadium, Lehigh University. Many members of the Goodman family graduated from Lehigh University. Alumnus Murray Goodman, cousin of Allan B. Goodman, went on to become a renowned shopping mall developer. Murray donated the funds for Goodman Stadium, believed to be located on the former site of the farm of Harry Blinderman (father-in-law of Edith Podberesky Blinderman and grandfather of Ann Beth Blinderman Klein). Lehigh University Postcard Collection, [LUPC LUPC0119], Special Collections, Linderman Library, Lehigh University, Bethlehem, Pa. Photograph by Lee A. Butz, Class of 1955.

Newer Perspectives: From Dr. Edwin Kay, My Friend and Neighbor

In the fall of 1964, I arrived at Lehigh as a graduate student in the math department. At that time, there was no hint of antisemitism. The department of about 15 faculty, five who were Jewish. Three of them were secular, and two were Orthodox. One of these moved to Allentown so that the family could be in walking distance of [the Orthodox synagogue there].

In 1971, I pursued (and caught) a second Ph.D. in Lehigh's psych department, then started as a faculty member there. With three exceptions, all the members were Jewish, including a Guggenheim heir. All of these faculty were secular.

I looked through Lehigh's 1978-79 school catalog, which lists the faculty. Of about 400, I can identify 73 as Jewish. I personally took advantage of the Religion Studies courses on Judaism by auditing courses taught by Larry Silberstein and Chava Weissler. Although I was an auditor, I was a serious student, attending all the classes, doing all the readings, and handing in all the assignments. Both Larry and Chava were excellent instructors. The students respected Larry and [in particular] loved Chava. Larry has a sterling scholarly reputation, and Chava is extraordinarily learned. Roger Simon was a driving force with Hillel (the Jewish students' organization found on many college campuses) for years, chairing the board of directors.

Then there's the Philip and Muriel Berman Center for Jewish Studies. [Larry Silberstein was the founding director.] The Hess Brothers (owners of the historic department store in Allentown) were a Jewish family, and Philip Berman bought them out. One day, I was out for a bike ride in Allentown and recognized pieces of art in Phil's yard. I asked him, "Where did you get the Henry Moore sculpture?" Phil was a stridently secular Jew.... He was interested in secular Judaism, the study of Judaism.

~

Edwin Kay and his wife, Jannie, were our near neighbors. When we first moved into the neighborhood, Jannie called me, sight unseen, and offered to host a breakfast at her house for the boys and me. Then she walked around the neighborhood and invited any other mothers and children she saw. I knew Jannie and Ed had spent two long stretches in Africa, first in Cameroon with the Peace Corps and then in Ghana and that Ed had taught there.

Chava Weissler, I knew as a kind person, a professor who had agreed to meet me for lunch to talk over my project sometime around 2011. It was Chava who had referred me to the work of anthropologist Barbara Meyerhoff.

Roger Simon was also extremely helpful for this project, speaking to me about local history and country clubs (a very interesting chapter in Lehigh Valley lore, though not within the Bethlehem city limits), sharing oral history interview recordings, and reviewing parts of this manuscript.

These are all terrific people, and I caught them at the tail ends of their careers. Each seemed so modest; it was hard to find out what I didn't know. I did a little more research for purposes of shining what I hoped would be "just enough" light on them in these pages. What I found only reinforced how important it is to look around us and ask the people in our lives what matters to them.

It turns out that, in addition to Ed's teaching, he and Jannie have been active in supporting development internationally: "Besides teaching at Ashesi (in Ghana), Professor Kay is currently working on a project with The Women's Trust Foundation in Pokuase (Ghana). Women's Trust was set up to support needy but brilliant girls financially so they can have access to a quality education. Currently, the foundation is supporting 63 bright young women." (Source: Asheshi University)

Dr. Chava Weissler is professor emerita of religion, culture, and society at Lehigh and held the Philip and Muriel Berman Chair of Jewish Civilization. She was honored during the Berman Center's Year of the Jews and the Arts. Identifying her as a folklorist and ethnographer of contemporary Jewish practice, Lehigh University posted, "Professor Weissler's courses took a folklore approach to the study of Jewish life and practice, with a focus on Jewish women, the Renewal Movement, Yiddish and classical texts, and popular practice...Her work creatively and critically examines Jewish texts in Hebrew, Aramaic, and Yiddish to ask, 'What does the female body signify?' and 'to whom?' ... Her work illuminates ethical and devotional literature, reading between the lines to show how to find women in the Jewish past even when they are difficult to see." This part, at least, wasn't a surprise since I had read her 1998 book, *Voices of the Matriarchs.*

Allan B. Goodman's fraternity, Sigma Alpha Mu, held this house party in 1959. Allan is shown back center, wearing glasses. Contributed photo.

Last but not least, an urban and social historian, Dr. Roger Simon is professor emeritus of history. According to Lehigh University, "He is particularly interested in organized labor and in Philadelphia and New York. He is the author of a monograph on ethnicity and neighborhood-formation in Milwaukee, *The City-Building Process*, and coauthor of a study of the urban adjustment of Italians, Poles, and African-Americans in Pittsburgh, *Lives of Their Own*. His most recent book is *Philadelphia: A Brief History*."

~

The University Social Scene: Back to Gordon Goldberg

When I asked Gordon Goldberg whether he met Jewish girls through social events as a Lehigh student in the 1950s, he didn't hesitate.

"What girls?" he joked. On a more serious note, he said, "There was what was called the Quad Cities—Reading, Allentown, Easton, and Bethlehem. They would have dances that alternated at the community centers. We went to all the social events. We dated. I was very shy. I loved to dance, but was shy when it came to asking a girl to go on a date. Petrified. I steered away from that sort of thing." Not forever, though. Gordon and his wife, Rose Lee, (of Allentown) enjoyed a long and happy marriage.

However, many of the Jewish girls of Bethlehem did date Lehigh boys. One woman said, "I wanted to have fun in high school. We all wanted to date Lehigh boys, and we did." The interest of the girls in the "Lehigh boys" caused chagrin among many of the local boys.

Gus Levin said, "The girls stuck it out with us until they were 16, then they didn't look at us 16-year-olds because they had 18-year-old Lehigh students to look at. There were a lot of girls from high school, smart girls. They would go out with the boys from Lehigh. A lot of them married boys from Lehigh."

Esther Hirshberg did. She said, "I met my husband the first day he came to Lehigh. He was a big athlete. This was in 1929. My sister's boyfriend was taking him to the bank to open an account. My husband came from New York, and they were going to the E. P. Wilbur Trust Company [in the well-known landmark Bethlehem "Flatiron" building]. I was still in high school, wasn't even graduated. I [later] went to school in Philadelphia, but we kept in touch. His senior year, he didn't want to leave without me. We eloped! We went to Elkton, Maryland, took off and got married."

So it went, decade after decade. Carol Herzon-Loney turned 16 in the 1970s, and she said, "When I was 16, me and my high school girlfriend, Kate, went to frat parties. We were 'townies.' We met students and got some boyfriends."

Some things had changed, though. For one, Lehigh began accepting female students in 1971, and Carol became a Lehigh student.

I Loved Being at Lehigh: From Carol Herzon-Loney

I never really thought about [the future] until I got to high school. I had taken a psychology class in high school and knew that I wanted to be a marriage counselor and sex therapist. I heard that Lehigh went co-ed. It was a good school and I had good grades. My G.P.A. was 3.75. I was treasurer of the National Honor Society, a Pep girl, in French Club, and the student activities director for the Student Council.

I applied to Lehigh. My parents said I could live on campus and be part of the student body. I was happy. If they hadn't agreed to that, I probably wouldn't have gone there. I wanted that college experience. I had a double major in psychology and social relations and a minor in humanistic perspectives in a technological society.

When I went to Lehigh, my friend Diane and I went to Hillel. We would go to breakfasts at the Jewish Community Center [Brith Sholom]. But Diane and I were the only girls. Lehigh was a male-dominated place. Most of the Jewish girls were from Long Island and I guess they weren't interested in Hillel. I don't think Lehigh had a very strong Jewish presence.

At the breakfasts, Diane and I ended up having to serve the food and clean up. We got very little help from the boys, so we stopped going. Diane was a chemist, so she was in the sciences where there would have been more Jewish men. She saw them a lot more often than I did over in the Humanities.

I loved being at Lehigh [during that time]. There were 500 women and 3,500 men when I got to Lehigh in '73. The ratio was 7:1. The social life was all about the fraternities. There were 33 frats [this takes into account all fraternities at Lehigh]. We went to parties, we would go to the Lehigh Lafayette games and there would be a big to-do, with cocktail parties and dinners at the houses.

When I started as a student, girls were not even considered part of the student body. They were called "coeds." There was resistance to women being there. By senior year, there was less resistance. The campus itself got used to the presence of women. My junior year is when some of the girls decided to form sororities. They didn't have a house, just got a dorm floor. They started to integrate into the Lehigh community.

~

About the time Carol matriculated, Dr. Harriet Parmet joined the faculty of Lehigh University as a professor of the Hebrew language. In the following decade, Phillip and Muriel Berman established their endowment. Through the Berman Center and a multitude of other sources at Lehigh, it became possible to hear world-renowned Jewish individuals speak at Lehigh, such as comic creator Art Spiegelman, cookbook writer Joan Nathan, and poets laureate.

All of these individuals visited Lehigh within my first year as the editor of the Lehigh Valley's Jewish newspaper. We were able to obtain hard-to-get interviews with several of these visitors and do press coverage of the visits of all. Sometimes it seemed as though the world came to Bethlehem.

Hebrew, Jewish Studies, and Elie Wiesel at Lehigh

Sitting along the low side balcony of Brith Sholom's sanctuary is where I first saw the woman with white hair and high color in her cheeks. She is Dr. Harriet Parmet. One Saturday, she was called up to the Torah and read a Hebrew prayer aloud. As she returned to her seat, she passed in front of me, her face aglow, and we shook hands, as was the custom.

At the *kiddush* (Hebrew for holiness, referring to the blessing over the wine, but it also refers to the luncheon after services), I admitted to Harriet, "When I go up to the *bima* (raised platform where the Torah is read), my knees shake."

Harriet responded, "So do mine! And you know it's not because of the Hebrew!" For we both experienced that same sense of awe when called to the holy ritual in front of an ark which has in Hebrew on its lintel words translating to: "Know Before Whom You Stand."

Later, Harriet agreed to speak with me regarding her time at Lehigh University. I visited her and husband, Sidney, in their Allentown home.

Drs. Harriet and Sidney Parmet in their Allentown home, circa 2012

Each in Our Own Pocket No More: From Dr. Harriet Parmet

I was the first one to teach Hebrew at Lehigh. I was also the first one to teach Jewish Studies and was involved in creating the Jewish Studies minor.

My mother was a Philadelphian; my father was born in Russia and came to Philadelphia. His father had died, and his mother remarried; things were very tough for him. My mother was a WAC (Women's Army Corp) in World War I, a medical technician and a graduate of William High School for Girls.

I grew up in an all-Jewish neighborhood in Philadelphia. We had off all of the holidays, not just the High Holy Days. I mean *shlosh regalim* (all the major holidays). It didn't matter whether you were of a religious ilk or not, no one was in school. The first time I encountered the world outside of that was when I entered Philadelphia High School for girls. I discovered this whole other world. Yet we still lived each in our own pockets, with little or no social interaction. I graduated in January of '46.

I went to Temple University where I had my bachelor's degree in English and my master's in Education. I went to Gratz College for a bachelor's in Hebrew Letters. You know about Rebecca Gratz of Philadelphia? She founded Gratz College. I taught Hebrew School all along.

I was from [the area called] Strawberry Mansions. I taught at Beth Israel on 32nd and Montgomery. It's not there now; it's a Black neighborhood and it used to be a Jewish neighborhood. I took my exam as was required and went to teach at Gillespie Junior High at 18th and Pike for five years until we moved. My husband is a dentist.

Is that why you moved to Allentown?

Sidney: She had to follow me. Harriet calls it her pioneer days.

Harriet: Anyway, we had our children and when the opportunity came to teach at Lehigh ... they were looking to introduce the Hebrew language and I applied, among others. I had the appointment and taught until 1994. Besides teaching, I did colloquia, inviting speakers. Alice Eckhardt and I worked together. Her husband was a minister, and she was involved with Holocaust Studies, and still is.

~

After working at Lehigh for many years, Harriet received her doctorate degree, also from Lehigh. A May 1998 Lehigh University Hillel Society photo shows her receiving her doctorate and labels her "Co-Founder of Lehigh's Jewish Studies Program."

When I asked Harriet if it was unusual for a faculty member to be female at the time she started, she replied, "There were a few."

She found Brith Sholom to be "a warm and welcoming congregation. Don't forget, when it was on the South Side, it was easy for me to slip in there."

Harriet explained that Lehigh became interested in having a Hebrew language program, even though Lehigh was originally an engineering school. "This was before the Berman [Center], before the establishment of Hillel. The dean of the college and the chairman of the Department of Modern Languages, Joseph Mower, were very favorably disposed to Jewish studies, very supportive."

"Remember, modern Hebrew was initiated well before the state of Israel. With the advent of Israel [in 1948], it became *de rigueur* (required by etiquette or fashion) for schools to offer Hebrew," she explained. "I had my Ph.D. from Lehigh, and with the advent of the Berman Center, it was a very affirming kind of thing because [the Jewish Studies program was] there before. I invited Elie Wiesel and I.B. [Isaac Bashevis] Singer."

"Elie Wiesel spoke at a convocation. They were each here in this living room. They were so warm, so *hamish* (Yiddish down-to-earth or homey) ... do you know the expression a *gleyzl tey*? It's Yiddish. All they wanted was 'a glass of tea.' That and a pencil and a little bit of paper for Elie Wiesel. The question came up with him, how would he feel speaking in a church? They went over it all and he said as long as it's not on the main pulpit, it's okay. It was quite an experience having him here, meeting him, having him as a speaker at the convocation. It was incredible because the whole chapel was filled. Elie Wiesel donated that which he was given for speaking."

Elie Wiesel, who was deported from Hungary to Auschwitz-Birkenau at the age of 15. He survived the Holocaust. He went on to become a writer, activist, and Nobel laureate, best known for his memoir, *Night*. Shown here with Harriet Parmet on his first visit to Lehigh University, to deliver the baccalaureate address at an ecumenical service, in 1985.

Harriet shared that the Jewish Studies program came about because Lehigh is a university, not a college: "They felt there would be a critical mass of all kinds of students. Hugh Flesher, a very close friend who was the chaplain for 15 years, was very much disposed to doing the program. As chaplain, he was influential with the higher ups. I worked with [Professor of Religion Studies] Alice Eckardt. Her husband, A. Roy Eckardt, was the Chair of Religion Studies. He was a minister. We had the Lehigh Valley Consortium of Colleges. Phil Berman offered a bounty to work on a dig in Northern Israel; we worked on Tel Akko [excavation on this site, a city in Biblical times] with [Israeli archaeologist] Moshe Dothan."

Harriet taught a popular Jewish Studies course. "It wasn't a required course, so everyone who took it wanted to be there," she recalled. "Some non-Jews took it because they were curious. Everyone cared very much about being there. Lehigh was mostly an engineering university; this was an elective. We did so much with so little, but I was never uncomfortable. I fought for acceptance. It was not automatic; it was very, very hard."

"It was a completely strange environment because I was going from undergraduate study to this completely different sea. [Before,] I had been in a religious school. It was different, moving to a secular world and creating academic courses that were viable and acceptable."

Then Harriet shared a powerful memory. "One student heard about an antisemitic incident that happened in Warsaw and said, 'I think that's ignorance.'"

Harriet's reply: "What do you think antisemitism is?"

Chapter 9
"Field and Fountain, Moor and Mountain, Following Yonder Star"
Weathering Changes

In 2014, in addition to publishing the newspaper, I was asked to develop a bi-annual magazine that had been a little-attended-to clause in my job description. It was during that process—when I was editing day and night, even in my dreams—that I finally began to see for myself what my middle son had long since noticed: Although it seemed I was doing everything my children and employer needed, there was nothing left over. My life was out of balance.

On weekends, I avoided social contacts in favor of rest, which proved elusive in a house full of active guys. Although I'd plotted out a timeline that would have me in that job until retirement, the truth finally dawned: I was headed for a breakdown.

My sense of self-confidence, which had at first increased as the newspaper's quality consistently improved and our advertising revenues grew, had taken a downturn. Practicing my craft and saving for college mattered, but maybe this wasn't the best way.

Meanwhile, people around me, including my husband, my community at Brith Sholom, and the new community at work were pleased and proud of me holding the role of editor. Making a change would mean standing up for myself and finding a good alternative.

I went to see my friend Betty Diamond, whom I had met through this project. By then, Betty was in her late 80s. Half her lifetime before, with the Steel on the decline and their South Side customers moving away, Betty and her husband, Gene, had closed their South Side shop, the Fabric Center, without a viable alternative for making a living. Yet I knew Betty had found a way forward.

"Betty, tell me more of your story."

Betty shared more of her personal story, and it was bound up in the story of Bethlehem. "The South Side was flourishing in the '50s and '60s because Bethlehem Steel was, too. After that, it was a matter of survival. When Bethlehem Steel was going full blast, there were a lot of people—a lot of families, a lot of workers. The South Side was a bustling area. With the demise of the Steel, it was the beginning of the end. It was in the '70s and '80s that we closed the Fabric Center. Things don't happen overnight."

Changing Winds: The 1960s to Mid '70s: When Everything Started to Collapse

"The very first time we went to Brith Sholom, Sandy Wruble approached me to join Hadassah," said Karen Bader. "Sandy was very persistent. So I joined Hadassah. I became a board member. All of a sudden, I discovered, I was on a committee, headed the committee, and then was President! It was a quick rise!

"I was the first one selling Giant (grocery) scrip (a fundraiser); I would take all the Giant scrip with me to the store and physically tackle people to buy it from me while they were in the store. Then I became Membership Chair for the Northeastern portion of Pennsylvania.

"Everything started to collapse as people found other things to do in the outside world. Hadassah and Sisterhood had met on alternate weeks. There were the same people in both, with the weekly meeting on Monday afternoon and a big monthly meeting. It was a tradition—Monday was 'meeting day'! Then Sisterhood and Hadassah grew apart. Meeting day conflicts developed.

"Health clubs became popular. Rather than walk around the neighborhood and do yard work, a lot of women would go to health clubs. Many women went back to work. Also—television."

Karen was the first to hint that the way more recent generations viewed the internet as leading to social breakdowns, so the previous generations experienced a loss of socializing due to the advent of television in most homes. Like the Internet, television (and newspapers and radio before it) brought into people's homes new information and awareness.

We Didn't Know from That: Phil Moskowitz

Until November of 1963, Phil Moskowitz must have thought life would just go on as it had started. Phil was born in Bethlehem in 1947, among the first of the generation that would come to be known as Baby Boomers. His family moved around a bit but came back to Bethlehem, where Phil got involved in Bnai Brith Youth Organization (BBYO). His mother taught, both because she wanted to and because the family needed the income. Life revolved around the Brith Sholom Community Center.

Phil went to Northeast Junior High, then Liberty High School. One day when Phil was in high school, a woman ran into his classroom and told the students the President had been shot.

"That was November 22, 1963," Phil recalled. "We were supposed to have a BBYO convention that weekend. Of course, it was canceled. I remember being riveted to the TV that whole weekend."

"I saw Jack Ruby shoot Lee Harvey Oswald," Phil said. "I remember being in the kitchen with my mom and dad,

Phil Moskowitz (center right, in white shirt) with his fellow summer Camp Retnec (Center spelled in reverse) counselors, circa 1962.

yelling, "Mom and Dad, Oswald's shot!" We just couldn't comprehend that.... The whole weekend was surreal. How do you make sense of that? You don't, not of something that doesn't make sense."

In a North Side Neighborhood "On the Edge of Rosemont": From Ann Klein

Ann Klein was born and raised in Bethlehem. The daughter of Martin and Edith Podberesky Blinderman ("The Border Was Always Changing," Chapter 3) and sister-in-law of Judy Aronson ("The Matchmaker," Chapter 7), Ann now lives with her husband, Jonathan, in Massachusetts but returns to visit relatives in the Lehigh Valley.

William Frankel was the rabbi when I was a kid and a teen; he and his family were well-liked by both the adult congregation and the children. This was in the 1950s and '60s Also notable was Aviva May. She was married to Stan May. She was Yemenite, beautiful, and bringing a warmth as

241

she taught us *niggunim* (Hebrew for melodies)—roots music that we hadn't heard before.

Bobby Gast functioned as a *gabbai* (one who provides support during the Torah service). He was young and handsome. For years, he led the service. He was an important figure and taught us lots of music, Yiddish songs. People thought I had a crush on him because I was sassy in his sixth grade class. He married a beautiful woman who looked like Marlo Thomas. There was a children's chorus, and my sister Gena and I both miss the tunes we learned as children.

Before the renovation [completed in 1963], there was dark wood in the sanctuary. From the child's point of view, it was warm and beautiful. There was always an organ. Things were kind of *hamish* (Yiddish for down-to-earth or homey). It was the melodies, the feeling, that I liked about synagogue.

Sometimes I was there four or five days a week: for Hebrew School, then on Shabbos for Junior Congregation led by our male Hebrew School friends Stan or Jeff Deutch, or Nevin Mindlin ("A Standout Star," Chapter 5). Girls were just beginning to have bat mitzvahs in my tweens and teens and, though we participated in Junior Congregation, the boys would lead.

The level of [academic] challenge and conversation at Hebrew School was often much higher than what we experienced at public school. Most of us really liked it, which I now know was unusual and amazing among Baby Boomers. We read *J.B.* by Archibald MacLeish in sixth grade! It was the story of Job.[9]

One thing about Hebrew School was you pretty much befriended everybody. Friendships between different types of

---

[9] The National Book Foundation spotlights the book for "sparking a national conversation about the nature of God, the meaning of hope and the role of the artist in society." (Source: NationalBook.org)

kids, from goody-goodies to rebels, were more common than they were in our larger public schools.

Because we were there much of the week, we gave up other activities like Scouts or sports. You'd think there would have been large scale resentment or rebellion, but I don't think there was. It wasn't all peace and love, and I'm sure there are grown-ups now who don't have such fond memories, but overall it felt like a more accepting atmosphere than public school. I think that because of outside influences, the Jews of Bethlehem had to pull together, and the place we knew we definitely belonged was at Brith Sholom.

Antisemitism was prevalent throughout my childhood and teens. There were overt, physical, and cruel incidents involving my sister and cousin in our elementary school. I was targeted verbally in junior high. By high school, I was [also] quite aware of the social exclusions that affected friendships and romances. Church and synagogue youth group participation were part of the social divide, but I understood that. I had many close non-Jewish friends, and although we joked about the pressures to conform to prejudiced norms, we pretty much accepted them.

The Junior League's annual holiday ball was an example of those norms. You had to be invited to attend, and no Jewish girl ever was. Jewish boys were sometimes invited, but according to hearsay, it was because extra boys were needed to be escorts. Most of my female friends were invited, and so was my non-Jewish boyfriend. I was not. If I were making a movie now, at least one of those people would have refused to go—I'd want it to have been my boyfriend—but in reality, he didn't refuse. Lehigh Valley was very "WASPy[10]" about social rank and hierarchy, very tuned in to the junior executives and the executives at the Steel company. Compared to other,

---

[10] White Anglo Saxon Protestant

more severe instances of bigotry surrounding our community and nation then and now, being left out of a dance isn't so terrible, but it certainly did affect me.

So even though the vast majority of kids in Bethlehem probably had parents working as laborers for the Steel, everyone participated in mirroring the hierarchy?

My neighborhood was Rosemont [considered affluent, on the West Side of Bethlehem]; we lived on the edge of Rosemont. There were junior executives and middle management on the way up.

One year at Brith Sholom, a Hanukkah decoration contest was held. I suppose it was intended to compensate for Jewish kids' feeling left out of the spirit of the [Christmas] season. I remember people from Brith Sholom coming to the house to see what we'd done.

My father made my dreidel costume from a large cardboard box. He used baling wire to make the point in the form of a dreidel. My head stuck out of a hole in the top, my arms stuck out of holes in the sides, and the box tapered with wire to a point somewhere around my knees, making it difficult to walk, though I could spin. When I first read about or saw Scout Finch in *To Kill a Mockingbird* trying to move in her ham costume, I knew how she felt.

Each year in elementary school, some Jewish child would be asked to explain Hanukkah to their classmates. I don't recall if we were actually asked or volunteered, but one of us would bring a menorah and dreidel to school. One specific woman teacher called it "the Jews' Christmas." We would try to find a way to correct that notion and told the class the actual story of the holiday. But at least four years after my attempt, that same teacher was still telling the class that my sister and her friend would be describing the Jews' Christmas. That was humiliating and enraging.

As an adult looking back, it's hard to understand why none of our parents took this on, or why they didn't volunteer to make a class visit and take the pressure off the kids. In those days, parents weren't very involved in schools the way they are today. Or perhaps they chose to pick their battles, and that wasn't the one to fight. But I also think about why that teacher refused to correct her mistake or change her opinion; her refusal was in itself an act of discrimination. This experience is one of the factors that led some Jewish kids in Bethlehem to become articulate representative Jews in later years.

In '67 or '68, my English teacher, who was also my school counselor, invited me and the president of the class to speak on a panel at First Presbyterian Church at a Junior League event to "address the challenges of youth." Under the influence of Bob Dylan, Joan Baez, and USY (a Jewish youth group), I was prepared to speak truth to power, which was not a phrase I'd heard yet.

My classmate and class president addressed the needs for a teen center so kids would not be hanging out at Illick's Mill, aka "the Mill, which had a reputation for fostering rebellious and/or illegal activities. I spoke about the larger problem of discrimination in Bethlehem. In my opinion, both issues were legitimate, but the reaction to our speeches differed.

I believe the *Bethlehem Globe-Times* reported what each of us spoke about that night. But the newsletter published by the sponsoring organization only reported what my classmate said. I obviously had struck a nerve, and my remarks were censored. I felt some satisfaction that my point had been taken, proven by the suppression of my speech. It was a subtle satisfaction, but a good lesson.

Overall, my Jewish education and experience taught me to raise questions and identify problems in order to fix or change things. I wasn't afraid to speak up or disagree with people or policies, though I certainly attempted to be professional and sensitive with my opinions. I thought that's what you were supposed to do, and I was confused and dismayed when I felt I was being perceived as a troublemaker.

I was always shocked that people who I knew agreed with me would stay silent. It is only now, past retirement and after years of learning more about life, that I have come to understand silence better and realize that my ability to speak up may have put others in a difficult situation, or that they might have had different, less public strategies for fomenting change. My ease in questioning authority was actually a gift from my parents and Jewish community.

New Perspectives: Only the Girls Were Confirmed

"We lived on Shakespeare Road [on the North Side]. I went to Governor Wolf Elementary, East Hills Middle School, and Freedom High School," said Carol Herzon-Loney. "There were only maybe four other Jewish children in East Hills. I didn't socialize a lot with other Jewish kids."

"I did go to Camptown—the Grove—for Jewish day camp," Carol added. "As I got older, I got a lot more involved with my grammar school friends, my friends from the neighborhood. Those were my friends. In my Hebrew School class, there were four boys and eight girls. That was it!"

"In 1968, I was a bas mitzvah, only the third girl in the Brith Sholom Community Center synagogue to be a bas mitzvah. It wasn't done before that. Then I was confirmed when I was 15 with the other girls in the class. It's funny, only the girls were confirmed. The boys just kind of wilted away."

A Fire at the Community Center

In 1970, Ray Bell was a graduate student at Lehigh University, just finishing his dissertation. He was getting married that December and working as quickly as he could in his office, which gave him an inside view of what was happening in the Bethlehem Jewish community. Many decades later, speaking

Brith Sholom's 1971 Confirmation class: Carole Schiff, Karen Cook, Judith Leenov, Carolyn Goldberg, Sandy Sonnenfeld, Susan Ungerleider, Carol Herzon, Rabbi Wasser (Source: *Brith Sholom Ad Journal, 1971*)

from his home along Prospect Avenue on Bethlehem's West Side, Ray recalled, "Lehigh University had rented almost all of the third floor of the Brith Sholom Community Center for the Lehigh Laboratory School. They also rented offices on the second floor. We used the swimming pool and the gym. Fewer than a handful of people came to pray every day."

Ray's wife, Elizabeth, said, "In those days, computers were the size of a room. We had punch cards and would sit at a keyboard and end up with a deck of data. There were racks; you would put your deck on the rack and pretty soon the technician would come out and run it. You'd wait for hours, and if there was an error, a mistake, or you forgot something, it was no good."

Ray had decks and decks of these cards filled with data to support his dissertation. Before the couple's wedding, he carefully locked up the data cards and three copies of his dissertation in his office on the second floor of the Center. Then he and Elizabeth went to Ohio, where her family lived, and got married on December 19. Afterward, they drove back to Bethlehem, arriving on the evening of the 20th.

Elizabeth recalled what they found when they got back to Ray's apartment. "On the bed, someone had left open a newspaper. We didn't look at it right away because we went out and got something to eat. It was only when we came back some hours later and looked at the headline that we knew anything."

At first, Ray said, "We thought it was a joke, that someone had pulled a prank." But they soon realized, "This was not a joke."

Raging Fire Rips Jewish Center
Bethlehem Globe-Times
Saturday, December 19, 1970
... A fire believed set to cover up an attempted safe burglary, ripped the Brith Sholom Jewish Community Center on Packer Ave this morning, destroying the offices, reception area, and some classrooms. "There is a very strong possibility of arson," Fire Chief August Sebastionelli said after he inspected the building.

Ray took up the story from there. "I'm pretty convinced it was antisemitic. I think the synagogue had been vandalized.... People broke into the offices on the second floor and into the sanctuary [on the fourth floor].... Then they set fires on the second floor and first floor. That's my understanding. The whole place was gone. My office was blackened.... I retrieved one deck of data; it was charred."

Elizabeth continued, "We had been planning to get on the airplane to go to England the next day, because I had never met Ray's family. Then I was going to come home and get a job. Well, we never went to England [that year]."

Instead, the couple sent a telegram to Ray's mother. Elizabeth brought it out:

> Happily married. Beautiful day. Returned to find school burned. Must stay and reorganize. Merry Christmas. Will miss being with you. See you in summer. Letter follows. Love, Ray and Elizabeth

Rather than getting a job, Elizabeth said, "I sat there rerunning data."

"It took eight months," Ray said. "The dissertation had been all set to defend, and we had to recreate it. " Ray then successfully defended his thesis and went on to a dual appointment as a professor of education and social relations for Lehigh.

With such a shared moment of adversity, Elizabeth said, "We feel this connection to the Jewish community. It was 40 years ago now that this happened."

Indeed, at the time of the interview, the Bells were preparing to celebrate their 40th wedding anniversary. Ray said, "On our drive home from Ohio 40 years ago, we stopped at a little town for the night and had dinner. All they had was steak and potatoes and salad. We're going to build a fire and eat the same meal we ate 40 years ago."

"Your Center Is Burning": Excerpted and adapted from an article by Betsy Glazier that appeared in the **Brith Sholom Ad Journal, 1971**

Fred Brown was going over some things in his office at about 7:00 that morning when one of his drivers dashed in the door. He had been riding up Carlton Avenue and noticed smoke coming from our building. Fred called the rabbi, President Sam Sheckter, and the fire department. Then he raced out to see for himself.

Murray Glickman stopped for some breakfast before opening his business for the day. "Hey," someone shouted to him, "your Center is burning." Murray alerted House

Chairman Leo Pozefsky, then ran up to Brodhead and Packer Avenues.

Word of the fire spread almost as fast as the blaze itself and before long a horrified group of members and friends had hurried to the scene to see what they could do to help. The mood was one of stunned disbelief. "Why the Center?" people asked. "Who could have done such a thing?" The questions still remain unanswered.

After initial shock had lessened, thoughts turned to the Torahs. Rabbi Wasser and Fire Chief August Sabastionelli made their way up the fire escape to the back door of the Temple (sanctuary). Chief Sebastionelli then requested one of his men to don a gas mask and enter the sanctuary. Following directions from the rabbi, he located the sacred scrolls. As he handed the first one to Rabbi Wasser, Gene Diamond dashed up the stairs to take it ... A human chain was spontaneously formed and the remaining scrolls were passed from man to man until they were all safely away from the building.

... Memories of the deep emotions evoked by this tragedy will always remain with us. Who can forget the determination of Sisterhood President Evelyn Brown as she somehow got into the kitchen to rescue the latkes for the children's Hanukkah party?

Who can forget the sight of grown men and women standing on Packer Avenue with tears streaming down their cheeks? Or the patience of those who spent hours sifting through the ashes trying to piece together bits of charred records?

How does one replace a home, a beloved structure, a center of the life of a people? You call in insurance adjusters, architects, and contractors. Somehow, the work begins ... We Jews in Bethlehem have a future. Our building [will be] restored. But the record of our past that we hold so dear, was irrevocably lost to us on that sad day.

Bethlehem firefighters respond to the fire at the Brith Sholom
Community Center; December 19, 1970. NB: Despite due diligence,
the origin of the photo is unknown; though replicated from the *Brith
Sholom Ad Journal, 1971*, it may have originated from the Bethlehem Fire
Department.

An Immediate Responder: Eugene Diamond

"My husband was alerted, and he raced up there, up the
block," Betty Diamond said. "Gene was so happy he could be
of help. The fire was heart-breaking. We were very worried
it would destroy the whole building, but it was fairly well-
contained. I think it was vandalism."

Ann Goldberg recalled, "We all learned about it and drove
down [to the Center that Saturday morning]. I remember
standing there in the parking lot and watching it burn. *Even
as we spoke, so many years later, tears welled up in Ann's eyes*. It wasn't
just smoke. The flames were soaring out of there. There were
those tablets on the front, maybe the flames were behind the
tablets? It could have been, memory's a funny thing."

"I felt shock, sadness, a feeling of vulnerability," Ann said. "It had looked like such a sturdy building. Gene Diamond went in and got the Torah scrolls and got them out. After that we had services at the Little Shul, across from Northeast Middle School. It was not our shul, but they graciously opened the doors to us. There was never any doubt in anybody's mind that it would be re-built. People felt loyalty to that building. People felt [re-building] was the right thing to do. I understand at one time there was a thriving community on the South Side."

Outpouring of Support

After the fire, the community received support from other people in the greater Bethlehem community.

From the Mayor: The Voice of the City

Excerpted from a letter to Brith Sholom from Bethlehem Mayor H. Gordon Payrow:

> At 7:25 a.m. on Saturday, December 19, 1970, our Fire Bureau received a call which notified men that there was a fire at the Brith Sholom Community Center.
>
> After the blaze was contained, people stared in disbelief at the boarded up building. Would there be no more Community Center?
>
> Of course there would be! As you prepare for the rededication of a building that houses people and events that mean so much to Bethlehem, please accept sincere congratulations from a grateful community.

"Like an Ice Cream Cone on A Hot Summer Afternoon": Excerpted and adapted from the Brith Sholom Ad Journal, 1971

> From the very beginning and through the reconstruction effort, the building committees

have been plagued by fiscal frustration. The first shock was felt during the insurance negotiations; insurance dollars were shrunk by depreciation formulae. ... The building committee sagaciously decided that reconstruction of the building as it was would also reconstruct fire and security hazards. The conflagration melted the aluminum façade like an ice cream cone on a hot summer afternoon. The glass entry was a prime target for stone-sniping vandals. ... Making changes compatible with the available funding required endless hours of negotiations, trading, deletions, additions. A new 20-year bonded roof has been installed for the entire building. This was done because the existing roofing was blistered, and insulation was found to be soaked with water. Watertightness is an absolute necessity for a minimum maintenance building.

"In Our Hearts"

Excerpted from a letter from Executive Director Edwin H. Frey to Rabbi Max Wasser on behalf of the Greater Bethlehem Area Council of Churches (formalized in 1968), that was reprinted in the Brith Sholom Ad Journal, 1971

August 20, 1971

Dear Max:

You and your people have gone through a distressing experience which you have translated into a triumphant event through dedication, hard work, and faith in the power of Almighty God....

We have a very warm spot in our hearts for you and your fellow-members.

We appreciate so much your cooperative participation on behalf of Brith Sholom in our various cooperative endeavors to serve the people of the community.

My best to you, as always.
Cordially yours,
Ed

Homecoming: Excerpted and adapted from an article by Helen Cook in the Brith Sholom Ad Journal

Arriving home is indeed good. Just as all wanderers hope and pray for their return home, we too have longed to be back; now, thank God, it is a reality. As we start the New Year 5732, we hope to stress our installation theme, *ve'ahavta*, "thou shalt love." Love can bring all people together. We must all pledge ourselves toward this theme.

Bethlehem Steel as my family first saw the shuttered giant in the early 2000s and next to it, running between the South and North sides of Bethlehem, the Lehigh River.

Crossing the River: A Move to the North Side

During the 1970s and early '80s, with the decline of Bethlehem Steel and, ongoing alongside this, the fortunes of the South Side, a number of long-time residents moved to the North Side. The Little Shul, Agudath Achim, had already moved. But there stood the hulking four-story, expensive-to-operate Center on its corner of Packer and Brodhead Avenues on the South Side. Parking was a problem; many young people were moving away from Bethlehem. There just weren't enough people filling the seats.

The Quarterback Rabbi: Excerpted and adapted from a speech by Bruce Smackey

In 1971, my wife, Ardie, our two daughters and I came to Bethlehem, and we joined Brith Sholom Community Center. In our first four years as members, our introduction to synagogue life witnessed the dismissing of one long-serving rabbi and the hiring of a replacement who lasted two years. The then-board of trustees formed a Rabbi Search Committee and received resumes from the Rabbinical Assembly of the Conservative Movement as well as resumes from Reconstructionist and Reform rabbis. Their resumes told the sad story of individuals toward the end of their careers. Finally, we were permitted to look at resumes of several upcoming graduates of Jewish Theological Seminary [JTS]—a pool of untested candidates for dealing with communal life from the pulpit—read *kvetching* (Yiddish for complaining) congregants and board members.

I called the director of placement at JTS and asked about several of the candidates. In a discussion of the off-resume credentials of the candidates, the director indicated that one particular candidate was quarterback of the undefeated JTS rabbinical football team. As a student, this rabbinical candidate had the strength to bring the team into the red-zone and—by his considerable tenacity—over the goal line.

That endorsement was good enough for the committee, and a pre-interview was arranged in New York City between Allen Juda and another congregant—David Trutt—and me.

We picked Allen Juda up outside Grand Central Station [in New York City]. The pre-interview was conducted with the rabbi sitting in the back seat as we drove back and forth to Long Island to visit my relative in a nursing home.

One of the questions I asked the then less than 30-year-old rabbinical student was, "Can you cope with a failure and how do you keep going forward?" His answer, understandably, wasn't explicit, but he stated that his interest was to be a congregational rabbi, he expected that there would be some failures, and he didn't fear the challenges he would face.

After several interviews with the Search Committee, the candidate Rabbi Juda and his then-fiancée Toby Keller (now Toby Juda) faced a final interview with 135 Brith Sholom congregants. Rabbi Juda became our rabbi in 1975.

The Rookie: From Rabbi Allen Juda

When I came, within the year or two before I was hired, they were thinking of merging with Bnai Abraham Synagogue in Easton. I don't know if there were formal discussions, but with the previous rabbi they had here—"Things were so bad," people said. That rabbi was here two years; in fact, when I came to interview, I couldn't look in his office because he had the office locked and wouldn't let anyone else in.

Look, it's a marriage, and that one wasn't a good fit. His behavior was very beneficial for me because, anything I did, people said, "This is so much better, or so much easier, than before." When you have a terrible experience, it works better for the next one. A good experience makes it tougher for the next one.

For a Potential Move, "Let Me See What I Can Do": Jerry Hausman and other leaders

At the time of the fire at the Center, Jerry and Florence Hausman briefly took the rescued Torah scrolls into their home until they could be safely placed in the ark of nearby Congregation Agudath Achim.

"We put them in the family room," Jerry said.

Although the congregation made a recovery via a rededication, having decided not to move the synagogue, it did little to solve the underlying problem. When Rabbi Allen Juda arrived in town, he recognized the dilemma as well: The congregants, including the Hausmans, had mostly moved to the North Side.

One day, Jerry stopped in for a visit at the Center, and Rabbi Juda said, "Jerry, if we don't do anything, we could die here."

Feeling grim, Jerry agreed. "Let me see what I can do," he said. Jerry called a friend who was vice president and treasurer of Lehigh University, along the southwest edge of which the Center was located. Jerry asked whether the university would want to buy the building.

The reply: "Get it appraised."

"We don't have the money," Jerry answered truthfully. Things were that bad.

"I'll pay for it," the friend said.

With other synagogue leaders, Jerry was deeply involved in the exploration of a move. He chaired the building of what is now Congregation Brith Sholom on West Macada Road. (His son Kevin later became president of Brith Sholom, making them the synagogue's only father-son presidents.) Jerry and his wife, Florence, went with Jack and Cecile Shaffer to the artist David Ascalon who created the sanctuary tapestry on the ark. They asked him to create the statue that now stands in the courtyard and the candelabra in front of the building, which became the symbol of the

Congregation Brith Sholom, on Bethlehem's North Side, circa 1986

synagogue's endowment fund. People pitched in any way they could.

Rabbi Allen Juda recalled, "Dr. Arnold Marder, a past president, oversaw a strategic planning committee that was crucial to the moving process. I believe he plotted the location of every Brith Sholom member around 1982-83 and that showed clearly that the vast majority of the congregation lived in north Bethlehem. I believe he was co-chair of the building committee."

One Brith Sholom member, Leo Pozefsky, shared these words about the move. He was aged, and there was a rhythm to his words, like poetry:

"When we moved to Bethlehem, I became a member of the *shul*.

We had two kids going to *shul* and a third one being born.

I got involved as a man of all work:

I served on the committees; I became the president,

not because of my Jewishness,

but because I was able to carry heavy furniture.
We were moving the *shul* to the North Side.
Who was going to supervise the move?
And carry books and chairs and desks?
Leo was very strong and Leo was very able."

~

When the congregation moved to its current North Side location on Macada Road, which was accomplished between November 1985 and early 1986, planners looked for a way to create a sense of connection to the new space. Rabbi Allen Juda said, "Taking some of the sanctuary windows was a very deliberate act of continuity."

As it had in 1924 with the establishment of the Center, the annual ad journal at the time carried the story of the past into the new location. Its feature "Phase I—Early Times" recounts the cornerstone laying, not of the Center, but of the 1897 building. The message for the community and future generations is put into perspective, not as the loss of the Center, the "home" that was so loved, but as part of a longer journey.

The article preparing the congregation for the new location closed, "The foundation of Judaism was set in Bethlehem of Pennsylvania. Phase I of our story is now complete."

~

In a series of actions that I have come to recognize as "a very Bethlehem story," the congregation brought hard evidence of their generative, or origin, story with them, as the ad journal recounts: "Careful scrutiny of the courtyard area of our new synagogue will locate the portion of the [1897] cornerstone that remains today. It was retrieved by Walter Oppenheimer some 30 years ago. Mr. Oppenheimer, a Hellertonian, saw it set as a curbstone at the Hellertown post office. He notified Rabbi Frankel, who then called the Hellertown Streets Department. It was then removed and given to the congregation." The cornerstone has since been moved to an indoor display case at the Macada Road location.

The cornerstone, with the year visible, as well as part of the original name, Brith Sholom Talmud Torah.

The congregational leaders, who had just a few years before decided on renovating the current space, had now changed course and gathered support for the move. It was a risk because the congregation felt such a sense of connection to the Center. Yet the Center had been called "an experiment" when *first* built. Would this *new* experiment to move the Center work?

When I asked Ann Goldberg how she had reconciled herself to the move, which many had resisted for a long time, she said, "When the community of respected leaders decided it was time to move, that's what we did."

Lighting the Way: Through Many Types of Changes

Betty Diamond was in her 40s and 50s when all of these changes on the South Side transpired. A person of determination, grit, and courage, Betty responded to this time of communal and personal loss, that of her and Gene's business, by looking for an opportunity, which then came calling, quite literally. The high school band leader phoned Betty to see whether she still had her connections in the fabric industry to enable the band to replace its uniforms at an affordable cost.

Betty did.

Fresh from the success of brokering that transaction, Betty reached out to other schools. She was soon operating a band uniform business out of her home. This was decades before home-based businesses became a happening thing.

Betty's story inspired me and bolstered my courage. At the beginning of 2015, I stepped down from my role as the editor of *Hakol*. The very next day, I had lunch with a *Hakol* predecessor and gifted graphic designer, Carolyn Katwan, also of Brith Sholom, mainly to talk over our past days at the newspaper. But I also needed to look to my future.

"Carolyn, could I hire you to design a business logo for me?" I asked. Of course, I had no idea how this should look.

Carolyn did. She reached out to me later with a beautiful swan logo beneath my motto "Everybody has a story to share" and also an unasked for and very much welcome job lead. That turned into a highly satisfying writing position with a wonderful firm, a role that finally afforded me the kind of work and the work-life balance I had always needed. And I would be working from home!

I thought, *Maybe I'll be better off mostly staying at home, limiting my interactions with people, which often felt a little stressful.* Of course, there should be exceptions. That much, at least, I understood.

~

By the mid-2010s, my children were reaching middle school and high school and wanted us to host a Hanukkah party. Yes, I agreed, that would be fun. We invited some friends with young children or from the neighborhood. Everyone would bring food and I made dozens upon dozens of latkes (fried potato pancakes), guests passing the platter hand to hand toward the buffet table. The crisp golden treats, slathered in applesauce or sour cream, would be quickly gobbled up. I carried a plate of doughnuts sprinkled with sugar outside to the kids, who were thrilled to be playing tag on one of the darkest nights of the year. As I stepped into their world, hands reached out from the darkness around me, emptying the plate. Making up for the lack of moonlight, I glimpsed, through the winter bare trees, "that star" shining on us from South Mountain.

One year, we welcomed a visitor. The Jewish Federation had arranged for the Valley's Jewish community to host a young Israeli woman to come as a *shlicha* (Hebrew for messenger or ambassador, in this case a sharer of culture). When we'd previously met for coffee, she said: "In Israel, on Passover, everything is closed. Here, nothing is. There, when Shabbat is coming, we feel it. We turn on the radio and we hear welcoming Shabbat tunes. It's the spirit of the day, of the holiday. Here, you need to make that choice: Will you send your kids to that most important soccer game of the year that comes on *erev* Rosh Hashanah? Here, you need to make more effort to stay connected. Yet when you do, there is a sense of a very connected community. When you decide to make that choice, you find it. Is there a 'Christian community of the Lehigh Valley'? No. When you are in the majority, the sense of community [may not be] that strong." At the party, she played with the children, taught them a few more words of Hebrew, and looked at the map of Israel with them. And, yes, it was fun.

~

Many things can change over the course of time. Among those raising their children in Bethlehem in previous decades, there came to be more awareness that their grown children would likely live elsewhere—that appeared to be the trend not only here but in American society at large. What this meant was that young people would need to be able to connect with an array of people.

Nurtured: From Toby Juda

We came here straight out of school. Bethlehem had no resemblance to anything I'd ever experienced. I'm from Milwaukee, which has 40,000 Jews. Bethlehem is more similar to Allen's (Rabbi Allen Juda's) background; he's from the town of Fall River, Massachusetts.

When I got here, I asked myself, "What am I doing here?" But we stayed, and I'm glad we stayed. I wouldn't have the children I do otherwise. They have small-town experience. Everyone matters. Bethlehem isn't big enough to have a mainstream. My children have experience in the way that everyone can affect the process. And there really is a lot of grassroots leadership here.

People said to me, "How will your children survive in a big city?"

Well, all three live in New York, and they're doing great. Their individualism was nurtured here. Who they are as a person was valued.

Sandy Wruble, Beth Tikvah, and Links to the Outside World

The Jewish community in Bethlehem also changed over time. Sandy Wruble of Brith Sholom was key to a project that had the effect of better connecting the Jewish community in Bethlehem with those of other Lehigh Valley cities. That project also provided something that many in the Valley-wide Jewish community needed. I visited Sandy at her North Bethlehem house and she gave me the scoop.

Sandy arrived in the area in 1970, because her husband, Norman Wruble, who had been working as an assistant principal in Middletown, New Jersey, accepted the position of principal at Saucon Valley [in Hellertown, near Bethlehem].

"We were happy because it was a little closer to our folks," Sandy said. Just in time, too, as Sandy explained:

"Wilkes-Barre where Norm's folks lived was hit by the flood in 1972. His father had already had a stroke and was living in a nursing home; Norm went up there looking for him, not knowing where he had been evacuated to. They lost everything. Norm moved them here and we found a house. We loved it, especially because it had a complete apartment downstairs. So they moved in with us."

Sandy described her career path. "I have a master's degree in speech pathology. I've worked in the schools and for Easter Seals. Home Healthcare of Pennsylvania was my last job [in that field], part-time when the children were young. I was driving up and all over to work with people who had had strokes. Norm didn't like me driving around like that.

"Then Rabbi Juda called. Leader Nursing and Rehabilitation Center [later called ManorCare] had opened up here in Bethlehem. The founder, George Leader, was the former governor of Pennsylvania. Some [from the Jewish community] in Allentown and Rabbi Juda met with him because there was a second building on paper. The rabbi and the committee met with Leader and got them to make one wing of the first floor for Jewish residents and provide space for a Jewish chapel and a kosher kitchen. This was the Beth Tikvah wing; it means 'house of hope.'" Jewish Family Service in Allentown worked with Leader Nursing Home on the project. Rabbi Allen Juda and Ruth Meislin were the co-chairs of the project.

"There were 31 beds in that wing," Sandy said. "Then they put in a dining room. This was in May of 1981. So Rabbi Juda called and explained what was happening. They needed a personal services manager and I was interested. Number one, I was getting tired of speech pathology; I was burnt out, and also I didn't like all that driving." Furthermore, Beth Tikvah was not far from Sandy's home.

For Sandy, the position was a wonderful way to work with people, including an extended version of the Jewish community—one that would include *other* Lehigh Valley cities, an early step toward forging a stronger connection with the local Jewish community beyond Bethlehem.

As Sandy said, "I did recreational activities and social work because I was the liaison between the Jewish communities of Bethlehem, Allentown, and Easton, the resident's families, and the rest of the place. I would reach into the community for help. Once a month, we would have a Friday night service, and I would ask various people to come and lead services. Steve Bergstein was one, Maur Levan, and Sam. I would vary the requests between Bethlehem, Easton, and Allentown.

"We would also have rabbinic visits; everyone had a week. The rabbis could visit everyone, or just people from their own city, whenever they wanted."

Bethlehem resident Ruth Radin, long a member of the Reform Congregation Keneseth Israel in Allentown, helped her mother move to Beth Tikvah. "At Beth Tikvah, there was a very strong sense of community that spanned the geographic divides across the Lehigh Valley," Ruth said. "There was a feeling that if anyone went there to visit a family member, they were an advocate for each Jewish person [who] was there. It wasn't just the eyes on the person you were visiting. We really had the sense that each other was caring. All of us would go and make sure everyone was happy, that their food was cut up.... It was a real sense of community."

Sandy said, "We were so successful that 10 years later we expanded it by 10 more beds. They added four doubles and two singles. We were close to capacity most of the time."

That didn't last.

"Our population started to decline," Sandy said. "Number one was the rise of assisted living, and it was cheaper. Two, the doctors didn't want to travel to Bethlehem to see one patient or two, and the family would say, 'Well my mother went to that doctor for 20 or 30 years and doesn't want to change. She'll go where the doctor goes.'"

Sandy continued, "And three, a lot of people didn't want to go to Bethlehem from Allentown to see their loved ones. They put them where it was convenient, saying, 'My mother wasn't kosher for her entire life.' I would say, 'Maybe she wasn't kosher, but does she like ethnic food, being surrounded by other Jewish people, and having holiday services with everything that goes with it, like gefilte fish?'"

~

Just as Sandy realized the downsides of driving all over Eastern Pennsylvania as a speech therapist, it wasn't long before I realized the problem with my new work-from-home situation. True, my writing career had evolved. I had the job I'd been hoping for, plus I was still doing contract work for the Federation, this time on sustainable terms. But I was also isolated. Although I wasn't lonely, the regained school-day solitude, which had been my choice, no longer felt as "comfy" as it once did. The truth is, we need other people. But there was something more to this story.

All the years of working at the Jewish newspaper, I had experienced belonging in so many forms: I had belonged *in* an organization (Federation). I had belonged *to* a staff serving the Lehigh Valley Jewish community. I felt I belonged *with* my congregation because, although I was doing little at the time to pursue my research project, many friendships had resulted.

In the case of that former job, I had decided it was time for me to exit that particular role and leave. Belonging can have a life cycle, too. I was experiencing the nature of belonging *through* that very process of going in and out of belonging.

I was starting to see belonging's true colors. Belonging isn't black or white, either/or, yes or no. It's not gray, either. Belonging is really *all* colors, *all* stripes, like the Biblical

Joseph's coat. Consider how many degrees of belonging and *not* belonging there are, including being cast out from belonging, that Biblical Joseph experienced before ultimately saving the very people (his own brothers!) who had sold him into slavery. Joseph, too, moved in and out of belonging, as did all his kin when they resettled in Egypt. Although at first they were welcomed, eventually they were enslaved before making their Exodus under Moses's leadership.

There's that shifting again, just like with those seemingly immovable mountain ranges. As long as we're alive, there's always the possibility of movement when it comes to belonging.

You know what else I realized? The collected stories of the Jews of the Christmas City and their lessons about belonging needed to be shared with other people.

"The Jews' Christmas"

When Laura Bochner attended grade school in Bethlehem, a full century after the days of Yehoshua Gilles, whose burial the town treated as a spectacle, she often found there would be craft projects to do at Christmastime. Laura said, "I didn't really mind. I always had the option to make other crafts. My teacher would ask me if I wanted to do my own thing. I didn't want to be the one kid doing something different. Some aspects of Christmas I can appreciate without getting too much into theology."

That sentiment holds true for many Jews in Bethlehem and for a variety of reasons.

"Christmas! I know I'm Jewish, but—I don't care—I like Christmas," Elaine Phillips said. "I love the music and the beautiful decorations. I love the spirit of Christmas. It should be that way all year long. This is Bethlehem! It's a beautiful thing, we drove around the city to show the kids the Christmas lights."

Many interviewees spoke of how they love Christmas songs. Gordon Goldberg enjoyed the songs, if not the meaning behind them. Gus and Zelda Levin volunteered on Christmas at the St. Luke's Hospital gift shop, knowing they would be needed that day because Christian volunteers would be celebrating the holiday. Rabbi Allen Juda said, almost to himself and in a tone of wonder, "I was the rabbi of the Christmas City."

Likewise, there's something poignant and ironic in Nevin Mindlin's describing the time of his father Morris's passing as "*erev* Christmas"—Nevin's very wording suggesting the connection he felt to both who he is as a Jew and the place in which he grew up.

Others felt differently. Morris himself and others refused to sing Christmas carols in school. Not everyone loves the Christmas tree on the plaza by City Hall, nor, in recent years, the menorah for Hanukkah, preferring clear separation of church and state.

"What I went after was the crèche (the display of statues of baby Jesus in the manger, with Mary and Joseph) at City Hall," said a contributor who asked not to be named. "If you read the Pittsburgh v. ACLU (American Civil Liberties Union) decision, it says those are unconstitutional. I went after the city with the help of the ACLU, with Stefan Presser [from ACLU]."

(Anonymous showed me a letter from Stefan dated October 20, 1989:)

"...I certainly admire your persistence in this matter. Unfortunately, given ACLU's limited resources which now include our challenge to the Commonwealth's Christmas display because of its inclusion of Latin crosses,...[the ACLU won't pursue the matter further]."

Anonymous continued: "Bethlehem's response to the ACLU was to place four [statues of secular] carolers in the vicinity of the crèche. I am being generous when I say vicinity...

"Locally [the challenge was not] very popular. I remained anonymous through the whole thing. I was genuinely frightened by the possibility [of exposure]...It gave me tremendously bad nerves."

Why?

"It's [seen as] un-Christian. Since then, I've heard very well-meaning people who just don't understand what it's like to have religious symbols thrust down your throat, and [taxpayers are] paying for it! They sing Christmas carols in school. It's offensive.

"When I was growing up [elsewhere, not in Bethlehem], we had to say a prayer every day; this was before [Madeline Murray O'Hare] brought suit around 1960. She was a strident atheist.

"First of all, we had to say the Lord's Prayer every day. Then there were carols. There was a policy on Wednesday afternoons of releasing students from school [if they] went to churches for religious instruction. The only ones left were the Jews. I guess [the teachers] resented us, otherwise they could [have gone] home."

Did this influence you to challenge the crèche?

"Maybe in some ways. I just have these libertarian ideas... Actually, the answer is yes because when the Supreme Court decision came down [outlawing] school prayer ... I was really happy. Imagine if they made us say Muslim prayers. It was like turning off the air conditioner. I feel so much better without the noise."

What do you make of the menorah Bethlehem's taken to displaying near the Christmas tree each year recently?

"I say, 'Why a big menorah? That's wrong!' What really complicates the issue is Hanukkah is an historical event, not a religious holiday."

Growing Up Jewish in the Christmas City

Yet because of Hanukkah's close time proximity to Christmas, this relatively minor holiday would often figure into the Christmas conversation at school, its own sort of fraught cultural event. Recall Ann Klein's words that she "did a talk one time ... about 'Growing up a Jew in the Christmas City.' It was unique and challenging." Ann added, "Overall, my sister Gena and I grew up liking the Christmas season's spirit, decorations and festivities. Despite being in a minority group, and experiencing antisemitism, I think our strong Jewish identities actually allowed us to enjoy the events around us. Our parents modeled humor and tolerance, we sometimes shared celebrations with non-Jewish friends and neighbors, and we learned to cope with the reality of being different. Maybe we accepted being members of a minority group better than people who grew up in large Jewish communities. Or maybe we just enjoy Christmas because it's pretty and it's the solstice for everyone, no matter what light you shine."

Ann and Laura, and similarly my son Jacob in his elementary school became, in effect, Jewish ambassadors to the general community. Having a positive role, a space, a positive place in the city of Bethlehem's story, on some levels feels good, their stories suggest. This isn't the same as everyone "knowing their place" (and staying in it) as John Angelucci recalled of the 1920s on the South Side. Everyone no longer "just knows" (or seems to care) who is Jewish.

But then there was Anonymous and the ACLU and others through the years who raised concerns about things like major tests on Jewish High Holidays.[11] Recall Ann Klein's frustration that "some teachers refused to acknowledge that

---

[11] For many years, the Bethlehem Area School District has included one High Holiday (either Yom Kippur or either day of Rosh Hashanah, depending on how the weekends fall) on its list of school closures.

[Hanukkah] wasn't the Jews' Christmas." These situations speak of being misunderstood, outnumbered, or just feeling different.

What's also different in Bethlehem is that this city that seems to value hard work and individualism, nevertheless had the temerity and foresight to reinvent itself for marketing reasons during the 1930s, calling itself the Christmas City. The city offered an experience that encouraged visitors. The side effect is a unique experience for the people living here, including those who are Jewish. Having grown up in the Christmas City means something special to my sons.

Bethlehem is named for the origin story of the Christian religion. However, even as this community story project came to a conclusion, I still puzzled over what the generative, or origin, story was for its Jewish community and where I might find it.

Then I realized: The opening pages of this very book refer to the 30th Anniversary *Brith Sholom Ad Journal, 1955* because the story of the community's founding is written there in the form of the history that Rabbi Frankel penned. The same story, or variations of that story have been shared on the ad journal pages over and over through the years! Despite being told, "We've been waiting for someone to do this," the joke was on me. *No one* was waiting. It was simply my turn. The absolutely wonderful Henry and Isabel Schiff even handed me an ad journal to help me get started! *That* is the origin story: the person to person connection that built a community.

Likewise, the 50th Anniversary *Brith Sholom Ad Journal, 1976* presented "a collection of stories, occasions, and photographs of the various events and individuals both living and dead, which formed Brith Sholom's character over the years." The Brith Sholom congregation has routinely used its ad journals to tell, re-tell, even re-shape its story in ways that highlight both continuity and change, thereby setting

Brith Sholom's ad journals through the years—part advertisement, part fundraiser, part directory, and part platform for telling and retelling the communal story. The early communal records having burned in the 1970 fire, these booklets are among the few community-published documents available; and most of these came from other congregants.

Like the stories these individuals recalled, these resources resided among many people. Pictured are, from the top, the 1963, 1971, 1976, and 2023 ad journals, each with its own version of the community history. The latter two, published 27 years apart, feature the same photo, of the 1924 cornerstone laying.

the stage for further change—and more continuity. Although Brith Sholom's story isn't the full story of the Jewish community of this city, it is a big part of that story. And this community, any community, needs its storytellers.

Be the Bridge

One time when my son Jacob was getting to the end of his middle school years, he went with me for my interview of our neighbor Edwin Kay, who with his wife, Jannie, had welcomed our family when we first arrived in Bethlehem.

After hanging out for a while, Jacob opened a coffee table book about bridges, studying several of the photos until Ed paused in our conversation and looked at the book with Jacob for a few minutes. Like others I'd talked with, Ed understood that our little get together was not just about himself and sharing his life story. He pointed to a photo of a stone bridge with an underpass like a doorway that appeared to have no support in its arch.

Ed asked Jacob, "Do you know why the bridge is arched?" The two of them talked it over. Ed said, "It has a keystone. Why does it have a keystone? The stones lean one against the other with a keystone at the top. They hold each other up, and then it's very, very strong."

~

Much has changed in the years since my family arrived. Bethlehem Steel has lost its original meaning here. The sociologist and anthropologist Jill A. Schennum wrote about deindustrialization and reasons why this happened in her book, *As Goes Bethlehem*. Back then, my family witnessed the machine sheds standing empty for many years, windows missing, mechanical contraptions exposed to the elements. These could be seen via bus tours of the facility, led by former steel workers.

Today, the smoke stacks continue to reach up into the sky, only now with colorful accent lights beneath them rather than flames above. They still contribute to Bethlehem's distinctiveness, but in new ways. The area at their feet has been converted to SteelStacks, an entertainment venue and gathering place for public or private events, located on Founders Way.

Though there are a number of shops on the South Side's Third Street, this is largely due to a revitalization. Before that, many of the little shops on the South Side had given way to malls located outside the city. Over the decades since Ann or Irving, Gordon or the Lehrich brothers grew up here, the Jewish population had decreased dramatically. The Little Shul is no more, and Brith Sholom has decreased in size if not vitality. Many churches have closed their doors. But some things don't change.

Generation to Generation

The 50th anniversary ("Jubilee Year") *Brith Sholom Ad Journal, 1976* opened with a memorial of one of the key founders, as Robert Black eulogized his grandfather, Morris Black: "[Here is] a classical example of a man with modest means and very little formal education who achieved success in life through hard work and by earning the respect of others. I well remember sitting on his lap as he recounted the story of his beginnings in this country."

The preceding page in that journal listed and memorialized many of the rabbis, cantors, and presidents up to that date. The next page opened with a reference to "The past is prologue." The content that followed, however, mixed past and present: Leah Schiff and Florence Hausman write of the Sisterhood's latest events, then list all of the Sisterhood's past presidents.

The journal's text then cited four preceding histories, with a hint of repudiation: "We are, of course, indebted to the people who scrupulously gathered and wrote these meaningful reminiscences of our community's past.... Following is a year-by-year chronicle of the more memorable occurrences in our congregation from 1963 to the present."

I realized: This is what people—*all people*—do. And this is what is so wonderfully fascinating about the fluidity of the spoken (and in the case of the ad journals, the written) word: We tell and retell our stories, working with the past, as if it's the clay beneath the riverbed of our lives, in order to help us live and navigate into the future.

The chronology that followed that *Brith Sholom Ad Journal, 1976* statement seemed to vacillate between the tried and true (a father-son dinner) and the new ("an original 'rock' service at Sisterhood Shabbat"). It recapped the loss of valued artifacts in the 1970 fire, chronicled the Yom Kippur war (1973) when Israel's neighbors all attacked during this most solemn holiday, and then made the leap to the big news of the "role of women strengthened by the granting of high holiday ark openings, followed by giving of Aliyot (ritual participation in going up to the Torah) to women at Sabbath and holiday services." The ad journal thereby told the story again and even highlighted the benefits of adopting new ways (strengthening women's roles in the service).

In so doing, the ad journal laid the groundwork for a much bigger change: Shortly after this 50th anniversary jubilee, the congregation made the difficult decision to leave its beloved Center on the South Side and build itself a new synagogue on Bethlehem's North Side.

Though I often pointed to my article for the *Bethlehem Press* at Hanukkah of 2010 as the beginning of my own journey to "tell the story" of being Jewish in the Christmas City, my jumping-in point traces more accurately to the congregation's Hanukkah party a few days later, when I was asked to participate in the communal Hanukkah candle-lighting for Brith Sholom's 85th anniversary.

Our whole family attended; my sons ranged from seven to 12 years of age. At the celebration, Bethlehem native Ron Black, another of the grandsons of cofounder Morris Black, lit a candle, then handed me the *shamesh* (Hebrew for helper, meaning the candle used to light the other candles). That done, I gave the *shamesh* to an even more recent newcomer for her to light the next candle.

The next day, I wrote up the event for the *Bethlehem Press*, and have not stopped writing since. That Hanukkah was indeed a cultural event, as so many before it had been, but for me it led to much more than lighting a candle.

Lighting a Hanukkah candle in 2010 with, from left: David Caine, Phil Moskowitz, Lisa (Friedman) Collins, Ron Black, and Cary Moritz.

Chapter 10
"O Morning Stars, Together[12]"
Sharing Our Story

My children are all grown now. They became bar mitzvahs at Brith Sholom. They joined the confirmation class led by Rabbi Michael Singer, who arrived in 2014. A couple of the boys took their turns leading junior congregation and the youth group USY. Then it was out into the world!

I spent my found time during their college years getting more involved at Brith Sholom, serving on the Board, and steering the newly needed Security Committee. My career developed, and I appreciated the wonderful people I met through my work. Then in 2023, just as the congregation's centennial was approaching, the Board elected me president.

For my first annual Rosh Hashanah speech, I spoke about the congregation's original president: "Aaron Potruch was an entrepreneur. He put up buildings in Bethlehem, helped bring about the Brith Sholom Community Center. But when I went to find his descendants, there were none. It was kind of sad. Reflecting on Aaron, I realized, there are all kinds of legacies.

"Aaron's real legacy, and that of other people too, was this community. For them, having straggled or streamed into town from all over the world, a united community was a very big deal. It still is.

---

[12] From the Christmas carol "O Little Town of Bethlehem."

"Especially at a time when we hear a lot about groups coming apart and things breaking down, having this place where people can and do come together *means something.*"

That message resonated. After the speech, congregants and visitors ranging from teens to nonagenarians came up to me smiling. For a little while, through story, we had transcended our singular existences. That's what story helps us do. Together, we had entered into the collective sense of belonging to what is, despite the nominal subject of Aaron, our story. The many had become one.

~

This legacy and sense of connectedness with each other and Bethlehem became all the more important just two weeks later due to "October 7th" and its aftermath. Much of the world quickly transmuted its shock at the initial attack against Israel to rage or disappointment at Israel's response. Expressions of antisemitism, already at an all-time high worldwide, escalated.

Yet quietly over the course of time, Bethlehem in Pennsylvania had grown more culturally diverse and more embracing of that diversity—with, for example, nearly a quarter of the population identifying as Hispanic or Latino and active city support of many sub-communities—if not yet very racially diverse. Many religions and houses of worship were represented and have quite a history in Bethlehem.

~

In 2024, Brith Sholom's centennial year opened January 1 with an immersive 1920s-themed party. When it was my turn to speak, I stood up in my flapper dress with a sparkly blue "fascinator" in my hair and shared fun vintage photos through a gigantic projection of the wall showing what those early years would have looked like—48 stars on the US flag! Today's often-congested bridges still in their construction phases! An airport that could be recognized only by flying down to see "Allentown" painted on the shed roof! A

Middle East map showing not Israel, but the British empire. Bethlehem's Main Street at Christmas ... about the same.

Approaching the nearest table, I asked for a volunteer to read a few lines of a story from the slide. So it was that we "heard" Henry Schiff—though he'd passed on eight years before—recalling the just-built synagogue, his parents volunteering, and how he kept out of reach of the kids at school.

With help from a volunteer at the next table, Esther Hirshberg—"the girl in the hat!"—"spoke" to us across the years. Allan B. Goodman read the words of his beloved grandfather, who at Brith Sholom's 50th anniversary had been the last surviving original board member—an incredible instance of cross-generational, outside-of-time connection for us all. The effect was electric; we could feel the room holding its breath so as not to miss a single word.

My youngest son, who was seated in the back at the former kids table (though most were now young adults) later said, "It was like I was really hearing the first people talk about their lives." For a March 10 "main event," I asked that same son, who had been the baby we set up the crib for when we moved to Bethlehem and who was by this time a college student, if he would help out with the program.

It was his second year at the community college, and he was studying media production. Mid-semester projects were already coming due. While many filmmakers would have needed six months and quoted a high price, when I (as I thought) calmly asked my son whether a short film was something he might want to do for the experience and a very modest fee, he agreed. Later, he shared his real motivator: "I made the film because I could tell you really wanted me to." It was a win all around. When he arrived in Documentary Filmmaking the next semester, he was glad he had done the project, too, but again, that was later. The few weeks he had available for the project hardly gave him time to pause and think.

At the time I asked the question, I had not yet even contacted the people we might interview. These turned out to be three individuals who grew up in Bethlehem in the 1930s through 1950s. All of them made themselves available on short notice for the sake of this communal endeavor. What a thrill to sit in the dining room of Allan B. and Mary Goodman, no longer on my own interviewing, but with my son just over my shoulder filming this "off-camera interview," with his whispered reminder, "Mom, don't wave your hands in front of the camera!"

We met with Bob Black; he invited us into the Morris Black kitchen showroom for a fun interview. Jane Spitzer instructed my son to bring down her wedding album from a high closet shelf. Yes, hers was a love story, and there were many in the memories these three shared, about growing up and marriage, about parents and community, about Bethlehem.

After the interviews, the hard work began. My son needed to edit with extra efficiency once he discovered the school lab would be closed for a full week before the event. The result, a 16-minute professional documentary, completed "soup to nuts" in less than a month, debuted before 150 people as part of a gala event.

The young filmmaker was again seated in the back. He went through all the nerves of opening night. He felt the relief of resounding applause, amplified because he was where it mattered most: Brith Sholom. Bethlehem. His home. Because he grew up here.

~

For Mother's Day, Ann Klein shared her story ("On Rosemont Avenue"), including memories of the Civil Rights Movement—"we talked about it at school and at home, and around our dinner tables; it mattered to us"—and her college years during the Vietnam War. She recalled John F. Kennedy's visit to Bethlehem and her surprise that many people booed him.

The reaction of a number of our young people to Ann's memories of that decade was also a surprise: "I never knew so much happened during the 1960s!" Storytelling does so much more than a school lesson can ever do. And we can all take part, sharing our stories within our families and out into our communities.

Through the rest of that year, the community's story continued to unfold with a gathering in the *sukkah* (Hebrew for this temporary harvest hut) and a Hanukkah/New Year's Eve party. I knew the congregation's annual ad journal had been an invaluable resource for this project. So, in my president's message in that year's ad journal, I documented—for some future researcher—the ways we celebrated. That message concluded the seven-part story we'd collectively shared for the centennial. We did this through many storytellers: orally, in writing, with pictures, and on film. The storytelling happened at holiday services, parties, and even through a program Rabbi Allen Juda led in the very place where this journey began—our very own "ground zero"—up at the cemetery.

~

During the autumn of the centennial, well into the second half of my two year term as president, my beloved father died. All that had happened in Bethlehem—my personal journey, the storytelling—prepared me to deliver one final gift to my father, his eulogy. I traveled to my native Missouri and found that things I had been noticing in Bethlehem were true elsewhere, including in the life my father lived: That there are all kinds of legacies. That beauty, meaning, and strength are to be found in stories of everyday life. That these can be preserved and shared through storytelling. All we need to do is to shine our own very bright light on them.

On returning to Bethlehem, I decided this time around to follow the Jewish mourning rituals. I gave myself a reprieve from some of my duties for the designated 30 days. Some but not all, because just a few weeks later, I again stood before the Brith Sholom congregation. Again, it was Rosh Hashanah, my second as president. Having spoken of Aaron the previous year, my 2024 speech tapped into where we were in the progressive storytelling: I told of the 1970 fire ("Your Center is Burning"), this time in the words of some of the women of the community. In the *Brith Sholom Ad Journal, 1971*, "Mrs. Edward Cook"—Helen—described the good feeling of coming home after the rebuilding.

I realized that my home was no longer in the Midwest. Home is where I am, in Bethlehem. Across boundaries, time, and space, a good story brought us together.

Acknowledgments

Thank you to the many people in, neighboring, or originally from the Jewish community of Bethlehem who shared stories for this project. Although there were too many memories shared to include in a single book, there is tremendous value in having told the stories and reflected on a lifetime of memories. The fact that the process seemed so meaningful to everyone who participated, and certainly to me the listener, documentarian, and story quilter, is proof of this project's key message: Sharing our stories matters and is important.

It took 15 years for this project to come to fruition. Prior to the publication of this book, and over the course of quite a few years, more than two dozen contributors passed on. Each of these individuals was unique and very much valued. They live on in my memory and those of their loved ones, and in some ways on these pages. I feel deeply grateful they shared their stories with us. They are: John Angelucci, Arnold K., Marilyn Bergstein, Alan Black, Edith Podberesky Blinderman, Bob Born, Jean Mindlin Deutch, Betty Diamond, Herb Gilles, Gordon Goldberg, Ervin Gross, Shirley Gross, Jerry Hausman, Esther Hirshberg, Robert Kroope, Ira Lehrich, Gus Levin, Zelda Levin, Nevin Mindlin, Harriet Parmet, Sidney Parmet, Mel Phillips, Leo Pozefsky, Ruth Radin, Henry Schiff, Lew Schor, Bruce Smackey, and Shirley Stein.

I strived for accuracy and sought reviews of contributions by the contributors, their descendants, or subject matter experts wherever possible; any errors in the historical sections or in how the individuals' stories are presented are entirely my own.

The Index By Last Name was made possible through a generous gift by Rabbi Allen and Toby Juda, in honor of their children, Adam, Aaron, and Tamar, who grew up in Bethlehem and at Brith Sholom. Many thanks!

Thank you to Chief Adam Waterbear DePaul and Ken Raniere for reviewing pages on the precursors of modern Bethlehem of which they have a rich store of knowledge. I also thank Rodney Frey, professor emeritus of ethnography at the University of Idaho. In my effort to learn how to tell this community's story, I scoured the country for others doing work in some way similar. Professor Frey, who worked extensively within the cultures of Inland Northwest indigenous tribes, graciously provided guidance and encouragement.

Many thanks to my editor, Jennifer Bright. True to her name, she has illuminated the path to publication for me and many other authors via her incisive editing and the brilliance of her publishing company, Bright Communications. Many thanks for helping to make my longtime dream of bringing this project, as it was envisioned, into reality.

Thank you to my memoir writers' group which for the last several years has included Flo Morton, Tony Nauroth, Alicia Ruiz-Orbin, and our leader Jerry Waxler. Jerry discerned much sooner than I did that, in the course of my quest, I had become part of this story too. Our little group met monthly for years. With seemingly infinite patience, my fellow writers provided their reactions and feedback on so many of the chapters of this book, reviewing some over and over again.

To the many friends who read parts or as "beta readers" all of the manuscript and provided feedback and to still more who offered moral support: "Thank you. I appreciate you!" Last but not least, I send out my infinite gratitude to my family, without whom this book would not have been possible.

Sources Cited

Alexander, Nome. "Who are the Lenape?" *Whitehall Historic Preservation Society*. Whitehall, Pennsylvania. Museum Exhibit. Viewed December 15, 2024.

"A Brief History of the Moravian Church," *Moravian Church of America*, https://www.moravian.org/2018/07/a-brief-history-of-the-moravian-church/. Accessed December 21, 2024.

"Brief History of William Penn," *ushistory.org*, https://www.ushistory.org/penn/bio.htm?srsltid=AfmBOoq-L6-ciW5-T4FGKQIL7oaUMwoSs6UxWvxQCqIYArQvIRW AARiM, accessed October 24, 2024.

"Broad Street, at Christmastime Bethlehem, Pa". n.d. Though undated this appears to be mid-20th century. Postcard by the Bethlehem artist and printer J. Carroll Tobias. https://preserve.lehigh.edu/digital-special-collections/postcards/broad-street-christmastime-bethlehem-pa.

Brooks, Phillips. "O Little Town of Bethlehem." 1868. Christmas carol.

"Burial of Mr. Gilles: Hebrew Ceremonies Observed," *Bethlehem Times*; April 17, 1893.

Brith Sholom Ad Journal, [Year] shown with various dates, cited in text, and referring to either Brith Sholom Community Center or Congregation Brith Sholom. NOTE: This title is used for consistency and readability, although the ad journals have a variety of specific titles, such as Congregation Brith Sholom [YEAR] or The Rededication Journal [Year].

"Celebrated the Passover," *Bethlehem Times*, April 3, 1893.

"Christmas Lighting-Hill to Hill Bridge." n.d. This bridge replaced a covered bridge and was constructed in 1921-24. https://preserve.lehigh.edu/digital-special-collections/postcards/christmas-lighting-hill-hill-bridge.

City of Bethlehem website. https://www.bethlehem-pa.gov/about/history.html, accessed March 25, 2019.

City-Data website. http://www.city-data.com/forum/general-u-s/610456-definition-large-medium-small-city-3.html, accessed June 27, 2019.

"*Compana sobre compana*" ("Bells upon bells"), a traditional Andalusian Christmas song https://www.pbs.org/wgbh/christmas-tabernacle-choir/concert-2017/campana-sobre-campana/, accessed August 13, 2025.

"Cornerstone Laying at Jewish Community Center Building Sunday," *Bethlehem Globe-Times.* June 16, 1924.

"Diversity, Inclusion, & Equity at Lehigh," Lehigh University website, https://www2.lehigh.edu/diversity-inclusion-equity#:~:text=Lehigh%20does%20not%20tolerate%20discrimination,or%20gender%20identity%20or%20expression, accessed March 24, 2022.

Edelman, Todd M. *Broadening Jewish History: Toward a Social History of Ordinary Jews.* Oxford: The Littman Library of Jewish Civilization, 2011.

"Faculty Profile: Prof. Edwin Kay," *Asheshi University*, Feb. 7, 2011. https://ashesi.edu.gh/faculty-profile-prof-edwin-kay. Accessed May 3, 2025.

Frankel, Rabbi William. "History of the Early Jewish Community of Bethlehem," *Brith Sholom Community Center Anniversary Year Book.* Bethlehem: Brith Sholom Community Center, 1953.

Frey, Clifford. "Red Letter Day in History of Jews in City," *Bethlehem Globe-Times*, March 31, 1924.

"From Rival Synagogues: Two Hebrew Factions Clash and Try to Settle in a Squire's Office." *Bethlehem Times*, Feb. 25, 1892.

"Furnaces, Bethlehem Steel Works, South Bethlehem, Pa." (1–). (n.d.). (1–). https://preserve.lehigh.edu/digital-special-collections/postcards/furnaces-bethlehem-steel-works-south-bethlehem-pa.

"German Troops Occupy Hungary," United States Holocaust Memorial Museum. https://encyclopedia.ushmm.org/content/en/timeline-event/holocaust/1942-1945/german-troops-occupy-hungary, accessed August 31, 2025.

Goodman, Harry M. "Recollections of an Original Board Member," *Congregation Brith Sholom.* (Undated.)

Gruber, Franz Xaver. "Silent Night." 1818. Christmas carol and UNESCO "intangible cultural heritage."

"Happily married ..." Telegram to Mrs. E. J. Bell from Ray Bell, undated.

Hawkins, David R. *Power vs. Force: The Hidden Determinants of Human Behavior.* California: Hay House, 1995.

hooks, bell. *Belonging: A Culture of Place.* New York and London: Routledge, 2009.

Hopkins, Jr., John Henry. "We Three Kings." Circa 1857. Christmas carol.

Hurston, Zora Neale. *Dust Tracks on a Road.* Thorndike Maine: G. K. Hall & Co., 1942.

Hurston, Zora Neale. "Halumuhfack," audio recording, *Library of Congress.* https://www.loc.gov/item/flwpa000014/. June 18, 1939.

"J. B." National Book Foundation. https://www.nationalbook.org/books/j-b/. Accessed April 13, 2025.

"Jewish Center Gives Program," *Bethlehem Globe-Times,* undated, presumed Dec. 1926.

"Jewish Center is Dedicated: Banquet Held," *Bethlehem Globe-Times,* Dec. 6, 1926.

"Jewish Population in the United States by State (1899-Present)," *Jewish Virtual Library,* https://www.jewishvirtuallibrary.org/jewish-population-in-the-united-states-by-state. Accessed July 5, 2021.

Karabel, Jerome. *The Chosen: The Hidden History of Admission and Exclusion at Harvard, Yale, and Princeton.* Boston and New York: Houghton Mifflin Company, 2006.

Kaufman, David. *Shul with a Pool.* Hanover, New Hampshire: University Press of New England, for Brandeis University Press, 1999.

Kranzley, Glenn. "Raging Fire Rips Jewish Community Center: Arson Suspected, Safe Damaged, Cash Missing," *Bethlehem Globe*, December 19, 1970.

"The Late Josiah Gilles," *Bethlehem Times*; April 22, 1893.

"Lebenslauf," *The Moravian Experience.* https://www.moravian.org/bcm/wp-content/uploads/sites/2/2020/03/Lebenslauf-Overview.pdf, accessed March 25, 2022.

Levering, Joseph Mortimer. *A History of Bethlehem, Pennsylvania (1741-1892).* Bethlehem, Pennsylvania: Times Publishing Company, 1903.

"Making Jewish Heritage in the Present: A tribute to Dr. Chava Weissler, Lehigh University, Emerita" Lehigh University. Dated November 12, 2024. https://bermanctr.cas.lehigh.edu/events/new-location-making-jewish-heritage-present-tribute-dr-chava. Accessed May 3, 2025.

Martin, Michael W. "Adeste, fideles: O Come, all ye faithful," Thesaurus Precum Latinarum Treasury of Latin Prayers https://www.preces-latinae.org/thesaurus/Hymni/Adeste.html, accessed Aug. 12, 2025.

"Men of Bethlehem" (Pamphlet.)Published by Fred L. Shankweiler. Assisted by Frank T. Boyle. Bethlehem, Pennsylvania, 1918.

"Morning Star O Cheering Sight" The Moravian Church. Text: Johann Scheffler (1657). Tr. Bennet Harvey, Jr. (1885) Tune: Francis Florentine Hagen (1836) https://www.moravian.org/2018/07/morning-star-o-cheering-sight. Accessed May 3, 2025.

"Nanticoke Lenni-Lenape: An American Indian Tribe," *nanticoke-lenape.info*, accessed July 20, 2021.

Novak, Steve. "The story of the Bethlehem star, shining on the Christmas City for 80 years," Lehigh Valley Live, December 7, 2017. https://www.lehighvalleylive.com/bethlehem/2017/12/bethlehem_star_christmas_city.html, accessed September 1, 2025.

"O Christmas Tree' lyrics: how does the much-loved festive carol go?" BBC Music Magazine. Dec. 10, 2024. https://www.classical-music.com/articles/o-christmas-tree-lyrics, accessed Aug. 12, 2025.

"O Little Town of Bethlehem," https://www.hymnsandcarolsofchristmas.com/Hymns_and_Carols/Notes_On_Carols/o_little_town_of_bethlehem.htm, accessed February 17, 2021.

Peck, M. Scott. *The Different Drum: Community Making and Peace.* New York: Touchstone, 1987.

Probyn, Elspeth. *Outside Belongings.* New York and London: Routledge, 1996.

"Roger D. Simon," Lehigh University. https://history.cas.lehigh.edu/faculty-staff/roger-d-simon, accessed May 3, 2025.

Schennum, Jill A. *As Goes Bethlehem: Steelworkers and the Restructuring of an Industrial Working Class.* Nashville, TN: Vanderbilt University Press, 2023.

Schlereth, Thomas J. *Victorian America: Transformations in Everyday Life, 1876-1915.* New York: HarperCollins Publishers, 1991.

Sklare, Marshall. *The Jews: Social Patterns of an American Group.* New York: The Free Press, 1958.

Soderlund, Jean R. *Lenape Country: Delaware Valley Society Before William Penn.* Philadelphia: University of Pennsylvania Press, 2015.

"Star of Bethlehem, Main Street, Bethlehem Pennsylvania, 2008." Photo by and (c)2008 Derek Ramsey

(Ram-Man), GFDL 1.2 https://commons.wikimedia.org/wiki/File:Star_of_Bethlehem_Main_Street_2382px.jpg via Wikimedia Commons

"Steel Works, Bethlehem, Pa.", Lehigh University Postcard Collection, [WPC0195], Special Collections, Linderman Library, Lehigh University, Bethlehem, Pa. 1908. https://preserve.lehigh.edu/digital-special-collections/postcards/steel-works-bethlehem-pa.

Stolarik, M. Mark. *Growing Up on the South Side: Three Generations of Slovaks in Bethlehem, Pennsylvania, 1880-1976.* New Jersey: Associated University Presses, Inc, 1985.

Tatu, Christina. "Black history in Bethlehem is focus of library's project," *The (Allentown) Morning Call*, August 11, 2020.

Taylor, Jane. "The Star." 1806. Poem later set to music, now known as the song "Twinkle Little Star."

"Two Synagogues Merged in One," *Bethlehem Times*; May 2, 1892.

"View of the Lehigh Valley, Allentown, Pa". 1907. https://preserve.lehigh.edu/digital-special-collections/postcards/view-lehigh-valley-allentown-pa-0.

Wade, John Francis (1711-1786), *"Adeste, Fideles"* ("O Come, All Ye Faithful"). Christmas carol.

"Walking Purchase, The; August 25, 1737, *State Historical & Museum Commission.* https://www.phmc.state.pa.us/portal/communities/documents/1681-1776/walking-purchase.html. Accessed Dec. 15, 2024

Weissbach, Lee Shai. *Jewish Life in Small-Town America: A History.* New Haven, Connecticut: Yale University Press, 2005.

NOTE: With the understanding that unpublished interviews are normally only cited in text or in notes, the names of the approximately 100 narrators and interviewees for this project are not included in the bibliography because the transcripts are unpublished and intended to remain so. Additionally, some prefer to remain anonymous or be identified by first-name only. Narrator names appear in the text with their narratives, or not, according to their wishes. Those whose surnames are used may be found via the Index by Last Name.

Index By Last Name

This index is not meant to be exhaustive, but rather to aid the reader in easily finding individuals who contributed or who are particularly highlighted through what is being shared.

A
Angelucci, John, 112, 121-122
Aronson, Judy, 171-174, 241

B
Bader, Karen, nee Sophie Rosenbaum, 108, 153-157, 158, 239-240
Bader, Morris, 156
Beilin, Jacob, "J.G.," 55-57, 59, 78, 79, 165
Bell, Elizabeth, 247-249
Bell, Ray, 246-249
Berger, Sam, 51
Bergstein, Marilyn, 26-29
Bergstein, Steve, 26, 215, 266
Black, Alan, 176, 178
Black, Ben, 175, 179
Black, Ben, 175, 179
Black, Bob, 280
Black, Leah, 175-179
Black, Linda, 31, 175
Black, Morris, 30-31, 33-34, 44, 78, 132, 175, 274, 275, 280
Black, Neil, 175, 179
Black, Robert, 274, 280
Black, Ron, 31, 175, 275-276

Blinderman, Ann Beth, 166, 173, 174, 192-193, 195-196, 241-246, 270, 280-282

Blinderman, Edith Podberesky, 13, 63-69, 102, 166, 173, 174, 178, 193, 195, 241

Blinderman, Martin "Marty," 68-69, 241, 244

Bochner, Laura, 191-192, 267, 271

Born, Bob, 35-37, 113, 120, 201-203, 216-217, 224-226

Born, Ross, 37, 217

Born, Sam, 34-37, 152, 201-203, 216-217

Bratspies, Nan, 57

Brisker, Cecilia Coleman, 159, 167-168

C

Caine, David, 277

Cohn, Rachel "Ray" Glasawitzki, 27-30, 44

Cook, Helen, 254, 283

D

Deutch, Bernard, 225

Deutch, Jean Mindlin, 86, 108, 124-125, 127, 223, 225

Diamond, Betty, 6, 33, 57, 175, 239, 252, 260-261

Diamond, Eugene, 57, 239, 250, 252, 261

Diamond, Gene, 250

F

Fink, Ann, 173, 174

Frankel, Anna (Podberesky), 63-64, 66, 194, 195

Frankel, Emma, 192-193, 194, 195-196

Frankel, Sam, 196

Frankel, William, Rabbi, 23, 24, 41, 96, 241, 259, 271

Friedman, Harry, 104, 146

Friedman Collins, Lisa, 277

G

Gandel, Abraham Reverend, 145, 211-212

Genel, Florence, 104, 108, 160, 170
Genel, Victor, 104, 108, 170
Gilles, Barry, 21
Gilles, Herb, 20-21, 188
Gilles, Max 19, 21, 30
Gilles, Yehoshua, 17-23, 76
Glasawitzki, Morris 26
Glasawitzki, Suzy 26, 215
Glazier, Betsy, nee Korson, 137-142, 143, 214, 249-251
Glazier, Harold, 86, 139-141, 143, 210-211, 211-212, 212-214
Glazier, Morris, 74, 79, 137, 139, 212
Goldberg, Ann, 41, 184-189, 252, 260, 274
Goldberg, Carolyn, see Katwan, Carolyn
Goldberg, Esther Molly, 198-199, 200
Goldberg, Gordon, 51, 99-100, 115, 118-119, 198-201, 225, 230, 268, 274
Goldberg, Harry, 198-199
Goldberg, Ken, 186-187
Goldberg, Mel, 185, 187
Goldberg, Rose Lee, 201, 230
Goldblat, Casey, 184
Goodman, Allan B., 279, 280
Goodman, Ben, 60, 78
Goodman, Gertrude, 211
Goodman, Harry M.,78, 88, 165
Goodman, Mary, 280
Grace, Eugene Gifford, 38, 130
Grace, Marion Brown, 46, 130
Gross, Ervin, 47-51
Gross, Julius, 215
Gross, Shirley, 47-51

H
Hausman, Florence, 257, 274

Hausman, Jerry, 41, 82, 114, 119, 150, 208, 209, 257
Heilbronn, Elsa, 134-136
Hirshberg, Esther, 55, 79, 80, 83, 101, 165, 231, 279

J
Juda, Allen, Rabbi, 57, 60, 81, 84, 85-86, 106-107, 131, 145-146, 167, 212-214, 215, 256-257, 258-259, 264, 268, 281
Juda, Toby, 256, 263

K
K., Arnold, 162-163, 197
K., Barbara, 162-163, 197
Kaplan, Anna, 180, 183
Kaplan, Fannie, 180
Kaplan, Herman, 180, 181-182
Kaplan, Irving, 100, 102, 105-106, 119-120, 180-184, 219, 274
Kaplan, F. Shirley, 100, 180, 181, 182, 183
Kaplan, Lynne Rita, nee Blinderman, 183-184
Kaplan, Nathan, 180-181, 182, 183
Katwan, Carolyn, nee Goldberg, 247, 261
Kay, Edwin, 226, 227, 228, 272-273
Kay, Jannie, 227, 228, 272-273
Klein, Ann, see Blinderman, Ann Beth
Klein, Jonathan, 241
Korson, Betsy, see Glazier, Betsy
Korson, George, 137, 138
Kroope, Nathan, 55, 59-61
Kroope, Robert, 55, 59, 60-63, 87, 89, 97, 109-110, 223-224
Kroope, Sylvia, nee Garfinkel, 62
Kuhn, Karen, 33

L
Lader, Jacob, 10-11, 109, 272-273
Lehrich, Art, 133

Lehrich, Betty, nee Perkin, 135, 166-167
Lehrich, Henry, 115-118, 131-132, 135-136, 166-167, 182
Lehrich, Ira, 85, 100, 114, 131, 132, 134, 135
Levan, Doe 209
Levan, Maur, 266
Levin, Gus, 55, 72, 81-82, 86, 143-144, 161, 166, 218, 230, 268
Levin, Zelda, 54-55, 140, 143, 161, 166, 269
Loney, Carol Herzon, 231-232, 246, 247

M
M., Carol, 81, 222-223
Makagon, Gert, 92
Makagon, Lou, 210-211
Meislin, Ruth, 265
Merkin, Natalie, 166, 173, 174
Mindlin, Jean, see Deutch, Jean Mindlin
Mindlin, Lil, nee Schwalb, 108, 123, 125, 126, 127, 128, 129
Mindlin, Morris, 108, 123-127, 128, 129, 137, 214, 225
Mindlin, Naomi, 126
Mindlin, Nevin, 44, 123-126, 129-130, 242, 268
Mindlin, Tillie, 220, 222, 223, 225
Moritz, Cary, 277
Moskowitz, Phil, 83, 240-241, 276
Mowitz, Abraham, Rabbi, 169-170
Murman, Judy, 89

P
Parmet, Harriet, 232, 233-237
Parmet, Sidney, 233-235
Perkin, Betty, see Lehrich, Betty
Perleman, Rebecca, 31
Phillips, Abraham, 57, 58
Phillips, Elaine, 69, 72-74, 267
Phillips, Maurice, 57

Phillips, Mel, 69, 72-74
Phillips, Sarah, 44, 57, 58
Phillips, Sol, 57
Podberesky, Anna, 55
Podberesky, Isadore, 55
Porath, Esther, 136, 138, 214
Porath, Jonathan, Rabbi, 41, 136-137, 138
Porath, Tzvi, Rabbi, 136, 214
Potruch, Aaron, 44, 59, 78, 79, 81, 87-90, 101, 134, 165, 277-278, 282
Pozefsky, Leo, 48, 250, 258

R
Radin, Ruth, 186, 266
Rosenbaum, Isak, 153-156
Rosenbaum, Rosalie, 153-156
Rosenbaum, Sophie, see Bader, Karen
Rosenberg, Willie, 170, 215, 216
Roth, Leon, 32-34, 44
Roth, Lila, 34

S
Schiff, Charles, 90, 92
Schiff, Henry, 13, 54, 84, 88, 90-96, 97, 99, 101, 165, 182, 271, 279
Schiff, Isabel, nee Kaplan, 13, 83, 94-96, 100, 159, 178, 272
Schiff, Leah, 216, 274
Schiff, Lena, nee Berkowitz, 90-92, 165
Schor, Lew, 125
Schwab, Charles, 38, 51, 193
Schwalb, Martin, 44, 107
Schwartz, Renee, 173, 174, 216
Sell, Anton, 59, 78
Shaffer, Irv, 35, 37, 152
Shaffer, Jack, 35, 37, 152, 216, 217-219, 257

Silberstein, Hani, 168, 169
Simon, Roger, 227, 229
Singer, I.B., 235-236
Singer, Michael, Rabbi, 277
Smackey, Bruce, 216, 255-256
Sonnenfeld, Martin, 118, 140, 216
Sonnenfeld, Nathan, 70, 71
Spitz, Joe, 146, 147, 152, 159, 178
Spitzer, Jane, 280
Stein, Shirley, 47

T
Trotner, Bob, 103-105, 108, 168-171
Trotner, Ida, 169-171

W
Wasser, Max, Rabbi, 250, 253
Weinberg, Marsha,166, 173, 174, 185
Weissler, Chava, 227-229
Weissman, Abraham, 96-101, 120, 136
Weisz, Ann, nee Gandel, 145
Weisz, Bill, 145-146, 159, 211, 212, 216
Wiesel, Elie, 233, 236
Wruble, Norman, 263-264
Wruble, Sandy, 159, 239, 263-266

Last names withheld
Laszlo, 146-152, 159, 190, 203-210
Ruth, nee Adams, 150-151, 152
Sam, 52-54, 146-152, 190, 203-210

"Then the traveler in the dark thanks you for your tiny spark…"
This lesser known lyric of "Twinkle, Little Star" illuminates
the now-stilled but ever iconic presence of today's Steel Stacks, an
entertainment venue and gathering place where it is now possible
to access close up views of the blast furnaces via the Hoover Mason
Trestle. The trestle's well-lit horizontal walkway can be seen in
this photo.
The former narrow gauge railway for many years transported iron ore,
coke, and limestone and is now repurposed into an elevated linear park
standing 46 feet high.

About the Author

Jennifer Lader is a writer, community builder, and storyteller. Growing up in her native Missouri, Jennifer was fascinated by the people she found through books, especially the creation stories of Indigenous peoples. She pursued her need to uncover the stories of the origins of culture, earning a bachelor's degree in anthropology at Grinnell College. For her master's degree in public administration at Syracuse University, Jennifer focused on how people can work together. Her message is simple: Listen to the people around you. Join a community. Make it stronger by sharing what you uniquely bring. A former editor of a regional Jewish newspaper, Jennifer's work has been recognized with a Keystone Press Award and the prestigious Simon Rockower Award from the American Jewish Press Association. This is her second book.

Share Your Story!

What story came to your mind when you read the story of this community? Write it here! Become part of this book. Better yet, if you hope to write a community story of your own, Jennifer offers the following resources: Her first book, *Six Word Lessons for Writing Your Community's Story* is available on Amazon and offers step-by-step guidance on how to develop a well-researched and communally supported project. Other support for your project can be found at <u>jenniferlader.com</u>.

www.ingramcontent.com/pod-product-compliance
Lightning Source LLC
Chambersburg PA
CBHW061601120626
46550CB00004B/1573